312 8/36

The Ideal Ministry

The Ideal Ministry

By
HERRICK JOHNSON, D.D.

Professor of Homiletics and Pastoral Theology, Auburn Theological Seminary, 1874–80; McCormick Theological Seminary, 1880–1906

NEW YORK   CHICAGO   TORONTO
Fleming H. Revell Company
LONDON   AND   EDINBURGH

SECOND EDITION

New York: 158 Fifth Avenue
Chicago: 80 Wabash Avenue
Toronto: 25 Richmond Street, W.
London: 21 Paternoster Square
Edinburgh: 100 Princes Street

To the memory of my beloved wife, who walked with me through all the years of my ministry, sharing with me its joys and sorrows, its trials and triumphs; whose songs of trust have winged the feet of the hours, and whose " voice in the twilight" has made many a piece of my patchwork seem worth while, this " Ideal Ministry" is most lovingly dedicated.

H. J.

Foreword

IDEALS are inspirations, incentives to effort, calls to come up higher. They fill us with a blessed discontent of the past, and stir us with an eager longing to do better things. They make a dead level impossible in any calling. Of all men, the man in the ministry is the one who should have ideals. The ideal "consecration," the ideal "life," the ideal "stewardship," the ideal "Church," the ideal "kingdom,"—he can tolerate nothing less than these. They are set before him by his Lord.

For the attainment of these God-appointed ideals, one of the God-appointed means, and the chief, is the ministry of the Word of God by the man of God. And in the prosecution of this ministry, the ideals of it we hang up in our sky, if worthy, though they may shame our past, will nevertheless prove incentives to higher things. So that idealizing in the ministry is not theorizing, nor ballooning, nor getting lost in the clouds. It is lifting a standard. In the reverent use of apostolic words, it is "forgetting the things which are behind, and stretching forward to the things which are before, and pressing on towards the goal unto the prize" of an ideal ministry in Christ Jesus.

That this book may be helpful to such a ministry and stimulative to homiletic effectiveness, is the hope and prayer of the author.

7

Contents

PART ONE

THE IDEAL MINISTRY

PART TWO

RELATED IDEALS

Contents

PART THREE
THE SERMON

PART ONE
THE IDEAL MINISTRY

I

THE IDEAL MINISTRY—ITS PERMANENT
FUNCTION : PREACHING

SYLLABUS

Introductory.—Certain great ideas have given the gospel ministry its peculiar glory. The great winners and builders of souls have been dominated by these ideas. One of these determining ideas is *preaching* as the permanent function of the ministry.

1. The dictum of a certain school of art as to whether it shall "preach."
2. What Christ intended for His Gospel.
    - (*a*) He meant it should be preached.
    - (*b*) He meant the living preacher.
3. What preaching really is.
4. Other agencies help tell the story, but preaching is the norm in gospel evangelization.
5. Some signs that seem to forecast the decadence of preaching.
6. Over against these is the living Christ saying to the living Church, "Go ye into all the world and preach the Gospel to every creature."
7. From this high premise these things follow:
    - (*a*) When preaching is out of date, Christianity will be out of date; for the word preached and the living Christ are tied together for all time.
    - (*b*) No modern device of human wisdom, no social settlement or sociological movement can supplant the preaching of the Word.
    - (*c*) By this sign we conquer. The order is the King's, and is backed by all of heaven's authority and power.
    - (*d*) If the sermon has become a "back number," the fact of preaching is not what's the matter, but the *kind* of preaching. The divine command is, "Go ye into all the world and preach." Let the answer be, in Rome or Athens, in town or country, in the seats of high culture or in the heart of pagan continents, "'As much as in me is,' always and everywhere, I am ready to preach."

I

THE IDEAL MINISTRY—ITS PERMANENT FUNCTION : PREACHING

IN every calling there must be belief in its great value before there can be intense ardour in its prosecution. It is not in the nature of mind to be stirred deeply by what it deems a trifle. Patriots are not born of low ideals. The things for which a man is willing to die are great things to *him*. The poet thinks no other art like his; he calls it divine. So, too, the painter and the sculptor; they have exalted conceptions of their work. Hence they come to their canvas or marble all aglow, with an enthusiasm that burns within them. And the canvas and the marble catch their spirit, and glow and breathe and speak under their touch. If an artist thinks meanly of his art, it will be mean art that is born in his studio. So, a conception of the gospel ministry as merely a respectable means of livelihood—a kind of bread and butter conception—will beget a tame ministry. If it is thought to be godlike, the godlike will appear in the heavenly doing.

It behooves us, therefore, at the very outset of our discussion, to inquire what those vital features of the gospel ministry are that set it apart from every other ministry, and that stamp it as superior to every other ministry. And if we find there are such features, then to grasp these several ideas, to weigh them, and

13

to come under the spell of their charm and power so that they shall cease to be mere intellectual beliefs, and become vitalized spiritual forces, is to be on the sure road to an ideal gospel ministry.

What, then, are those ideas, unique and matchless, transcendent in their worth and of eternal consequence, that give the gospel ministry its peculiar glory and sanctity? They are:

Its permanent function; its supreme aim; its ruling spirit; its subject matter; its preeminent business; its central theme; its eternal sanctions; and its cooperating agent.

The ambassadors for Christ who have hitherto come nearest to an ideal gospel ministry have been stirred the most mightily by these ideas. This has been the characteristic mark of their stewardship. They have widely differed in many respects—physically, intellectually, temperamentally, emotionally. The giants in Israel that have done great things for God—that have had wide hearing and multiplied victories—have not all been *intellectual* giants. Some have been distinguished for wide scholarly research; some have had a soaring imagination; some have been logic on fire; some have been signally endowed with sanctified common sense. What strong contrasts between Paul and Peter, Augustine and Chrysostom, Calvin and Melanchthon, John Knox and John Bunyan, Spurgeon and Beecher, Brooks and Moody, Finney and Whitefield, Jonathan Edwards and Gypsy Smith! But these all, and a multitude more of winners and builders of souls, were alike in this—they intensely believed in, and were supremely dominated by, the several ideas that are here named as stamping and distinguishing the ideal gospel ministry. Let us consider them in the order named :

The Ideal Ministry—Its Permanent Function : Preaching.

1. " Thou shalt not preach " is the first and great commandment of that school of art which believes in "art for art's sake." " Go ye into all the world and *preach* " is the last command of Him who came to seek and save that which is lost. The dictum of the art school is open to challenge. The order of the King admits of no debate. And it makes preaching the permanent function of the gospel ministry.

If the exclusive business of art is to " hold the mirror up to nature," if art is to " exhibit alike the vices and virtues of the age," " but must not take sides "; if " the moment a moral or an immoral intention obtrudes itself, that moment the artist begins to fall from grace as an artist "; and if in art " *all* things are permissible in their place and proportion," [1] then art, of course, must not and cannot preach. It is merely imagination's drag-net for the good and the bad, the clean and the filthy, the pure and the vile, the angelic and the devilish. All the weird witchery of evil and subtle seduction of lust that appears in nature and society may be put upon canvas, provided the canvas is true to its mission as " a mirror," and provided the vicious and the virtuous are given their due proportion.

But that this would play havoc with morals, we all know. There is a great deal in nature and life that should not be seen in a mirror. Why should not art

[1] John Burroughs, "Thou Shalt Not Preach," *Atlantic Monthly*, August, 1899.

preach, if it will? It has glorified, to many a soul, a truth of God. But let it beware how it preaches, lest it change the truth of God into a lie. If, as the author already quoted says, "Dante makes hell fascinating by his treatment," then Dante not only preaches, but puts a false tone in his colouring; for he and the divine Artist do not agree. Christ makes hell dreadful and damning by His treatment.

2. Whether, however, this dictum of art, "Thou shalt not preach," is accepted or rejected, there can be no shadow of doubt as to what Christ intended for His Gospel. (a) He meant it *should be preached.* He commanded its preaching. He bade His disciples to "go into all the world and preach." "Make disciples of all nations" is His final and perpetual charge. By "the foolishness of preaching" salvation cometh. "Preach the word" is the apostolic injunction. Along this road the Church has pushed to her world-wide conquests. She has gone everywhere, preaching the Gospel. And through all the ages since Christ first called men to Christian ambassadorship the preaching of the cross has been to "them that are being saved," "the power of God."

As it was in the beginning, it is now, and ever shall be. The Founder of Christianity made no mistake when He staked its triumphal progress down through time and its victorious consummation at "the end of the world" on "the foolishness of preaching." He chose the agency in full view of the puissant forces and changed conditions of these later centuries.

(b) And He meant the *living preacher.* "Go ye into all the world." He knew, as no one else knew, the might of truth in personality. The consummate flower and power of revelation was *He Himself—God, manifest in the flesh.* Prophecy! teaching! vision! type! earlier theophanies!—what were these compared with *Him!* How they faded away in the presence of the glory and power of truth embodied in His divine person; and that person " in the flesh," face to face with men, sympathetic to their need, sorrowing with them, touched with the feeling of their infirmities, the Spirit of the Lord upon Him, anointed to preach the Gospel! Here is the perpetual warrant for God's great ordinance of gospel proclamation.

3. *To be like Christ, to stand in His stead and speak in His behalf, sensible of a divine commission, persuaded that we are His ambassadors, not by infallible sacerdotal selection, not by the market law of demand and supply, but by immediate, internal, and effectual call of God; and thus persuaded, to take the truths of Holy Scripture and unfold, illustrate, amplify them for enlightenment and persuasion, and under the guidance of the Holy Spirit, to have them intensified by profound personal conviction, fused in the fires of one's own soul, poured upon waiting ears and hearts from lips touched with God's altar-fire, and accompanied by every possible adjunct of effective posture and gesture and voice—this is preaching.*

4. Other agencies that help tell the story. Symbol and sacrament do indeed preach for God. Music and architecture, by their rhythmic song and silence, make proclamation of the everlasting word. The wheels of organized Christian activities help spread the Gospel. The ubiquitous press with its prodigious enterprise, scattering its leaves as the drops of the morning, wings the divine message to millions. Cross-signed lives and

transformed characters tell the story of redemption. And surely the Bible, without note or comment, brings Christ to many a soul. But no one of these, nor all of them, is "preaching" in the official sense of Christian ambassadorship, and in complete obedience to the great commission. The full-orbed glory of the meaning of the Master, in bidding us preach His word, we do not see until we see a living man before living men with the nameless and potent charm of intense personality so crowding into his speech, as he preaches Christ crucified, that it becomes the power of God. The total of human personality cannot be represented by white paper and black ink. The total of truth cannot be preached save in and through personality. The man behind the word; the word in the man; truth in and through the person—this is the norm in gospel evangelization.

It would seem, therefore, as if the business of preaching were to be the conspicuous and absorbing business of the Church of God until the end of the gospel age.

5. Yet we cannot shut our eyes to some signs in the sky, seeming to forecast the decadence of preaching. Dr. Storrs, not long before his death, in two notable articles,[1] discussed "The Future of the Protestant Pulpit in American Society," and noted impressively the facts that looked like prophecies of waning power. He named as some of these: the preacher no longer regarded as speaking oracularly; the doubtful or critical attitude of mind towards the preacher and his words; the prodigious multiplication of objects of absorbing interest; the ever-hastening

[1] *The Independent*, April 20 and 27, 1899.

rush of our modern life ; the dense massing of population in our cities ; the break in the continuity of city
church life through increasing exodus into the country
each year for a period of weeks and months ; the lessened power of copious and sonorous public speech—
this decline in eloquence being marked at the bar and
in parliament and assembly as well as in the pulpit ;
the Sunday newspaper, as attractive to multitudes as
a novel of society or a drama on the stage ; and the
recent criticism of Scripture, conveying the impression
of its uncertain authority, and making pulpit teaching
less commanding than it was.

Now some of these points might well be challenged,
some might be shown to be ephemeral, some might be
given an opposite significance, some might demand,
not abstention from preaching, but change of method
and a study of adaptation.

6. But concede their validity, give them all their
full weight, and over against them we place the old yet
ever-present need of man, the cry of the soul, the
sense of sin, the ineradicable responsibility of personality, the human conscience, the unchanging conviction
of the truth of immortality, the unbridged gulfs in any
evolution without God, the history of Christianity, the
historic Christ, the resurrection of Jesus Christ from the
dead, and the present immanent living Christ ! And
to meet this need and answer this cry, and take sin's
burden off, and restore the divine image to personality,
and make the bird in the bosom sing sweetly, and
prove that it is blessed to die, here is this living Christ
saying to His living Church, " *Go ye into all the world
and preach the Gospel to every creature.*"

7. *From this high premise these things follow :*

(*a*) It follows, that whatever the signs of the times, whatever the adverse conditions, whatever the dark problems of city life, whatever the results of modern criticism, if it should ever come to pass that preaching is out of date, then it will have also come to pass that Christianity and Christ are out of date; for in this last command of the Master the word preached and the living Christ are tied together for all time. The divine order is, "Go preach My Gospel," and the divine promise is, "Lo, I am with you alway, even unto the end of the world."

(*b*) It follows, secondly, that no modern device of human wisdom, no possible agency of any sort can supplant the preaching of the Word or subordinate the preaching to any other means of gospel conquest. And by preaching is meant not simply, nor chiefly, printing Bibles, or holy living, or the use of chant and ritual, but the public, authoritative, personal proclamation of the truth of God to men by a living man. Such preaching as Paul meant when, facing corrupt Corinth, he said to the Christians there, "I am determined not to know anything among you save Jesus Christ"; or when facing imperial Rome, he said, "As much as in me is, I am ready to preach the Gospel to you that are at Rome also"; or when itinerating the pagan provinces, he went everywhere triumphing in Christ Jesus. Such preaching as Peter's—not so much when he wrote his two epistles of consolation for the world's bruised and broken hearts, but rather when under the power of God at Pentecost he poured his ardent spirit down the channel of public speech and won three thousand souls to Christ. Such preaching as Timothy was charged with when he was apostolically enjoined to "*preach the Word; be instant in season, out of season; reprove, rebuke, exhort with all long suffering and teaching.*" This is New Testament preaching. It is no hazy thing, as if it were a misty and mystic conglomerate of all influence for Christ. We know what it is. It has a boundary. It can be defined. It is God's chief instrument of conquest. And history shows us that fidelity to it marks the rising Church; that infidelity to it marks the falling Church. Nay, more: it is the test and sifter of all modern panaceas that are offered to heal the world's bleeding hurts. You may know the nostrums by this unfailing sign: Do they make conspicuous and luminous the preaching of the Word? Do they set forth Christ crucified as the only power of God unto salvation? If they do, they are of God.

But look at the so-called "social settlement," that is silent in all its public speech as to the gospel settlement for sin. Look at the sociological movements that swell with reform and shrink to the last degree of littleness at any thought of spiritual regeneration, so that there is no room for the new birth in their remedial agency. Look at Christian Science, that preaches more often the word of a woman than the word of the Master. There is danger even in some of our best-meant devices of gospel propagandism that they subordinate, and so dishonour, God's ordained method of reaching and saving men, by retiring the preaching of the Word and bringing to the front with bustling activity and iterated emphasis the loaves and fishes of a mere material and social life. We want clean streets, and fine parks, and good drainage, and

municipal reform.   But Paris has all these.   Is Paris
any nearer clean hearts ?

Mark this, O ye heralds of God ! You cannot
hasten the millennial glory by making the Church of
Christ a vast soup-kitchen, or club-house, or lecture-
ship platform, with a gospel attachment.   The New
Testament is a message.   First of all, and oftenest of
all, it must be delivered.   Go, preach.

(c) It follows thirdly, that *by this sign we conquer.*
How could it be otherwise ?   The order is the King's.
And it is the one distinctive order that He distinctly.
backs by a limitless amplitude of power.   " All authority is given unto Me in heaven and on earth.   Go
ye, therefore, into all the world and preach.   Go ye,
therefore, and make disciples of all nations."   How
can preaching fail with such backing ?   Shame on the
Church that will fly to other measures in despair of
this !   There ought to be no standing-room on earth
for a preaching coward.

Men of the ministry, do we really believe Christ is
behind this thing ?   Do we believe His hand is on all
heaven's forces, and earth's, too, as He bids us go and
preach ?   Then never shall we be lured or driven to
anything that will make it seem as if we were trembling for our pulpit throne.   Let us plan for and welcome organized activity, helpful adjunct, Christian endeavour, men's clubs, social pact, help for God's poor,
the enthusiasm of comradeship.   But in the midst of
all these let us set preaching, chief, supreme, regnant,
and give it our utmost toil, our consuming zeal, our
heart's blood, as the heaven-ordained instrument and
agency by which salvation cometh.   If we find we
cannot " raise the dead in thirty minutes "; if the

dense population of a great city confronts us with its awful problems and its dark despair and its seething mass of pollution, making the case look desperate for truth and righteousness ; if a hostile criticism looks up at us with conscious authority, threatening to lessen the authority of God's Word and to make the pulpit seem " a piece of antiquated lumber" that has had its day and should cease to be, God forbid that we should run to the wish-wash and tow of some modern reformatory device of man to get our case.   Let us preach on ; that's our business ; that's the King's business.   We are not going to raise these dead souls, thrice dead and buried in the godless worldliness of our modern life ; we are not going to pierce this blackness of darkness of city pollution with the radiant beams of transforming day ; we are not going to answer the critics and make defense of the truth—by *abandoning* preaching and running to " settlements," and soup-kitchens, and carpenter shops, and sanitariums, and bath-houses, and sacred concerts.

(*d*)   It follows, fourthly, that, if the sermon has become a back number, the *fact* of preaching is not what's the matter, but the *kind* of preaching.   And we may have to tear our kind to shreds and trample it under our feet, and cry to God for another kind, before the dead come forth, or the city's stench grows sweet, or the critics join both in intelligent and believing acceptance of the Word of God as the only infallible rule of faith and practice.

When the preacher, charged to feed the flock of God and to rescue the perishing, gets a chief reputation for scholarship, and no reputation whatever for spiritual power—when the consuming joy of such a preacher is

to go on long and eager microscopic research in matters of speculative interest, but of no practical value
—then look out for a theological mummy. We shall
have him—plenty of him—dead and dry.

But do we not want scholarship in the ministry? O
yes, we want the finest scholarship. An empty mind
has only one gift—what Spurgeon once called "a
hideous gift"—the gift of saying nothing at great
length.

But does not this advocacy of "preaching" as the
permanent, conspicuous function of the ministry tend
to narrowness? By no means. We are running no
tilt against breadth of scholarship in the ministry. We
want broadness; but we want it of a particular kind.
Surely not the blanket and barn-door variety that
keeps forever broad and flat; but the kind that can be
focussed and concentrated and made to bear mightily
on the brains and hearts and wills that wait upon the
preacher Sabbath by Sabbath to hear what message
he has from God. Let special fondness for this or
that study be tested by the help the study renders in
achieving the supreme aim of preaching, or in master-
ing and making effective its subject-matter, or in doing
its preëminent business. And let the curb and bit be
put resolutely on any linguistic bias, or delight in
philosophic speculation or passion for antiquarian research, from which the preacher returns with reluc-
tance to his God-ordained work of ministry, as if it
were a monotonous drudgery, which he would fain get
through with as soon as possible, that he may go back
again to his favourite fields of study. "Go ye into all
the world and *preach*," is the divine order. Let the
answer be: In Rome or Athens, in town or country,

in the seats of high culture or in the heart of pagan continents, in the palaces or in the slums, "as much as in me is," always and everywhere, I am ready to preach.

II

THE IDEAL MINISTRY—ITS SUPREME AIM:
PERFECT MANHOOD IN CHRIST JESUS

SYLLABUS

1. It is in aim that secular and sacred public speech radically differ. Secular public speech aims to move the will. Sacred public speech aims to move the will Godward.
2. Scriptural confirmation :
   (a) This is what Christ gave Himself to the Church for (Eph. 4 : 11, 12).
   (b) This is the exact meaning of the "Great Commission" (Matt. 28 : 19, 20), Go ye and *make* and *teach* disciples. Rescue men from spiritual death, and build them up in spiritual life.
3. While this is being done, many other things will be done: Social conditions will be revolutionized ; governments will be made pure ; clean homes and streets and politics will be the universal order ; the kingdom of heaven on earth will at last witness, in its completeness, to the manifold wisdom of God.
4. The God-appointed means for all this is the *Preaching of the Word*, constituting the ministry of *Reconciliation* and the ministry of *Sanctification*. No other ministry for a man of God or a church of God.
5. Two things made impossible by the presence of this supreme aim —
   (a) That the sermon should be prepared with only the sermon in view.
   (b) That one should think lightly of homiletic toil.

II

THE IDEAL MINISTRY—ITS SUPREME AIM: PERFECT MANHOOD IN CHRIST JESUS

THE supreme aim is perfect manhood in Christ Jesus. The preacher's finished work is not a finished sermon, but a Christlike soul. He constructs a sermon that he may reconstruct a man. Salvation is his weekly purpose; not reformation, not social improvement, not intellectual uplift, not æsthetic delight, but salvation in its broad Scriptural sense.

1. It is just here that sacred public speech differs radically and fundamentally from secular public speech. Secular public speech aims to move the will. Sacred public speech aims to move the will Godward. This is its vital function and distinguishing characteristic—persuasion to a divine life and to growth in that life, "unto the measure of the stature of the fullness of Christ" (Eph. 4 : 13).

True preaching is thus the truly divine art; for it ties to art this supreme exalted aim of transforming men into the divine image.

The speech of the pulpit that does not have this in view is not preaching. It may be learned in exegesis, critical in commentary, profound in philosophy, and richly historical, and so be instructive. It may have wealth of illustration and imagery and beauty of rhetorical form, and so be pleasing. But this is only

to be at the level of any other art or authorship,—
contributive of instruction or pleasure. It is not a true
gospel ministry, unless the vital function of persuasion
to divine life is in it as an end distinctly aimed at.

This is not disparaging instruction nor ignoring
emotion. It is only insisting on a certain use of instruction and emotion.

Preaching is teaching—it must give instruction, of
course. Truth must be unfolded. Mere hortatory address is beating the air. Of Christ who claimed to
be divinely anointed to preach the Gospel it is said in
Scripture, " He opened His mouth and taught." Alas,
some of His professed representatives in the pulpit
never get beyond the open mouth. But to teach is
vital. The point of emphasis now is the *kind*. It
must be oratorical teaching, looking beyond mere instruction. The *will!* The *will!* To be forevermore
reaching and moving the will, so that it shall be more
and more like the will of God—this is the end of all true
gospel ministry ; the function of every sermon.

Preaching must also give pleasure. It is an art—
the divinest of arts. It must be exhibitive of rhetorical and moral beauty. But the differentiating feature
of sermonic art is that it does not stop with pleasing
the æsthetic sense and kindling emotion. It looks on
beyond the emotion and, through that, strikes at
character. Not art for art's sake—to give pleasure ;
but art for the soul's sake—to give more likeness to
Christ. Not the mere art to win by, but to win to
godlike things.

So it is ; a true gospel ministry means, first and last
and always, perfect manhood in Christ Jesus—both
rescue work and constructive work, freeing men not

only from sin's penalty but from sin's power and sin's pollution until at last they are complete in Christ. And so it is, winning souls and building souls are alike and forever the work of every man who has the care of souls.

2. Mark now the Scriptural confirmations of this truth:

(*a*) The Scriptures expressly declare that this is what Christ gave Himself to the Church for—" that He might present it to Himself, a glorious Church, not having spot or wrinkle or any such thing " (Eph. 5 : 27). And the Scriptures expressly declare that this is what God calls men to the ministry for : " for the perfecting of the saints, unto the work of ministering, unto the building up of the body of Christ " (Eph. 4 : 11–12). The Westminster Confession of Faith embodies this biblical idea in its declaration that " to the Catholic visible Church Christ hath given the ministry for the gathering and perfecting of the saints in this life to the end of the world " (Confession, Ch. XXV : 3).

(*b*) And this is the exact meaning and scope of the great gospel commission (Matt. 28 : 19–20). There are just two things in that last command the official ambassadors of Christ are told to do. They are to go into all the world and " make disciples," and they are to " teach " these disciples " what Christ has commanded."

The first is rescuing men from spiritual death. The second is building them up in spiritual life. This is comprehensive of the entire work of the gospel ministry ; the sum and substance of the great gospel commission.

3. Of course, while this twofold work is being done,

many other things will be done—many glorious
things. Social conditions will be revolutionized;
governments will be made pure and peaceable; righteousness will increasingly prevail; ethical values will
have wider and wider recognition; clean homes and
clean streets and clean politics will come to be the
universal order; and the kingdom of heaven on earth
will at last witness in its completeness to "the manifold (the *variegated*) wisdom of God." Christ will
then see to the full of the travail of His soul—see it
in its complete and splendid realization—and be satisfied; and all creation will join in the anthem: "Glory
be to the Father and to the Son and to the Holy
Ghost." This will be the final and blessed consummation.

4. But meanwhile, and down to "the end of the
age," the God-appointed means to the attainment of
this mighty triumph is the *preaching of the Word*. And
this constitutes that double gospel ministry so often referred to in Holy Scripture—namely, the ministry of
reconciliation and the ministry of sanctification.
There is no other ministry for a man of God or a
Church of God.

As to the ministry of reconciliation or the work of
rescue: We are under the order of the great commission to "make disciples." We are bidden to go
out and "compel" men to come in. In the spirit of
our blessed Lord we are "to seek and save the lost."

As to the ministry of sanctification, or the work of
structure, Paul tells us it is proclaiming Christ;
"admonishing every man and teaching every man in
all wisdom, that we may present every man perfect in
Christ Jesus."

5. Mark now how the presence of this supreme aim in preaching makes two things impossible :

(*a*) It makes it impossible that a sermon should ever be prepared with only the sermon in view, for the end is not a new sermon but a new man, and the sermon is a means to that end. How has it been with the world's great orators ? Surely they did not have great orations in view, but living men and mighty issues, when they prepared their immortal speech. And Raphael was not intent on a magnificent picture, so much as on a lofty ideal, that should stir and uplift human hearts, when he painted the Sistine Madonna. Tempted and overborne of the devil must be the preacher who deliberately sets about to prepare sermons as such, with no reference to the work they are to do. He must beware of an idolatry of sermons—fine sermons, show sermons, great sermons. Sermons are tools.

(*b*) A second thing made impossible by the presence of this supreme aim in preaching is the thinking lightly of sermonic toil. Sermons are tools, indeed. Nevertheless, what work they do! And, therefore, what tools they ought to be! How exquisitely tempered and fashioned! How fitted to the needs and conditions of that pliant, and yet resistant, and sometimes defiant element upon which sermons are to do their work—the spirit of man! Unlike secular discourse, which aims at influencing for a particular measure—to secure a vote, a verdict, a present impression, or an elevation of taste or judgment—sacred discourse strikes at the very seat and soul of character. A new creature in Christ Jesus is its first and last and supreme intent. And this is Redemption's intent. And thus the sublime purpose of God's whole plan of salvation crowds itself into every true sermon. Tie that idea to sermon-making—have it distinctly associated with every effort of gospel ministry—let it be grasped all along the process of pulpit preparation—and a " fire in the bones," a passion for souls, is as sure of birth as day is when the sun comes forth out of his chamber.

III

THE IDEAL MINISTRY—ITS RULING SPIRIT: LOVE

SYLLABUS

Love in God gave birth to the wondrous plan. Love in Christ gave up everything to give us everything. Love in the Holy Spirit leads him to brood and strive even where He is grieved and resisted. Love is the whole law ; love is the gift of gifts.

Faith must work by love.

Truth must be spoken in love.

Eloquence is " sounding brass " without love.

Knowledge is " nothing " without love.

Self-sacrifice, even to the giving of one's body to be burned, is of no profit if love be absent.

" Truthing it in love " is the very heart of the gospel ministry. It is Jesus coming unto His own, when He knew His own would not receive Him. It is standing in Christ's stead, with Christ's spirit, beseeching men to be reconciled.

This love is a growth. We cannot resolve ourselves into it or get it by a spasm.

Association, meditation, contemplation—this is the secret.

III

THE IDEAL MINISTRY—ITS RULING SPIRIT : LOVE

IT is preeminently the spirit of love—an absorbing love for Christ and truth and men. Love gave birth to the plan of redemption, and love floods the whole scheme. God so loved the world that He gave His only begotten Son to die for it. Christ so loved the world that He gave up everything to give us everything. The Holy Spirit so loved the world that He came to stay in the midst of it pollution and here He broods and broods even where He is grieved and wounded and rejected. The whole law is in this: Thou shalt love the Lord thy God with all thy heart, and thou shalt love thy neighbour as thyself. Clearly, love is the commanding commandment. Love is the gift of gifts. Faith, Hope, Love, these three, but the greatest of these is love. An ideal gospel ministry— any real gospel ministry—is impossible without it. It is an atmosphere—pervasive, vital. The man who seeks to give this Gospel to dying men must have faith, but it is a faith which " worketh by love." He must speak God's truth, but he is to be always heard "speaking the truth in love." He must be profoundly in earnest, but his earnestness is to be by the constraining power of love. And his work of ministry will be true and Christlike as it is bathed with a supreme affection.

It is true of no other vocation as it is of this. A

37

lawyer can make a great legal plea without love.   It
is a matter of intellect, pure and simple.   What saith
the law ?   A physician may be a great practitioner
without love.   Keen, thorough, searching diagnosis of
diseases is not dependent on a state of heart.   Hear
Paul on this matter.   He was the apostle of brains,
scholarship, high culture.   He could mass arguments
and drive truth home by logical process, as could few
men of his own time or of any time.   Well, this
trained intellectual athlete takes the things that are
prized most among men—eloquence, knowledge and
self-sacrifice—and he says of eloquence :   "Though I
speak with the tongues of men and of angels and have
not *love*, I am become *sounding brass !* "   And he says
of knowledge :   "Though I know all mysteries and
all knowledge and have not love, I am nothing."   And
he says of self-sacrifice :   "Though I bestow all my
goods to feed the poor and give my body to be burned,
but have not love, it profiteth me *nothing* " (1 Cor. 13).

And this was no mere theory with this mighty man
of God.   He did not carry it about with him as a
patent, for occasional exhibition.   It dominated all his
thinking.   It coloured all his preaching.   It was the
secret of his power.   Many are accustomed to look
upon the apostle as intensely fond of the austerities of
rigid and relentless doctrine, and of choice the enthusiastic champion of the harder and severer side of
truth.   But while he was indeed a great reasoner, he
was also a great lover.   While he grappled with great
doctrines, he also got a deathless hold of men's hearts.
The truth is, no man of all the apostles felt more
deeply, loved more devotedly, gave himself to Christ
and His Church and souls with a greater passion of

affection than Paul. His love sometimes glows and burns in his epistles until everything else seems consumed in the fiery flood of it. Now it bursts forth in a very riot of tumultuous passion; now it calms itself in a deep of almost infinite tenderness. He warned men night and day, but he warned them with tears like his Master. He was swept out to men and into them, as by a passion for their welfare. He poured out such treasures of desire, such passionate longing, such deep, strong, tender, self-surrendering love as nowhere else has expression in human language, except from Him who "spake as never man spake." Whether he wrote to Ephesus, or Colosse, or Thessalonica, or Philippi, or Rome, it was all one way. His love, his yearning, tender, tearful love and sympathy, broke out everywhere.

You, young men in the ministry or on your way to the ministry, who are ambitious, and rightly ambitious, to be great scholars, great reasoners, great intellectual forces in the kingdom of God, here is your model— *Paul!* In logical force, in mental grasp, in sweep of reason and imagination, he had no equal in the apostolate, and has had scarcely an equal among men. But listen! To the Church in Thessalonica he writes: "Being affectionately desirous of you, we were well pleased to impart unto you, not the Gospel of God only, but also our own souls, because ye were become very dear to us," and "ye know how we dealt with each one of you as a father with his own children" (1 Thess. 2:8, 10). And to the Church at Corinth he writes: "I seek not yours but you. . . . And I will most gladly spend and be spent for your souls. If I love you more abundantly, am I loved the less?"

(2 Cor. 12 : 15).   Think of the tears this man shed, of
the prayers he poured out of his yearning heart—
prayers richer and deeper than his arguments—think
of his joy in being a fool for Christ's sake, of his willingness to be "all things to all men" that he might
win some.   Love and sympathy bent him to every
need of human nature.   Henry Ward Beecher thus
paraphrases Paul's noble avowal: " I know how to
fit myself to every sinuosity and rugosity of every
single disposition with which I have to deal.   You
cannot find me a man so deep or so high, so blunt or
so sharp, but I would take the shape of that man's disposition in order to come into sympathy with him, if
by so doing I could lift him to a higher and a nobler
plane of life."

"Truthing it in love"—this is the heart of gospel
ministry ; this is the ruling spirit in all true preaching
—the distinctive quality without which both messenger and message are as light without heat, as body
without soul.   It is the reaching out of the heart to
bless others, whether they be lovely or unlovely.   It
is Jesus coming unto His own, when He knew His
own would receive Him not ; pouring into the world's
heart the great and mighty passion of sympathizing
and suffering love, that He might glorify its baseness
and change its enmity to friendship.   It is standing in
Christ's stead, with Christ's spirit, to beseech men to
be reconciled.

Tempered by an affectionate tenderness, then, must
all preaching be, to reach and move men.   And this
rare, godlike quality is a growth.   Its dominance in
the soul must come by cultivation.   We cannot resolve ourselves into it.   We cannot get it by a *spasm.*

But it belongs to preaching as fragrance to the violet, as beauty to the rainbow, as guilelessness to Jesus. Cold and hard and repellent is a gospel ministry without it. God pity the students of His mysteries who go to their work with little or none of the glow of this love in their hearts. They can preach the hard things of revelation, the severest truths of God, with acceptance and power, with this ruling spirit in them, dominating their speech, glorifying their calling, and giving even to "the terrors of the Lord" a tearful pathos. But they will be as those who beat the air if they have it not.

Is it asked how the spirit of love may be deepened and developed until it completely possesses the preacher? Association, meditation, contemplation— this is the secret. Be often at Calvary. Stay near the cross. Look up into the face of the Crucified. If you would be moulded into the image of His divine passion—*bathed* in the spirit and power of His sacrifice—this is the way. Nothing will so stir and feed this divine and holy love and bring it to supremacy in the soul. " The immediate intuition of the great Atonement arms the preacher with a wonderful tenderness and power of entreaty. Other doctrines are powerful, but this carries him beyond himself, and fills him with a deathless affection for God and the soul of man." [1]

[1] Homiletics," Dr. W. G. T. Shedd, p. 255.

IV

THE IDEAL MINISTRY—ITS SUBJECT-MATTER: THE WORD OF GOD

SYLLABUS

What to preach, a more vital matter than when, or how, or by whom.

I. Three things, fairly considered, go far to settle this question of what the man of God is to talk about in his official ministry.

    (a) His position—a herald.

    (b) His commission—to preach the Gospel.

    (c) His aim—to make men like Christ.

II. Mark the vast variety of Holy Scripture.

III. Hence the folly of tampering with Holy Scripture:

    (a) By unduly spiritualizing Scripture.

    (b) By using Scripture by accommodation.

    (c) By resorting to shifts and twists to get an "up-to-date" message.

IV. From these promises four things follow:

    (a) What a text for a sermon should be:

        Never a pretext.

    (b) What fidelity to the text will secure:

        (1) The greatest variety

        (2) The best exegesis.

        (3) The most Scriptural instruction.

        (4) The most honour to the Spirit.

    (c) What selecting and announcing a text is doing:

        (1) It is virtually saying, "I bring you to-day the Word of God."

        (2) It is determining the leading of God's spirit.

        (3) It is selecting a remedy best adapted to the actual need.

    (d) What the minister needs in determining this varied Sabbath ministry.

    To choose texts wisely he must "walk with God."

IV

THE IDEAL MINISTRY—ITS SUBJECT-MATTER : THE WORD OF GOD

WHAT to preach is a more vital question than when, or why, or by whom. If the supreme aim of an ideal gospel ministry is perfect manhood in Christ Jesus, then the thing that will make that manhood is the thing to preach : When Jesus said to His disciples, "Ye shall know the truth, and the truth shall make you free," He did not mean the truth as it is in philosophy or science or the stars. When Jesus prayed, " Sanctify them by Thy truth," He did not mean any truth, for He added, " Thy word is truth." And "preach the Word," is the repeated and positive injunction of prophet and apostle and Jesus.

I. Three things, fairly considered, go far to settle this question of what the man of God is to talk about in his official ministry. They are : his office, his commission, his aim.

(*a*) The preacher's *office :* He is called in the Word of God a herald, a proclaimer, a public messenger. The herald does not create his message. He carries the message of the power that sends him forth. He is simply the medium by which the message is transmitted. He is to explain the message, to render its true meaning ; but it is utterly beyond his province to add to, or to take from, the message with which he has been entrusted. The preacher is God's herald. And as such he has God's message to deliver—neither more nor less. He is also called in Scripture an *ambassador*. An ambassador represents his government; has his instructions; knows his government's wishes. To go beyond them, means instant rebuke or recall. The preacher is an ambassador for Christ, his King, the King of kings. He is shut up to his instructions. What the Word of God authorizes him to preach, that he is to preach. Anything else is recreancy to a great trust.

(*b*) The preacher's *commission :* It is found in the last words of instruction given by Jesus to His disciples: " Go ye, make disciples of all nations, teaching them to observe all things *whatsoever I have commanded you*." And again : " Go ye into all the world and *preach the Gospel* to every creature."

That this is what all preachers for all time are to teach is evidenced by the added words of Christ: " Lo, I am with you alway, even unto the end of the world " (Matt. 28 : 20). So every man commissioned to preach has his instructions. He is to go everywhere, as those early commissioned heralds and ambassadors went, " holding forth the word of life." It was this that whole cities " came out to hear." It was this that " mightily grew " and " prevailed." It was this that " was not bound." It was this that was " living and active and sharper than any two-edged sword, piercing even to the dividing of soul and spirit " (Heb. 4 : 12). It was this that led men to cry out, " What shall we do to be saved ? " And it was this that answered that cry and gave them a Saviour.

As then, so ever since, and now and forevermore.

It is the Gospel alone that is the power of God unto salvation, to every one that believeth. And not the Gospel as a social cult, or an ethical value, or civic reform, but the Gospel as a salvation from sin and death, whose centre and soul is the Lord Jesus Christ, whose symbol is an uplifted cross, whose rectifications go to the very roots of character, and whose issues are everlasting. And this points straight to the third of the three things that go far to settle the question as to what the man of God is to talk about.

(c) The preacher's *aim* : It is, as we have already seen, the *Gospel's* aim—perfect manhood in Christ Jesus. He is to search for and find his man, and then build him up in Christ. Not all truth can do that. The truth of science, the truth of art, the truth of any social cult, might make a man learned, artistic, a paragon of polite breeding, but it could not take his sin away, or free him, by so much as one guilty stain, from sin's pollution, or loose him the slightest from sin's power, or lessen, by one day or hour, his sentence to sin's final and eternal doom.

The divine order is Preach the Word! Preach the Word! The subject-matter of all true gospel ministry is Holy Scripture : the Word of God.

II. Mark the *vast variety* of Holy Scripture. "Is not My word like fire, saith Jehovah, and like a hammer that breaketh the rock in pieces ? " (Jer. 23 : 29). It is "sharper than a two-edged sword, piercing even to the dividing of soul and spirit and quick to discern the thoughts and intents of the heart" (Heb. 4 : 12). It is a high tower, whereunto we may continually resort. It is a shield against the fiery darts of the adversary. It is a balm in Gilead, kept by the Good

Physician for sin-sick souls.   It is God's comfort to all
that mourn, "giving a garland for ashes, the oil of
joy for mourning, the garment of praise for the spirit
of heaviness " (Isa. 61 : 3).   What want is there it
cannot meet ?   What burden is there it cannot lighten,
or help to bear, or take away ?   What sin is there for
which it has not expiation and atonement ?   What
sorrow is there it cannot heal ?   How its doctrine of
God's fatherhood has brought the wandering prodigal
back to the Father's house !   How its doctrine of forgiveness has hushed feuds !   How its uplifted cross
has drawn men !   How its divine ὀργή thundered from
the pulpit, has arrested some persecuting Saul, breathing out threatenings and slaughter and led him to cry
for mercy !   How this sword of the Spirit, which is
the Word of God, has cut clean through many a
Pharisaic refuge of lies and shown the whited sepul-
chres to be full of dead men's bones and all unclean-
ness !   There is not a kind of man, or a state of heart,
or a twist of conscience, or a sophistry of reason, or a
pride of intellect, or a lust of the flesh, or a hell of
hate, or a rottenness of social condition to which the
subject-matter of Holy Scripture has not made successful appeal.

III.   Hence the folly of tampering with Holy
Scripture.   If this is the varied, diversified, many-
sided subject-matter of Holy Scripture, placed by
the Holy Spirit to the hand of every minister of
the Gospel—what possible justification can there be
for the mutilations, the twists, the perversions, the
accommodations of God's Word, and even the substi-
tutions for that Word, that, alas, are all too common
in pulpit discourse !   There has thus been generated a

liberty in the use of Holy Scripture that has degenerated into a lawless license.

(a) By unduly spiritualizing Scripture. From Jacob's crossing his arms over two of Joseph's children to bless them, has been drawn the subject: "There is no blessing but under the cross." Some spiritualizing is justifiable; God's Word warrants it. Some temporalities of the Old Testament are typical and prophetic of the spiritualities of the New Testament. Jesus Himself spiritualized ordinary events: "Behold, a sower went forth to sow." To go as far as the Scriptural record goes is well. But men have gone wildly beyond and spiritualized everything. Origen was wildly extravagant here; and he has had many imitators. Even Augustine was very often at fault. He is represented as spiritualizing the bread, the fish, and the egg which Christ supposes a child to ask of a father. "The bread," gravely says Augustine, "is charity; the fish is faith, which lives amidst the billows of temptation, without being broken or dissolved; the egg is hope, because though the egg is something, it is not yet the chicken."

But we need not go to the fathers for this absurd allegorizing. Swedenborg ran riot at this business. Fondness for novelty, the desire to appear original, the temptation to draw spiritual lessons from everything, have conspired to perpetuate this attempt to make God's Word mean what it does not mean.

(b) And the use of a text by accommodation is another way in which topics have found an unwarrantable place in the ministry of the Word. Even Dr. George Campbell, author of "Sacred Eloquence," took a lie of the devil—"Ye shall be as gods, knowing good and evil " —and from that text discussed the future glory of the Christian. The appearance of Jesus walking in the garden at the break of day on Easter morning has been used as a basis for discussing "the benefits of rising early and taking a walk before breakfast." And in my own knowledge, the words so full of pathos and tears—" And when He drew nigh He saw the city and wept over it"—were the text for a sermon on "the relative advantages of city and country life."

With such inexhaustible riches of subject-matter as are in the Word of God, what possible justification can there be for accredited heralds and ambassadors of Jesus Christ resorting to such shifts and twists of Holy Scripture to get an up-to-date message for the times! Vinet goes not one whit too far in saying : " No human book has in this way been so tortured and sported with as Holy Scripture." Indeed, such frivolities of imagination, such vain conceits, and freaks of foolish fancy, such utterly unwarranted liberties, would never have been tolerated in connection with any other book. Think of a company of lovers of Shakespeare sitting at the feet of a lecturer announced as an exponent of the text of this dramatic genius, and the lecturer taking such liberties with that text as ministers are known to take with the text of Holy Scripture! The Shakespearean exponent would either be hooted from the platform or be left to talk to vacant seats. Hear the weighty words of Austin Phelps, that prince of rhetors, who gave such glory to Andover: "One abuse invites another; one abuse justifies another; the principle of a slight abuse is the principle of an extreme abuse."[1] And here is Burton's

[1] Phelps! "Sacred Rhetoric," p. 109.

wise and witty word on textual fidelity : "How far
may we use texts and passages rhetorically rather than
exegetically ? Does the Bible like to be dragged in to
assist oratory in that way, even though it be sacred
oratory ? Is it sacred oratory, with these devices
scattered along through it ? And when you come to
preach from a text, may that text be made to do a
duty it never thought of till you got hold of it, and
had a present and particular good you wanted to accomplish by its teaching ? Of course anybody can
see that we must not stand up and squarely say,
'Dearly beloved, this text teaches so and so,' when it
does not. We may say : 'It suggests to me the following twelve heads,' and then go on to make our
whole discourse on those twelve heads. There is no
lying in that ; but how must that text feel all this
while ? Doubtless, it is flattered that an educated and
cultivated and religious man is so crammed with suggestions by its humble self. At the same time, must
not that text be mournfully remarking in its own mind,
now and then : 'But I have a meaning of my own (so
I always supposed) a God's meaning ; and on the whole
I should be pleased if you would make a thirteenth
head on that, and let me serve to that extent, as my
original self ; and not as a mere suggestor.' "[1]

IV. From these premises four things follow.

(a) What the text which is placed at the head of
a sermon should be. *Never a pretext*—but a true
word of Scripture, the surface of which is to be
pierced, the secrets of which are to be unlocked, the
thoughts of which are to be unfolded, and the lessons
of which are to be practically applied.

[1] Burton : "Yale Lectures," p. 339.

(*b*)   What this fidelity to the text will secure: Fidelity to the text will secure the greatest variety in preaching, the best exegesis, the most Scriptural instruction, the best honour to the Spirit, and, hence (the conditions being in all respects the same), the most success in winning and building souls.

(*c*)   What selecting and announcing a text is doing : Here are some of the things it is doing.   It is virtually saying to the people, " This is the Word of God I bring you to-day."   It is interpreting God's providential dealings with His people week by week.   It is determining the leadings of God's Spirit Sabbath by Sabbath. It is choosing the spiritual food best fitted to meet the present actual spiritual need of the flock of God.   It is selecting the remedy most perfectly adapted to the changing symptoms of the diseased and sin-sick souls committed to his charge.

(*d*)   What the preacher needs in determining this varied Sabbath ministry :   He needs care and prayer at this initial point in the work of the week.   He needs familiarity with Holy Scripture.   He needs knowledge of the people to whom he ministers, and sympathy with them.   He needs a spirit quick to catch every breath of the Divine Spirit, and to take instant note of the wise and gracious direction of that Spirit.   *To choose texts wisely one must walk with God.*

V

THE IDEAL MINISTRY—ITS PREEMINENT BUSINESS: PREACHING CHRIST

SYLLABUS

Introductory.—The Jews and the Greeks of Paul's day were types of two permanent classes, showing two distinct tendencies, to be met now as then, not by signs nor by wisdom, but by preaching Christ.

1. Our times in special need of a clear understanding of the meaning of the phrase, "Preaching Christ."

    (a) Christianity has so won its way that men are wearing its name without possessing its essential spirit.

    (b) Another spirit of the times voices itself in the cry, "Back to Christ." Give us less doctrine and more Christ—less Paul and more Jesus.

2. To preach Christ according to the Scriptures is to preach Him as *God and man, perfect in both natures, God manifest in the flesh, the supreme gift of divine love and the power unto salvation from sin and endless death, by atoning, expiatory sacrifice, through faith.*

    (a) Before all else, in preaching Christ, there must be a true conception of the *person* of Christ.

    > He is a man—a *perfect* man, knowing no sin. And He is God as well as man—God manifest in the flesh.

    (b) What brought Him here? Two things : a great love and a great purpose. He is therefore to be preached as the supreme gift of divine *love* and the power unto *salvation.*

    (c) But salvation from what? From sin and endless death. This must be preached if Christ is preached.

    (d) And to save how? By *atoning, expiatory sacrifice.* Salvation is by this road and by no other. Preaching a divine incarnation, for divine instruction and example and sympathy, *if it stop there*, is not apostolic preaching.

    (e) And to save through what instrumentality? Through *faith* alone.

V

THE IDEAL MINISTRY—ITS PREEMINENT BUSINESS: PREACHING CHRIST

WE have seen that an ideal gospel ministry must have for its subject-matter, "all Scripture." But while "every Scripture inspired of God is profitable for teaching, for reproof, for correction, for instruction which is in righteousness" (2 Tim. 3 : 16), is not some Scripture so fundamental to faith, so vital to spiritual life, as to demand first and chief place in any true gospel ministry? The inspired record of the early Christian Church gives us complete answer to this question. That record bulks large with one thing—*preaching Christ*. "Every day in the temple and at home, they ceased not to preach Jesus the Christ" (Acts 5 : 42). Philip went down to a city of Samaria and preached Christ (Acts 8 : 5). Saul was scarcely a convert when straightway he preached Jesus, that He is the Son of God (Acts 9 : 20). "We preach Christ crucified," Paul said to the Church at Corinth,—"Christ the power of God and the wisdom of God" (1 Cor. 1 : 23, 24). And as if that were not enough he added, "I determined not to know anything among you save Jesus Christ and Him crucified" (1 Cor. 2 : 2).

Clearly those early preachers made it their preeminent business to preach Christ. And the business of their day, is the business of our day. The times have changed, but the desperate needs of dying men

55

have not changed. The blessed truths of the Gospel
of the Son of God have not changed. The Jews and
the Greeks of Paul's day were types of permanent
classes of men. They showed two distinct tendencies
which have had manifestation ever since, leading to a
false, one-sided materialism, and a false, one-sided
rationalism. They are present to-day—active, bold,
aggressive in their demands. And to-day, as in apostolic times, these two tendencies are to be met, not by
signs nor by wisdom, but by *preaching Christ.*

1.   Our times in special need of a clear understanding of the meaning of the phrase "preaching Christ."

(*a*)   Christianity has so fought and won its way to
the world's recognition, that men are wearing its
name without possessing its essential spirit. There is
abroad an unmistakable desire on the part of men to
be counted as Christians. They hotly resent the
charge of "infidelity"; and the answering chargé of
"bigotry" rings through the air. Thomas Buckle,
Herbert Spencer, and lesser lights, with similar tendencies, have been classed as in the Christian ranks of
our age. Men who look upon the Bible as they look
upon Plato's Phædo or the Koran of Mohammed, do
not hesitate to call themselves Christians. Men who
boast of being members of no sect nevertheless claim
to be Christians. We hear those who are fond of declaring their faith in the absolute religion, indulging
in a style of negation concerning definite religious
truth that leaves no ground to stand on. They do not
worship the Bible nor yet Christ, they say. They do
not go to church. What of that ! The great thing is
to be a Christian. We have an absolute Christianity,
a broad church Christianity, a liberal Christianity, a

Christianity not willing to assert that Christianity is the only true religion ! Verily we need to reproduce and bring out boldly the sharp outlines of the old faith. Can a man believe anything, and yet preach Christ ?

Still another spirit of the times voices itself in the cry, " Back to Christ ! " " Give us less doctrine and more life ; less Paul and more Jesus ! " Surely, there is imperative need that we understand what it is to preach Christ. If an ideal ministry is to follow apostolic example and not know anything among men save Jesus Christ and Him crucified, these vague notions and this hazy indefiniteness as to what this phrase, " preaching Christ " means, must give way to exactness of thought and precision of speech. Let us grasp its scope, its true significance, its vital facts and truths. Let us weigh our words as those who are buying the truth. The very innermost substance and soul of the preacher's message are here.

2. To preach Christ according to the Scriptures is to preach Him as *God and man, perfect in both natures, God manifest in the flesh, the supreme gift of divine love, and the power unto salvation from sin and endless death, by atoning, expiatory sacrifice, through faith.*

(*a*) Before all else there must be a true conception and presentation of the *person* of Christ, if He is to be Scripturally preached.

He is in the Christian system, and the soul of it, as no personality ever was in a cause. " I am the Way ; " " I am the Truth ; " " I am the Life ; " " I am the Door ; " " I am the Light of the world ; " " I am the Resurrection and the Life." " Come to Me." " Believe in Me." " Follow Me." " No man cometh to the Father but by Me." It were easier to untwist all the beams of light and to get at and expunge one of the colours fixed there of God, than to get the person of Christ out of the Gospel.

But what kind of a person is He who is so inseparably connected with this Gospel that if you take Him out you take its heart out ?

He is a man—a tempted, tried, suffering man, touched with the feeling of human infirmity ; a real man of body, soul and spirit, of flesh and blood. Otherwise, He could not die, and so meet and conquer death. " Since the children are sharers in flesh and blood, He also Himself in like manner partook of the same " (Heb. 2 : 14).

He is a perfect man. If there is human flaw in the Man of Nazareth, He is just like other men, and the whole scheme fails. If He ever sinned, He needs a Saviour, and cannot be the sinner's Saviour. He claims for Himself freedom from sin : " I do always those things that are pleasing to the Father " (John 8 : 29). " The prince of the world cometh and hath nothing in Me " (John 14 : 30). He is tempted, but never yields to temptation. He bids men repent, but He never repents. He is the Lamb without blemish— the Just One, harmless, undefiled, separate from sinners.

But He is God as well as man : God manifest in the flesh—a divine incarnation. He claims equality with the Father. He asks men to trust Him as they trust God ; to honour Him as they honour God. He does not invite discipleship ; He commands it. He lays His hand upon all the dearest and most treasured loves of the human heart, and demands a superior love, saying : " He that loveth father or mother more

than Me is not worthy of Me." He claims divine pre-
rogatives. He accepts without rebuke the glowing
confession of Thomas, " My Lord and my God."

Clearly he who preaches the Scriptural historic
Christ must preach Him as a divine-human personality—God manifest in the flesh.

(*b*) But what was behind this strangely constituted
personality ? What led to this marvel of marvels—God
manifest in the flesh ? Two things—a motive and a
purpose. The motive was *love ;* the purpose was *salvation.* The love was for a lost world ; the salvation
is from sin and death.

Here then are two things more that must be
preached, if Christ is preached.

First, He must be preached as the supreme gift of
divine love for a lost world. The sufficient and
blessed warrant for this is that deep word of Scripture : "God so loved the world that He gave His
only begotten Son, that whosoever believeth on Him
should not perish, but have eternal life " (John 3 : 16).
"Jesus Christ tasted death for every man." We cannot preach Christ according to the Scriptures without
preaching Christ's " whosoever " invitation. We cannot preach Christ according to the Scriptures without
preaching the love of God as sufficient for, as adapted
to, and as taking every legal obstacle out of the way
of, every sinner of all the world, and as on these
grounds to be freely offered to every sinner of all the
world. If Christ is preached, this love of God will
have no limitation of race or caste or colour.

But a second thing must be preached, if Christ is
preached. Christ must be set forth as *the power unto
salvation from sin and endless death.*

If love was the motive of the marvellous manifestation—God manifest in the flesh—the *purpose* was *salvation*. The angel said to Joseph concerning the child that was to be born of Mary, "Thou shalt call His name Jesus, for He shall save His people from their sins." He was given to the world " that whosoever believeth in Him might not perish." His own great, solemn, assuring, authoritative word is : "I know Mine own and Mine own know Me, and I give unto them eternal life, and they shall never perish." Jesus Christ is a *Saviour*.

He did not come, therefore, simply or mainly, with a system of education or of reformation, but with a system of salvation. The gospel system of ethics is transcendently above any other ethical system, and to those who are in Christ it is an ideal rule of life. If, however, the Gospel is simply a scheme of morals to correct men's conduct then the divine incarnation was superfluous. But the Gospel is infinitely more than a code of ethics. It is a supernatural, rescuing force, not of the world nor of the ruin in the world ; but a power from without, from above. It is God moving in the midst of the ruin, come in the person of Christ to seek and save. And to save, not from misfortune so much, not from trouble, not from ignorance, not from sorrow, but from *sin*, the fountain and source of all these ills ; and from endless death as the penalty of sin. Sorrow is the badge of all the race, and Christians must wear it, like all the rest. But the Gospel sanctifies sorrow, gives the conquering spirit in sorrow, and makes joys flash from the very swing of it.

To preach Christ, therefore, is to preach Him as a

Saviour from sin—God manifest in the flesh is the power unto salvation from sin and endless death.

But to save how?   After what manner?   Through what instrumental agency?   On what ground? Where does the gospel record put the power of Christ to save?   The answer is clear and unmistakable. Holy Scripture does not leave this vital matter in even the least shadow of doubt.

Christ is a Saviour from sin and death *through His atoning, expiatory sacrifice*.   It is Christ as *crucified* that must be preached if He is to be preached according to the Scriptures.   The salvation is a salvation through suffering.   The redemption is a redemption by blood.

Preaching God manifest in the flesh as a divine teacher, with divine credentials, come to teach divine truth and to exhibit divine life : preaching that satisfies itself with presenting the divine assumption of humanity, for divine instruction and divine guidance and divine example and divine sympathy, *if it stop there*, is not apostolic preaching.

Eloquent laudation of the character and life of Christ will not suffice.   The added recognition of Him as a divine incarnation, leaves still a mutilated Gospel. Even the presentation of His *death*, as the sacrifice of *love in innocence*, and as an expression of suffering sympathy, is not enough.   The " moral " theory of the atonement is a truth of the atonement, but not the whole truth.   There must be recognition of Christ's death as an *expiation for sin*.

So, the sacrifice of the cross is not merely suffering in behalf of others.   Many a mother has suffered even unto death, in behalf of her wayward, sinning child.

Many a father has broken his heart over the cry, "Where is my wandering boy, to-night?" But no amount of a father's suffering or a mother's sorrow has ever taken away a child's *sin*. This is the difference between the sacrifice of Christ and all other sacrifice—and the difference is immense. Between the two a great gulf is fixed.

Just one thing more is involved in this preeminent business of preaching Christ; namely, that He be preached as the power of God unto salvation, only and solely "*through faith*." He that *believeth* shall be saved. The justifying righteousness of the Son of God must be so presented that it shall be apprehended by *faith*, as the first act of the sinner, antecedent to penitence and love. No right feelings can have birth in a sinner's heart, save as they are awakened by appropriate objects. A crucified Christ alone can waken penitence for sin and love for the Saviour. Faith alone can accept Christ as crucified—looking believingly to Him as the Lamb of God which taketh away the sin of the world. Faith is the root of love. We cannot love aright where we do not trust. And penitence is the tear in the eye of faith.

Christ must therefore be so preached that His *justifying righteousness* shall be offered to faith and accepted by faith—not offered to penitence; not to love. If the sinner wait for penitence and love he will wait in vain. Faith is the hand of the heart that reaches out and takes. Free justification without any antecedent whatever, save its acceptance by faith—this is the vital necessity in preaching Christ. He that *believeth* shall be saved. Trust is the entrance-gate to eternal life. Not prayers, nor tears, nor works; not self-denials; not walking miles on a Malabar coast with spikes in one's shoes, nor swinging with hooks in one's living flesh as the pagan heathen do; not giving up outward flagrant sins and going to church and contributing to good causes, as the Christian heathen do.

> "Just as I am without one plea,
>   But that Thy blood was shed for me,
>   And that Thou bidst me come to Thee,
>   O Lamb of God, I come."

This is "the way" that must be preached, if Christ is preached.

Let us again hear the sum of the whole matter: The preeminent business of an ideal ministry is preaching Christ as God and man, perfect in both natures, God manifest in the flesh, the supreme gift of divine love, and the power unto salvation from sin and endless death, by atoning, expiatory sacrifice, through faith.

If less than this, it is not in entire and absolute fidelity to Jesus Christ. If less than this, the truth may have been preached, but not the whole truth.

But is there not something that holds supreme place in this preeminent business of preaching Christ? Is there not *a central theme* so vital, so profound, so far-reaching, so transcendently important, as to have no rival in the claims it makes for conspicuity, emphasis, and indispensableness in God's plan of salvation for lost men? We must find our answer in Holy Scripture.

VI

THE IDEAL MINISTRY—ITS CENTRAL
THEME: CHRIST CRUCIFIED

SYLLABUS

1. In the preeminent business of preaching Christ there is a central theme, so vital and far-reaching as to have no rival in the claims it makes for conspicuity and emphasis in God's plan of salvation. That theme is *Christ crucified*.

    Throughout both the Old and New Testaments runs a crimson thread.

    (*a*) The first word of Messianic prophecy points to a suffering Redeemer, and the first word of the New Testament is "Behold the Lamb of God." And the song of the ransomed heavenly host is, "Redeemed by blood."

    (*b*) The *incarnation* was in order to crucifixion.

    (*c*) The *resurrection* points back to the crucifixion. Christ could not stay in the tomb and be a Saviour.

    (*d*) The *ascension* is another witness. Christ must not die again, if He would prove Himself Lord of life and death.

    (*e*) His ceaseless *intercession* has its sole warrant in His crucifixion.

2. By this sign the Church has conquered. Not by an ethical Christ, or a sociological Christ, or a civic-righteousness Christ, but by a *crucified Christ*.

    (*a*) It was this the early Christians lifted aloft after their Lord ascended to glory.

    (*b*) It was this that made the Reformation host invincible.

    (*c*) It has been this that has studded history with the mighty triumphs of redemption.

3. This is not only the indispensable condition of an ideal gospel ministry : it is the *crucial test of any* gospel ministry.

VI

THE IDEAL MINISTRY—ITS CENTRAL THEME: CHRIST CRUCIFIED

A CAREFUL reading of the Scripture makes it clear that there is a central theme, holding unrivalled place in the Word of God, and that this central theme is *Christ crucified*. It is upon this truth and fact that Holy Scripture puts the emphasis with singular and marvellous iteration. Prophet, apostle, and Jesus Himself point to the *sacrifice* as the central fact in the redemption scheme.

(*a*) The bloody sacrifices of the Jewish ritual were types and symbols of what should be at the end of the ages, when Christ should be manifested to put away sin by the sacrifice of Himself (Heb. 9 : 26). Isaiah tells us with pathos and tears of a coming Messiah as " a man of sorrows," " despised and rejected of men " : that it " pleased the Lord to bruise Him," to " make His soul an offering for sin," to " wound Him for our transgressions," and " bruise Him for our iniquities."

And this crimson thread that stretches through the Old Testament colours all the warp and woof of the New Testament.

(*b*) The first thing we hear from the lips of John the Baptist as he sees Jesus is this : " Behold the Lamb of God which taketh away the sin of the world." Paul tells us God set forth Christ Jesus to be a propitiation " by His blood "; and that we are "justified" "by His blood," and have "redemption through His blood." Peter assures us we are "redeemed with precious blood, even the blood of Christ." John speaks of the blood of Christ as cleansing us "from all sin." And what is the Lord's Supper but a sacrament wherein, as we eat the bread and drink the cup, we do "show the Lord's death till He come." Listen to Jesus Himself: "I, if I be lifted up, will draw all men unto Me." And the inspired writer adds: "This He said signifying by what *death* He should die." From Christ's own lips therefore we have the distinct avowal that it was by His death— not by His incarnation, nor by His doctrine, nor by His miraculous deeds, but by His *death*—that He was to have His redemptive power, and draw men to Him.

Look now into heaven with the vision of John of Patmos: "Who are these with white robes, and palms? These are they which came out of great tribulation, and have washed their robes and made them white *in the blood of the Lamb!*"

Catch the notes of the new song sounded out in heaven's hallelujahs: "Worthy art Thou, O Lamb of God, to receive blessing and power and glory and honour, for Thou wast slain, and didst purchase unto God with Thy blood men of every tribe and tongue and people and nation."

Go search the Scriptures, or God's book of Providence, or heaven itself for any other note of redemption, and you will not find it. Whom did the apostles constantly preach? Christ incarnate? Christ the great teacher? Christ the moralist? Nay, verily. Paul says, "We preach Christ crucified." And he

came to the Church at Corinth "determined not to
know anything else." To the materialistic Jews this
was a "stumbling block." To the rationalistic Greeks
it was "foolishness." They did not like it. And the
materialists and the rationalists do not like it now.
But to the saved then, and to the saved now, Christ
crucified is the "power of God and the wisdom of
God." "Far be it from me to glory," is Paul's
triumphant word, "far be it from me to glory, save in
the cross of our Lord Jesus Christ."

The cross, the blood, the death, the propitiation, the
sacrifice, the crucifixion—surely, it is upon this the
Word of God throws the tremendous emphasis.
Everywhere in these Scriptures the cross is lifted up.;
every page is splashed with the blood. Look where
we may, we find a sign-board pointing to Calvary and
the crucifixion. The four great facts in the gospel
record—the Incarnation, the Resurrection, the Ascension and the Intercession of Jesus Christ—that form
what may well be called the gospel quadrangle, have
as their centre an uplifted cross. They face that cross,
point to that cross, have no worth and no significance
apart from that cross. Take John's deep saying that
tells us of the incarnation : "In the beginning was
the Word . . . and the Word was God . . .
and the Word was made flesh." Why this marvellous
birth ? We are expressly told why. "Since the children are sharers in flesh and blood He also (Christ)
Himself in like manner partook of the same, that
through death He might bring to nought him that had
the power of death, that is the devil, and might deliver
all them who through fear of death were all their life-
time subject to bondage" (Heb. 2 : 14, 15). In other

words He was born that He might die. Incarnation
was in order to crucifixion.

Men, it is true, are saying differently. They are
making the incarnation and the life chief, and the
death incidental. They are magnifying the incarnation and minimizing the crucifixion.

Well, let us not abate the exceeding great glory of
God incarnate—God manifest in the flesh. It is the
wonder of the ages—an integral, essential part of the
divine and wondrous plan of redemption. It was a
stupendous act of divine condescension for God to
send "His own Son in the likeness of sinful flesh," as
the apostle puts it, but the condescension and humiliation are seen to go deeper far, when the apostle
adds that God sent His own Son in the likeness of sinful flesh as "*an offering for sin.*" This was the end,
of which the manifestation in the flesh was the means.
In other words, Christ partook of flesh and blood that
He might die, and, through death, bring the devil to
nought, and deliver the sinner.

There were other ends of the incarnation, beyond a
doubt. It hallows childhood. It tells mothers to
give over anxious thought about their dead babes.
Christ was a babe. Can He ever forget a mother's
love and kiss ? Did He not say, " Of such is the kingdom of heaven " ? The incarnation also hallows labour. " The son of a carpenter ! " What a world of
significance there is in that phrase ! How impossible
that true Christianity should have no sympathy for
the men that toil. The incarnation also gives " the
knowledge of the glory of God in the face of Jesus
Christ." It shows us a great High Priest, "touched
with the feeling of our infirmities." But all these ends

are secondary and subordinate. The chief, conspicuous, transcendent purpose of God manifest in the flesh was that through *death* redemption might come. "It behooved Him in all things to be made like unto His brethren, . . . to make propitiation for the sins of the people."

(c) The *resurrection* of Christ is another sign-board pointing to Christ crucified. As the incarnation looked forward to the crucifixion, so the resurrection looks backward to the crucifixion. Paul says, "It is Christ Jesus that died; yea, rather, that was raised from the dead." This makes it seem as if resurrection must come to pass, or crucifixion will be of no avail. And now that Christ has died, it certainly is an absolutely indispensable thing that He should rise again. For, if Christ be not risen, preaching is vain and faith is vain, and, reverently be it said, the cross is vain. *Jesus must not stay in the tomb !* The sepulchre must be emptied and emptied by Himself, in His own inherent power as Lord of life and death. Let us see why.

In the first place, Christ had committed Himself. He had said, "I am the resurrection and the life." He had said, "Destroy this temple"—meaning His body—"and in three days I will raise it up." He had also said, "No man taketh My life from Me. I have power to lay it down and I have power to take it again."

But there He is on the cross, in the hands of His enemies, after all His declarations of power. They are railing and jeering at Him. They are saying, "Let us see if no man can take the life of this impostor and blasphemer !" They are sneeringly re-

minding Him of what He had said: "Ha! Thou
that destroyest the temple and buildest it in three
days, save Thyself and come down from the cross,
that we may see and believe." He Himself cried out,
"My God! My God! Why hast Thou forsaken
Me?" Some other cries came from Him: "Father,
forgive them;" "Into Thy hands I commend My
spirit;" "It is finished." And He was dead. His
cause seemed lost. If ever on earth there was apparently utter failure, it was there at Calvary. They
took Him from the cross, dead. Suppose He had re-
mained there, dead; His body turning to corruption,
and nothing more heard of Him! Who would have
believed that He was Lord of life and death, if He
had died and turned to dust in the tomb like all the
rest of us? So He came forth from the grave in proof
of His divine mission. He was "declared to be the
Son of God with power by His resurrection from the
dead" (Rom. 1 : 4). The risen Christ points to the
crucified Christ, and says to all who belong to Him:
"I died that you might live; and, behold, I live that
you may never die."

But where is He now, this once born, and dead, and
risen Saviour? He is at the right hand of God. How
did He get there? Did He die again and go by
death's road? Never. That would have thrown
doubt on the resurrection. That would have made
the crucifixion an ordinary tragedy. That would have
left the incarnation a delusion or a dream.

(d) *Jesus Christ must not die again.* And He did
not. This is the way He went back to His Father's
house: One day "He led His disciples out until they
were over against Bethany, and He lifted up His hands

and blessed them. And it came to pass while He blessed them He parted from them; a cloud received Him out of their sight." He was taken up into heaven; and He "sat down on the right hand of the Majesty on high." How sweet and calm and simple and beautiful. Nothing spectacular. No parade. No gorgeous display. No retinue of angels. The glory was in the thing itself. It befitted the Lord of life and death. He had once been down in the valley of the shadow of death; He had entered its awful gloom. And having died, the just for the unjust, and made spoil of death and robbed the grave of victory, He must needs go home this conquering way. It was a way of power and victory. It hushed the jeers and ribald taunts of men who shouted at His cross, "He saved others; Himself He cannot save." And it cast a new glory on the crucifixion.

Mark the immediate effect upon His disciples. When Christ died they were disheartened. They knew not what to do. They "thought it had been He which should redeem Israel." And He was dead. They were filled with sorrow. Peter got back at his old trade, and went a fishing.

But when Christ ascended from Olivet, and they saw Him no more, were they sad and troubled? Did they have a shadow of doubt of His redeeming power? That ascension illumined the cross. It pointed to Calvary. It emphasized the crucifixion. Christ, "when He had offered *one sacrifice for sins forever*, sat down on the right hand of God (Heb. 10 : 12).

(*e*) And now for the last great fact in the redemptive scheme. Christ's intercession—which way does that point? The writer to the Hebrews says that Christ

" because He abideth forever hath His priesthood unchangeable. Wherefore also He is able to save to the
uttermost them that draw near unto God through
Him, seeing He ever liveth to make intercession for
them" (Heb. 7 : 24, 25). And the basis for this perpetual intercession is the *crucifixion*. " Once, at the
end of the ages, hath He been manifested to put away
sin by the sacrifice of Himself" (Heb. 9 : 26).

This is the ground of His plea before God. It is on
the basis of His crucifixion that He makes His intercession. "They are Mine," is the word of His heavenly
advocacy. "I bought them with My blood. I laid
down My life for them. I went into the blackness of
darkness of that crucifixion hour that I might save
them from the hour and power of darkness. Thou
didst covenant with Me, that if I should die they
might live. They are Mine ; and all things that are
Mine are Thine, and Thine are Mine. And I am glorified in them." If Christ had not died, and so pur-
chased redemption for His people, He would have no
case at heaven's court.

And so it is : Incarnation, Resurrection, Ascension,
and Intercession, all point to *crucifixion*. They all
join with John the Baptist saying, " Behold the Lamb
of God that taketh away the sin of the world."

Surely, surely, the central theme of an ideal gospel
ministry is *Christ crucified !*

2. And by this sign the Church has conquered:
Not by an ethical Christ or a sociological Christ, or a
civic-righteousness Christ, but by a crucified Christ.
The times of her aggressive spiritual force, when she has
multiplied her victories as the drops of the morning,
have been the times when she has lifted up the cross

and preached a crucified Saviour, and said to men—
burdened, troubled, weary, sin-sick—"Behold the
Lamb of God! Look and live! Believe and live!"

(*a*) It was so with those early Christians who saw
their Lord pass up to glory. When a cloud received
Him out of their sight they "returned to Jerusalem
with great joy," the Scripture record tells us. And
from Jerusalem they went to the ends of the earth,
"glorying in the cross," preaching "Christ crucified,"
who had entered into heaven itself now and forever
to appear before God in the behalf of those whom He
had "bought with a price."

Under the inspiration of this blessed belief they met
mad mobs, they faced wild beasts. When their bodies
were flung into the flames, they said to the quivering
flesh, "Be still, O flesh, and burn." And they died
with the prayer on their lips, "Lord Jesus, receive my
spirit." They went everywhere preaching Christ
crucified. They determined not to know anything
else among men. They gloried in nothing but the
cross (Gal. 6 : 14).

By and by, alas, the symbol of that cross came to
be substituted for the reality of it; penance took the
place of "the blood," the "crucified one" was hidden
beneath a mass of forms and rites and fasts and ceremonial observances. Jesus was crowded out by Jesus'
mother.

(*b*) Then the Protestant Reformation burst upon the
world. That moral and spiritual revolution was simply
a restoration of Christ to His supreme place in the ministry of the Word, as the crucified one. The doctrine
of justification by faith alone led the sinner straight to
Calvary ; and there, at the foot of the cross, he looked

up into the face of the crucified Christ and found a
Saviour.   And again the Church was mighty to the
pulling down of Satan's strongholds.

(c) So it has ever been. Call the roll of the men
of God who have cut wide swaths, who have been
conspicuous as winners and builders of souls—
Melanchthon, Knox, Luther, Edwards, Whitefield,
Spurgeon, Robertson, Finney, Maclaren, Hall, Moody
and a multitude more—and see whether the men
who have preached Christian ethics and Christian
socialism and Christian civics, and made these and
like topics central in their ministry, have been any
match, in spiritual power and spiritual victories for
the men whose central theme has ever and conspicuously been *Christ crucified!* Did a Gospel
of Christian socialism, or a Gospel of Christian
ethical precepts, or a Gospel of educational culture
ever turn any community upside down, or bring any
great multitude to Christ, or make any church a har-
vesting-place for souls? Never. They are impotency
itself, in the presence of the god of this world ruling
in an unregenerate heart. Are then a sociological
Christ and an ethical Christ and a civic righteousness
Christ of no value in the gospel ministry? Of absolutely no value whatever except as they are *adjuncts
to the crucifixion—fringes in the robe of Christ's
righteousness woven in the loom of suffering, side-
lights to that central sun that flung out from Calvary
its beams of light and life upon a world of darkness
and death.* Nothing but "Christ crucified" is "the
power of God and the wisdom of God. Is any *ideal*
gospel ministry possible without it? Is *any* gospel
ministry possible without it? Suppose every man

now at this preeminent business of preaching Christ
should challenge his own record as to the place given
in his ministry to "Christ crucified." If he should go,
in the light of God's word, and led by the Holy Spirit,
to a review of his past, what would he be likely to
find as distinctively and unchallengeably manifest in
his ministry of the Word; not impliedly manifest back
somewhere in the hidden depths of his own consciousness, but openly manifest to the sight of men?
Would it be that here is a man who intensely believes
"there is no other name under heaven given among
men whereby we must be saved" (Acts 4 : 12), and
who is determined not to know anything among men
save Jesus Christ and Him crucified (1 Cor. 2 : 2), and
who glories in nothing save in the cross of the Lord
Jesus Christ through which the world has been crucified unto Him and He unto the world? (Gal. 6 : 14).

3. Surely this is not only the indispensable condition of an ideal gospel ministry; it is *the crucial test
of* ANY *gospel ministry.*

But let us be swift to say, this is no narrow limitation of the gospel message. It is as high as heaven,
as deep as hell, as wide as the universe. The cross is
the radiant centre. Out from it stretch the radii.
However remote the circumference, lines drawn from
it anywhere verge towards the centre. The preacher
does not need and should not have any preaching to
the "times," or to the "occasion," that shuts out
Christ or hides His cross. The power of the ministry,
that shall meet the yearning and heart-hunger of men,
that shall uplift humanity and bring it back to God, is
not in rites and ceremonies, not in imposing ritualistic
forms, not in robed prelates and superfluous benedic-

tions, not even in organized agencies and wise plans and skillfully directed activities; nor is it in preaching to the day, nor in preaching science or philosophy— the power is not in any or all of these. Nor is the power so much in truths and doctrines; but in *the* truth and *the* doctrine. There is but one. All the wisdom, all the love, all the forgiveness and the tenderness and the patience and the pathos and the power of God are in that word—*Christ crucified*.

We may be sure this is not restricting preaching to any narrow field, nor compelling any monotonous repetition. This will be the apprehension only of him who has failed of comprehending the cross of Christ in its relation to God, and eternity, and the divine law, and the human soul, and duty, and destiny. "The maturest and ablest men in the Christian ministry will testify with tears of delight and thankfulness that the gracious mystery of redemption by the cross has ever more grown before the vision of their reverence and love until it has filled all things with its mournful, holy and infinite glory. They will testify further that the cross of Christ is the only key which can open the secrets of human history. Apart from that cross is confusion without hope, . . . a theology without religion, a temple without a God. . . . In holding up that cross over the whole field of human sin and want, the finest powers may be exercised and exhausted," evoking from men dead in sin, penitence, loyalty, service, devotion, sacrifice, and lifting them up to a life hid with Christ in God.

Moreover, to preach Christ is to preach all the perfections and glories of God Himself; for in Christ dwelt, and dwelleth, all the fullness of the Godhead bodily. The *glory* of God is seen nowhere else as in the face of Jesus, He being "the brightness of His glory and the express image of His person."

Power belongeth unto God, but in Christ is the exceeding greatness of His power manifesting itself not simply over inanimate material things, but over living souls—the highest and sublimest display of power.

Wisdom belongs to God. But to preach Christ is to preach God's wisdom in preeminence—His "manifold wisdom." For it is written, "Unto the principalities and the powers in heavenly places shall be made known through the Church the manifold wisdom of God according to the eternal purpose which He purposed in Christ Jesus."

God is glorious in *holiness ;* but His holiness finds its intensest and most transcendent expression at the cross. *Justice,* too, is God's essential attribute, but he who would set it forth to men must preach Christ crucified, in whom the inviolability of the justice of God has its chief expression.

But while Christ is the power, the wisdom, the glory, the justice, the truth of God, so that no preacher can dwell on these divine attributes without being led straight to Christ's cross for their climax and culmination, there are some divine attributes that cannot be known at all, with any clearness, away from Christ. The infinite pity, the boundless compassion, the matchless and exhaustless sympathy—nature is silent about these ; creation gives no sign. They can only be preached as Christ is preached.

To preach Christ to man as He is by nature, is to make profoundest exhibition of the illimitable need of man. Whence this august being, and why His tragic death, if man is not under a fearful condemnation! What balance is there for this power of an endless life with which Christ came, but this power of an endless death under which man is placed! Preach the law, and it is only man's schoolmaster to bring him to Christ. Preach duty, and it sends the sinner who cannot discharge it to Him who was obedient unto death for the sinner's sake.

And to preach Christ *to the believer* is to preach all the gifts and graces of godliness as they are of Him and in Him, who is made of God to every disciple wisdom and righteousness, and sanctification and redemption. Faith, love, joy, peace, humility, patience, gentleness, life itself, are all of *Him* as He is seen, appropriated, fed upon. Believers are complete in Him, built up in Him, transformed more and more into His likeness, as He is preached to them, and they behold His glory, and are changed into the same image from glory to glory. Endless are the sides and aspects in which He stands related to His people.

Preaching Christ, monotonous! Then infinite variety is monotonous. The preacher who thinks so should cry to God to open his eyes. For when the blind lead the blind, both shall fall into the ditch.

VII

THE IDEAL MINISTRY—ITS ETERNAL SANCTIONS: EVERLASTING LIFE AND DEATH

SYLLABUS

"Sanctions"—not in the ordinary sense of *approving*, but in the deeper sense of *enforcing authority*. No other speech of man save preaching has God behind it. No other is mighty with the power of endless life and death.

1. He who gave these sanctions their widest, deepest significance, is He who came to seek and to save.

2. His coming and the way of His coming are a proof of the limitless sweep of the two eternities.

3. He speaks with the same degree of positiveness of the one as of the other.

4. He makes the one as everlasting as the other.

5. But it was on the side of life and glory He loved most to dwell.

And He says with an infinite tenderness and pathos that the way we treat Him *makes the difference*—whether we become heirs of God to an inheritance incorruptible, or are paid the wages of sin, which is eternal death.

VII

THE IDEAL MINISTRY—ITS ETERNAL SANCTIONS : EVERLASTING LIFE AND DEATH

ANOTHER of the great and mighty ideas connected with the preaching of the Gospel, and that tends to uplift and glorify it as the ideal ministry, is the *eternal sanctions*. It will be understood that this word " sanctions," is not here used in the ordinary sense of *approving*, but in the deeper sense of *enforcing authority*. No other speech of men has God behind it. And no other speech of men is mighty with the power of endless life and death. Every other word and work is of man, and has to do with time. This is of God, and has to do with eternity, and goes far to decide it for every soul it touches. What other message is there that men dare carry on their lips to other men, and say to them, " This is a savour of everlasting life or of everlasting death to you ? If you believe the message you will be saved. If you do not believe it you will be lost."

1. First of all, let it be distinctly borne in mind that He who gave these sanctions their widest and deepest significance, is He *who came to seek and save*.

He did not come as a prosecuting attorney, representing government and law, to make out a case against us. But *seeing* the case against us, He came to provide a warrant and base for His unceasing and effectual advocacy in our behalf. He saw us " partakers of flesh and blood," and He came to be one of us, to assume our human nature, not to thunder accusations and send us on to perdition; but to die in our behalf, to destroy Him that had the power of death, and to deliver us who were otherwise doomed to eternal bondage. And it is this Lord Christ, Son of Mary and Son of God, come " in the likeness of sinful flesh," yet without sin, who speaks the most clearly and weightily and frequently of these eternal sanctions. From no other lips have they fallen so often and so unchallengeably. It is this lover of our souls, this seeker and Saviour of the lost, who tells us most plainly what it means to be lost. It is His parables of the Lost Sheep, and the Lost Coin, and the Lost Boy, and the Lost Rich Man that reveal with a vividness and intensity beyond the possibility of human language to surpass, not only heaven's deep concern for the lost, but *what a fearful thing it must be to be lost!*

2. Christ's coming and the way of His coming are a proof of the limitless sweep of the two eternities.

Why should He who came from God and went to God, and thought it not robbery to be equal with God, and who was the brightness of the Father's glory and the express image of His person—why should He walk that path of tears and blood until at last in utter anguish of soul the cry was wrung from Him, " My God! My God! Why hast Thou forsaken Me," if no great issues hung in the balance, and everlasting life and death are figments of the imagination! Why should Christ come " in the power of an endless life," if the power of an endless death is only a fancy or a dream. That anguish of Calvary must have some justification.

3. Christ spake with the same degree of positiveness of eternal death as He did of eternal life. His own representation of the final judgment is unmistakable: "These shall go away into eternal punishment, but the righteous into eternal life" (Matt. 25 : 46). To privileged Capernaum He said : "It shall be more tolerable for the land of Sodom in the day of judgment, than for thee." And beholding Jerusalem He wept over it, saying, "O Jerusalem, Jerusalem, which killeth the prophets, . . . how often would I have gathered thy children . . . and ye would not—henceforth your house is left unto you desolate." He said there would be at the last those applying for admission to heaven to whom He would say, "I never knew you ; " " Depart from Me ; " " The door is shut ; " "None of those which were bidden shall taste of My supper." If these are not finalities, then finality never found expression.

4. Christ represents the death and the life as alike everlasting. He applies to each the terms that mean " without end." Neither the words nor their setting indicate suspension of punishment, any more than suspension of reward. If the life continues right on, the death continues right on. If the life is spiritual, the death is spiritual. And spiritual death, here or hereafter, is not extinction of being, but of well being.

Moreover, the Gospel does not coin the punishment or make the sinner. Men are sinners. And there the punishment is. Hell therefore has not been built by the Gospel. There is a hell, Gospel or no Gospel. Does the headlight of the locomotive *make* the jaws of death into which the express train plunges because of a misplaced switch ? The danger is there and imminent.   And the headlight only tells the engineer he is swiftly approaching it.   Sometimes the telling is too late.   But the light of the cross flashed on the pathway of the sinner is never too late, if *heeded*. Heeding that light makes the difference.   What we do with Christ makes the difference—whether we become heirs of God to an incorruptible inheritance, or are paid the wages of sin, which is eternal death.

5.   But it was on the side of eternal life, its exaltations, its visions, its exceeding and eternal weight of glory, Christ loved most to dwell.   And here He put the infinite pathos.   In the parable of the talents we hear Him saying to each of the labourers who had gained *anything* by their talents, " Well done, good and faithful servant.   Thou hast been faithful over a few things, I will set thee over many things.   *Enter thou into the joy of thy Lord.*"   And the parable of the Pounds tells the same story : " Thy pound hath gained ten pounds ; *have thou authority over ten cities.*"   And in that marvellous picture of the last scene, painted with Christ's own pencil, hear Him saying to the righteous, " Ye blessed of My Father, inherit the kingdom prepared for you from the foundation of the world.   For I was hungry and athirst and in prison, and ye ministered unto Me."   And when they answer, Lord when saw we Thee hungry and athirst and sick and in prison ? The King shall answer, "*Inasmuch as ye did it unto one of these least, My brethren, ye did it unto Me.*"

What wonderful promotions ! What marvellous stimulants ! What awe-inspiring and restraining motives ! If everlasting life and death enforce anything, if the love of God and the wrath of God have any significance, if God is not playing with our hopes and fears, and if Calvary is indeed an infinite sacrifice instead of an ordinary death of an ordinary criminal, then there is nothing so deep and so high and so mighty as the Gospel's eternal sanctions. And preaching is weighty with the word of endless life and death.

"Who is sufficient for these things?" it may well be asked. Neither Paul, nor Apollos, nor Cephas, nor an angel from heaven alone, even though perfect manhood in Christ Jesus be the supreme aim of the ministry, and love its ruling spirit, and the Word of God its subject matter, and preaching Christ its preeminent business. There is still a *divine accompaniment, vital to spiritual power and victory.*

VIII

THE IDEAL MINISTRY—ITS COOPERATING AGENT: THE HOLY SPIRIT

SYLLABUS

Introduction.—In the prosecution of great worldly business enterprises, there is often a silent partner. In the business of winning souls and building them up in Christ, there is *always* a silent partner. "It is not by might nor by power, but by My Spirit, saith the Lord."

1. This silent but mighty cooperating Agent in preaching can never be seen, though He can always be consulted. His cooperation is through faith not sight.

2. His cooperation in the work of the ministry is assured by exceeding great and precious promises.

3. His specific cooperation in the construction and application of the sermon :

   (*a*) It marks the substantive difference between "preaching," and all eloquence born of the natural powers of man.

   (*b*) It is along the lines that are vital to spiritual power in the ministry.

   (1) In producing conviction of sin.

   (2) In begetting the new creature in Christ.

   (3) In exhibiting Christ for comfort, stimulus or rebuke.

   (4) In shedding abroad the love of God in the heart.

   (*c*) It starts with the selection of a theme or text, and continues throughout the entire construction and delivery of the sermon. Through the whole process the Holy Spirit may be, and should be, a cooperating agent.

VIII

THE IDEAL MINISTRY—ITS COOPERATING
AGENT: THE HOLY SPIRIT

IN the prosecution of great worldly business enterprises, there is often a silent partner. In the
business of winning souls and building them up
in Christ Jesus, there is *always* a silent partner. In
the worldly business, the silent partner is often the
most efficient. In the business of the kingdom of
God, the silent partner is *always* the most efficient.
Indeed there is no efficiency apart from Him. It is
"not by might, nor by power, but by My Spirit, saith
the Lord."

1. This silent mighty cooperating agent in preaching the Gospel, can never be seen, though He can always be consulted. He is never behind locked doors,
but we can never take Him by the hand. Communion with Him is always a blessed possibility: but
He will never say to a doubting soul, as Christ said to
doubting Thomas, "Reach hither thy finger." The
cooperation must be through faith, not sight.

In further confirmation, that the Spirit's cooperation is through faith, hear the Master's word to His
disciples while He was with them in the flesh: "It is
expedient for you that I go away. For if I go not
away, the Comforter will not come unto you. But if
I go, I will send Him unto you." Why expedient?
Clearly, His *body was in the way*. It *localized* the

91

kingdom, and the kingdom is by eminence a kingdom
of spirit, where locality is nothing, and life is everything. So it was better for the Spirit to come than
for Christ to stay. The touch of the hand is as
nothing to the sight of the soul.

2. The Holy Spirit's cooperation in the work of
the ministry is assured by exceeding great and
precious promises. "If I go," said Jesus to His
disciples, "I will send Him (the Holy Spirit) unto
you, and when He is come, He will convict the world
in respect of sin, of righteousness and of judgment.
. . . He shall guide you into all truth. . . .
He shall glorify Me for He shall take of Mine and declare it unto you (John 16 : 8, 13, 14). The Comforter
whom the Father will send in My name—He shall
teach you all things and bring to your remembrance
all that I said unto you" (John 15 : 26). "The love of
God is shed abroad in our hearts through the Holy
Spirit" (Rom. 5 : 5). "We know not how to pray as
we ought—but the Spirit helpeth our infirmity—maketh
intercession for the saints according to the will of
God" (Rom. 8 : 26, 27).

3. The Holy Spirit's specific cooperation in the
construction and application of the sermon.

Everything in the structure of a sermon may be
referable to human powers. But if it be genuine
spiritual discourse, it has come from natural powers
only as "enlightened, sustained and made adequate to
the result" by the Holy Spirit.

(a) This makes the substantive difference between
preaching and all eloquence born simply of the natural
powers of man. Even the commonest operations of
spiritual life, such as prayer or the reading of God's

Word, are profitable only as the Spirit has part in
them. We read the letter only, without Him to aid in
the reading; and prayer is empty and vain speech, unless He help our infirmities and teach us how to pray.
But this high and holy work of preaching, unfolding
divine truth, analyzing and developing Scripture texts
that are the very mind of God, "speaking as God's
mouth the infinite things of the Spirit,"—can it be
anything else than divine-human work? Take away
the cooperating agency of the Holy Spirit in the
analysis of the text, the preparation of the plan, and
the rhetorical construction and actual delivery of the
sermon, and what is it, what can it be, but simply
natural discourse—a *human* product, and not a *divine-*
human product? The mere use of the letter of God's
Word does not lift the discourse out of the natural
into the spiritual realm. It is only when He, the
Holy Spirit, preaches that we have true preaching.

(*b*) This cooperation of the Spirit is along the very
lines that are vital to spiritual power and victory in
the ministry of the Word.

(1) The preacher would produce *conviction of sin*
by his sermon. But this is the Spirit's specific and
exclusive office. He alone can do this initial thing in
the process of making a man a new creature in Christ
Jesus. So the preacher will seek the Spirit's guidance
in his choice of a tool suited to the specific need; and
His guidance also in the unfolding and application of
the truth.

(2) But suppose conviction is already wrought, and
the preacher is now after instant and absolute surrender—a new creature in Christ Jesus. "Except one
man be born he cannot see the kingdom of God."

But born *of whom?* The Holy Spirit! And straight to Him the preacher goes for His cooperation, in the preparation of the sermon that shall be adapted to bring to pass this great thing.

(3) But again; the object of the preacher may be to bring vividly to the sight and heart of a child of God some beauty or glory of Christ for his comfort or stimulus or tender rebuke. Here again the preacher comes upon a blessed office of the Spirit. It is the glory of the Spirit to glorify Christ. And so the preacher turns to the Spirit, and seeks His help in the making of the sermon that is designed to exhibit new beauty in Christ Jesus that we should desire Him.

(4) Or again, the preacher would magnify and make more potential in his people's hearts God's boundless love. And again he turns to the Holy Spirit for His special help in this blessed business; for he knows that " *the love of God* is shed abroad in our hearts *through the Holy Spirit.*"

(c) This cooperation of the Spirit in the preaching starts with the selection of a theme, or the choice of a text, and continues through the meditation on it, the elucidation of it, the construction of the discourse, and its actual delivery. It is not simply there, at the contact of the sermon with the hearer's heart in the public assembly that His aid is to be invoked and expected. Throughout the whole process He is a cooperating agent. Ignore this and we are left to naturalism in the most important department of ministerial toil. Let the preacher believe it, get thoroughly possessed with the conviction that in the entire ordering, as well as in the issues, of homiletic preparation for the pulpit the Spirit of God has a cooperating agency—that the mightiest agent in the universe is silently, constantly, lovingly working with him in all the process of the sermon, and in all the conduct of the public service, and what intensity of devotion will be given to it! A zeal, in temper with the Holy Spirit's zeal—which must be as Christ's was—will be the preacher's as he studies and analyzes and plans in the prosecution of his preparation for the Sabbath and the sanctuary.

THE SUMMARY

Let us now once more call the roll of this mighty succession that makes up the ideal ministry, and that stamps the proclamation of the Gospel as the transcendent work of this world. Preaching is its *permanent function;* bringing men to Christ and making them like Christ is its *supreme aim;* love is its *ruling spirit;* the Word of God is its *subject-matter;* preaching Christ is its *preeminent business;* Christ crucified is its *central theme;* everlasting life and death are its *eternal sanctions;* and the Holy Spirit is its *cooperating agent.*

THE SEARCHING INTERROGATIVES

Suppose now we change these affirmatives into interrogatives, and that they lie there on the study table of the man of God, and look up into his face for answer every week as he begins his work of sermonizing.

The first question that faces him is, What is my *permanent, paramount function in the pulpit?* It is preaching—first, and last and always—*preaching.* To this God has called me. I have been given a message, and I am to deliver that message; with every variety of style indeed, with every help of logic and illustration; but I am to deliver the message. Teaching is not preaching, unless it is *oratorical* teaching, aimed at the will. Instruction is not preaching, except as instruction means, first and last and always, *persuasion.* Exegesis is not preaching, though exegesis may be, and often should be, used in preaching. An exegesis, however learned and exhaustive and evangelical, is not a sermon, though it may contribute to the effectiveness of the sermon. Nor is commentary preaching. We may have whole pages and books of commentary, critically explaining the text, unfolding its meaning, freeing it from misconception, and yet have not one word of preaching. Exposition *and application;* enlightenment *and persuasion;* the intellect *and the heart;* the conscience *and the will*—these are the marriages that must take place in the purpose of the preacher, to constitute true preaching; and that must take place in the consciousness of the hearer to constitute effective preaching. " Is the sermon done ? " was the question asked of a hearer, as he stepped from the sanctuary. " No," was the answer, "it is only preached. It still remains to be done." The great thing in preaching is to get the sermon done, by getting it transmuted into character, and translated into life.

The second question supposed to look up at the preacher and to challenge answer, as he begins his weekly sermonic work, is this : *What is my supreme aim in this week's sermon ?* Is it to bring a sinner to Christ, or to make a Christian more Christlike ? It must be one or the other or both, to constitute true preaching. Distinctly is my sermon for next Sunday to be planned so as to secure, in some distinct and definite way, more perfect manhood in Christ ?

The third question facing the preacher, as he gets ready for next Sunday, is this : *Is love my ruling spirit* in the preparation of this sermon ? Love for God for whom I preach, love for the souls to whom I preach, love for Christ whom I preach, and love for the truth it is given me of God to preach ? How the mere ambition for literary fame, for eloquence of speech, for scholarly repute, for any kind of reputation whatever, born of this world, and time, would shrivel up and be consumed in the fire of this consuming love, if it were once and unchallengeably the ruling spirit of his ministry.

Another question that looks appealingly up from the study table into the preacher's face for answer, and that should have clear and unhesitating reply, is this : *Is my subject-matter the Word of God ?* Is it God's Word I preach to-day—a clear, unchallengeable, "Thus saith the Lord"? And it goes without saying that *the use of a Scripture text* is no answer to this question. For, as we have already seen, a text may be torn from its nexus, and made to mean what the Holy Spirit never intended it should mean, when He placed it in the Scriptures. The text of the sermon may be the very letter of God's Word, and yet the sermon preached therefrom may have no scriptural warrant whatever. How easy it is, in the interests of a good purpose, to twist the Word of God to suit that purpose. How every preacher should watch his soul, and cry to God to keep him from making his own will God's will.

Still another question that should have answer, in that first morning hour in the study: *Is preaching Christ my preeminent business?* Am I showing it in my weekly ministry? Does this sermon show it? Not that every sermon should specifically and technically preach Christ; but that a succession of sermons should show *trend*, and that all sermonic roads should lead to Christ.

And a question more vital if possible than all the others named, should look up in the preacher's face and get answer, viz., *Is the central theme of my ministry Christ crucified?* Is my preaching prevailingly pointing men to the Lamb of God which taketh away the sin of the world? The preacher knows. He can tell. If he has any doubt about it, his *record* will tell. Let him go back and see. Has the cross been often uplifted in his pulpit? Has he made it clear to his hearers, by every possible variety of representation, and by every pressure of argument and appeal, that there is none other name under heaven, given among men, whereby they can be saved?

Then there is the question as to the Gospel's *eternal sanctions;* the things that give authority to the message, and make preaching tremendous with the possibilities of everlasting life and death, as they are wrapped up in the Gospel's acceptance or rejection. Have these eternal sanctions any rightful place in the preaching bidden us of God? Did Christ make any room for them in the midst of His own marvellous, tender, solemn beseechings and warnings? Then we must make room for them in our preaching, or be recreant to truth and to Him. What place have we given them? Much place? Little place? *Any* place? No change of times or seasons, no feelings of love or pity or compassion, no conditions of refinement and culture can justify silence, where our blessed Lord has spoken—with divine and matchless tenderness indeed; with tears and a broken heart indeed; but He has spoken, and with a fidelity we must try to equal, if we would tell His whole story. We never can preach His *Gospel*, if we hide His *cross*. There is no heaven to the preacher who can be silent about hell! And the crucifixion was a butchery, if it is not a dreadful thing to be lost!

Blessed be God, there is another question looking up into the preacher's face, in the quiet of his study, as he begins his sermonic work. And he asks himself, *Who is with me in this mighty business?* And the answer comes from the Lord's own lips. He had told the disciples He was going away, and sorrow filled their hearts. And He said, I will not leave you comfortless. It is expedient for you that I go so that the Holy Spirit may come, and He will abide with *you forever*. And it will be His blessed business to "teach you all things," and to "bring to your remembrance all that I have said unto you." "He shall bear witness of Me." "He will convict the world in respect of sin, of righteousness and of judgment." "He shall guide you into all the truth." "He shall glorify Me."

And so the Holy Spirit is here. He is here to stay. He is the silent partner in this business of preaching. He is to take of the things of Christ and show them to us. All the riches of grace and glory in Christ inconceivable, He is to open to us. And our preaching is to be not by might, nor by power, but by the Holy Spirit: convincing of sin, convincing of righteousness, convincing of judgment, transforming men more and more into the divine image from glory to glory, until they are set before the presence of God's glory with exceeding joy. Should a sermon ever be prepared without the sermonizer's first asking and answering these questions? What is my aim in this sermon? What am I handling? What is my spirit? By what is my word enforced? Who is with me in the mighty business?

The ideal ministry indeed! How peerless its claims! How limitless its possibilities! How superb its permanent function! How lofty its aim! How godlike its spirit! What a Christ it preaches! What a cross it lifts up! What everlastingness it puts into its inescapable alternatives! And what a partnership with God it furnishes in the person and presence and power of the Holy Spirit!

These are the great and mighty ideas that are indissolubly connected with the work of preaching, that uplift and glorify the homiletic art, and that are fitted to arouse a lofty enthusiasm in its prosecution. What are mortal daubings on canvas when painting can be done with eternity for a background! What are Thorwaldsen's and Michael Angelo's chisellings in marble when sculptured souls, wrought into the very image of Christ, may be the immortal product of our toil! What is it to make poems and orations that shall kindle only natural emotions, when sermons may be made that shall put a new song in the mouth and a new joy in the hearts of redeemed millions—the song to be sung and the joy to be felt forever and ever!

PART TWO
RELATED IDEALS

IX
THE "CALL" TO THE MINISTRY

SYLLABUS

I. What is the "call" to the ministry?

    (a) It is of God ; not of man.

    (b) It is immediate ; not through a church or bishop.

    (c) It is internal ; the direct agency of the Holy Spirit on the heart.

    (d) It is effectual ; the called of God to the ministry get into the ministry.

  1. Argument from Scripture.

    (a) The call to the sacred office under Old Testament dispensation was God's exclusive prerogative.

    (b) Christ made it His exclusive prerogative while on earth.

    (c) In every recorded case the "call" was immediate, personal and effective.

    (d) The Church is to pray that He will continue to call.

    (e) Having ascended on high Christ answers this prayer, and continues to give the Church pastors and teachers.

    (f) The Scripture record, after Christ's ascension, shows that the "call" is now by the Holy Spirit, but still immediate, personal and effective.

  2. Argument from the nature of the case.

    (a) The supreme head of every government appoints the persons that represent it.

    (b) Difference between God's call to a spiritual office and His call to an ordinary occupation.

  3. Argument from the testimony of the Church.

    (a) Apostolic Church held that the "call" is by the Holy Spirit.

    (b) Church of Reformation so held.

    (c) Post-Reformation Churches characterized as evangelical have so held.

II. How is the "call" certified to the individual?

    (a) By the conviction that one ought to preach.

    (b) By the desire to preach.

    (c) By the possession of the natural qualifications—physical, intellectual and spiritual.

    (d) By the approving judgment of the Church.

IX

THE "CALL" TO THE MINISTRY

IS there a special call to the gospel ministry? How is this call certified to the individual? Very much more depends upon the answer to these questions than may at first appear. One's view of the ministry not only, but his fitness for it and his efficiency in it, will be largely determined by the view he takes of the call to the ministry, and of its proper authentication. If we hold that the divine call is through an infallible Church, whose voice is always and everywhere God's voice, then we have a ministry of priests whose authority consists in a certain sacred something that has come to them through the laying on of hands, and we are swung to the extreme of sacerdotal dogma. If we hold that the call is not, either in kind or degree, different from God's agency with reference to any other occupation, then we have a ministry that can be entered and left almost at will, and we are swung to the opposite extreme of license and the purest naturalism.

What is the call to the ministry? It is of God, immediate, internal, effectual.

It is of God, not of man—divine, not human.

It is *immediate*, not through a church or bishop.

It is *internal*, the direct agency of the Holy Spirit on the heart—not external, as in providential circumstances.

103

It is *effectual*. The called of God to the ministry get into the ministry.

1. ARGUMENT FROM THE SCRIPTURES

In proof of this special, divine call our appeal should be taken *first to the Scriptures*. Do they fairly warrant the view here taken ? To the law and the testimony.

It cannot be questioned that God exercised over the sacred offices of the Mosaic dispensation an exclusive proprietorship. He did not assign to the mass of His people their several occupations. But He did distinctly call and set apart certain persons to official spiritual service. It was " the word of the Lord " that came unto the prophets, and from Samuel to Malachi they spake as they were moved by the Holy Ghost. Aaron was named of God for the High Priesthood. And in Hebrews 5 : 14 it is expressly declared, " No man taketh this honour unto himself but he that is called of God as was Aaron."

When Christ was " made a High Priest forever," and " offered a sacrifice once for all," the sacrificing human priesthood was abolished. But the prophetic office, barring the predictive element, was perpetuated. While Christ abolished the priesthood, He established a ministry. He personally selected and called a certain number to follow Him. He gave them personal instruction, and charged them alone with certain spiritual and official functions. His final commission was twofold : they were to go into all the world and *make disciples*, and they were to *teach these disciples*. In other words, they were to bring men to Christ, and then to build them up in Christ (Matt. 28 : 19–20).

In proof that this evangelizing and teaching ministry
was not simply apostolic we have the promise added
to the charge: " Lo, I am with you alway, *even unto
the end of the world.*" To provide for the perpetua-
tion of this ministry, and in proof that the *agency of
the Lord is personal and vital in putting men into it,*
we have twice from Christ's lips this impressive command, " Pray ye the Lord of the harvest, that *He* will
send forth labourers into His harvest" (Matt. 9 : 38;
Luke 10 : 2). So this command not only lays permanent obligation on the Christian Church thus to pray,
but it just as truly indicates Christ's *exclusive prerogative* in sending men into the ministry. It is therefore
not lineal descent nor an infallible Church, but the
Lord Himself that designates who shall preach.

But how ? In what way ? Is His agency indirect
and providential ? Or immediate and spiritual ? The
Scriptural record after the ascension seems clearly to
indicate the latter.

The first point in proof is the call and appointment
of Matthias (Acts 1 : 15–26). One hundred and twenty
disciples were met together, and at the suggestion of
Peter they took the necessary steps to fill the place of
Judas. They selected the two men who probably alone
of that company possessed the requisite qualifications ;
i. e., men who had been with the disciples all the time
the Lord went in and out among them, and who could
thus witness to His life and death and resurrection.
They then prayed their ascended Lord that *He* would
show which of these two He had chosen. And giving
lots for them, the lot fell upon Matthias.

It is objected that this whole proceeding was without divine sanction, and simply another proof of

Peter's forwardness. In support of this objection it is said that the Holy Ghost was not yet given, that Matthias was never afterwards mentioned, that it excludes Paul from the number of the twelve. To this it may be replied : (1) The Holy Ghost had been given (John 20 : 22), though not in the copious measure and miraculous way of Pentecost; (2) If Matthias is never again mentioned, neither are most of the other apostles; (3) Paul was never numbered with the twelve as Judas' successor, but was distinct in his office as the apostle to the Gentiles.

In proof of direct divine sanction, we have (1) The fact that the record is spread out in the inspired narrative with great fullness of detail and without a hint or suggestion of disapproval. Is it at all likely that an *unauthorized* proceeding would here and thus be recorded? (2) After the death of Judas and until this choice of Matthias the apostles are called " the eleven " (Matt. 28 : 16; Mark 16 : 14; Luke 24 : 9, 33); after this choice, and before Saul's conversion, they are called "the twelve " (Acts 2 : 14; 6 : 2). (3) The inspired record expressly says of Matthias, " He was numbered with the twelve apostles." This, of itself, fixes Matthias' place, and so stamps his call as of God.

Paul also was directly called of God. Over and over he states this fact : that he is an apostle by the commandment of God (1 Tim. 1 : 1), by the will of God (2 Cor. 1 : 1), that Jesus Christ put him into the ministry (1 Tim. 1 : 12), that he received his ministry of the Lord Jesus (Acts 20 : 24). The Holy Ghost said (Acts 13 : 2), " Separate Me Barnabas and Saul for the work whereunto I have called them."

This was at Antioch where Paul was publicly ordained along with Barnabas as a missionary to the
heathen.

Furthermore we have this Scriptural statement that
when Christ ascended up on high, "*He* gave gifts
unto men," and "*He* gave some apostles, and some
prophets, and some evangelists, and some pastors and
teachers : for the perfecting of the saints ; for the
work of the ministry ; for the edifying of the body of
Christ" (Eph. 4 : 11, 12).

That this divine call is *effectual*, all these Scriptures
go to prove. They show not only that the Lord calls,
but that the call is specific and personal, always to
the individual, not general and to the mass. Hence, the
selection is proof of the divine wish and purpose, and
carries with it the idea of effectualness. Moreover,
every man called, of whom we have record in Scripture, was made *to obey the call*, though at first reluc-
tant and even opposed. Moses remonstrated until the
anger of the Lord gave an imperativeness to the call
that silenced his opposition. Jonah sought to flee the
divine call, and was landed in the belly of hell, till he
repented and gave the call heed. The record is of
obedience in every case. Whom God wanted to
preach His Word, He got to preach it.

We have, then, established by Scripture these
points : (*a*) That the call to sacred office, under the
Old Testament dispensation, was God's exclusive
prerogative. (*b*) That Christ made it equally His exclusive prerogative while on earth. (*c*) That in every
recorded case the call was immediate, personal and
effectual. (*d*) That the Church is to pray that He
will continue to call. (*e*) That having ascended on

high He answers this prayer and continues to give the Church pastors and teachers. (*f*) The Scripture record, after Christ's ascension, shows that the call is now by the Holy Spirit, but still immediate, personal and effective. The mode of the divine call has changed. The fact of the divine call remains. The call is no longer audible, for this is the dispensation of the Spirit. God, the Spirit, does not speak to the outward ear. His call is inner and silent, to the ear of the soul, but as immediate, personal and effectual as was Christ's when on earth.

Those who hold to the contrary must show some Scriptural authority for their belief. They should be able to point to some statement of the Word declaring a change in the divine method of getting a ministry.

2.   ARGUMENT FROM THE NATURE OF THE CASE

This argument is not used to *support* the Scriptural argument, but to show that the two are in perfect harmony. By a sound, enlightened judgment on the case, we are brought to the same conclusion, as we are by the Word of God.

The supreme head of every government appoints the persons that represent it. They are styled ministers, ambassadors, heralds. They stand in the name of the power appointing them; their business is not their own. They are called, chosen and sent. They never go merely of their own option. An ambassador without direct and sovereign appointment is an absurdity.

Now, the preacher of the Gospel is named an ambassador, a herald, a steward, a minister. But how can he be these without a commission, an appointment? And from whom but Christ, the head and king of the Church? Does not right reason demand that he who declares himself an *ambassador for Christ*, so that it is as if God spake by him and he were in his king's stead, must hold a commission consciously from his divine sovereign, or be guilty of blasphemous presumption!

In reply to this it may be said, Let it be granted that Christ calls men to the ministry to be His ambassadors: He also calls them to *other occupations*. God, in His providence, has a place and a work for every one of the subjects of His kingdom.

To this the sufficient answer is, There is a manifest difference between God's providential agency and His spiritual agency, and between ordinary occupation and a spiritual office. The spiritual office has been created by Christ, the work in it depends upon the immediate presence and power of the Holy Spirit, and the call to it is therefore manifestly different from the call to occupations that are solely of man. Furthermore, we do not pray that the Lord would send forth lawyers, physicians, merchants, mechanics. We are *commanded* to pray that He would send forth *ministers*. The supply for the former we know may be left to take care of itself. The supply for the latter cannot be so left. Yet why not, if God's agency is the same in either case? A spiritual call concerns itself with spiritual things. God, by His Spirit, calls to a spiritual office. A providential call concerns itself more immediately with temporal things. God, by His providence, calls to an ordinary occupation.

3.   ARGUMENT FROM THE TESTIMONY OF THE CHURCH

The voice of the Church is not necessarily and always the voice of God. But if the Church, in all her best ages and branches, has been agreed in holding the call to the ministry to be by the Holy Ghost, the fact does very greatly strengthen the conviction that this is the teaching of Scripture.

That the apostolic age so held is proved by Scripture. The form of a spiritual call to the ministry was maintained in the Church through the first centuries though the reality was ere long and often disregarded. This is clear from the forms of ordination used even after the development of a hierarchical theory of a priesthood. The words of the Greek Church were, " The divine grace which helpeth them that are weak and supplieth that which lacketh chose this godly deacon to be priest." " The Constitution of the Holy Apostles," a spurious work, whose date cannot be certainly fixed, but which doubtless appeared somewhere in the very early centuries, appointed this prayer for ordination, " Grant by Thy name, O God, who searchest the hearts, that this Thy servant whom Thou hast chosen to be a bishop," etc.

It early came to pass, as Chrysostom of the fourth century declares, that men were selected and advanced to the priestly dignity for causes which ought to have prevented them from passing over the pavements of the Church. Hence monasticism, the best life of the Church hidden in monasteries, through the corruption of the priesthood ; monks called by eminence religious ; the clergy called secular or worldly, not having taken upon themselves the vows of poverty. The *sacerdotal*

idea had become dominant, the sacraments, being
exaggerated and perverted, and the preaching and
teaching function almost wholly set aside. Growing
out of this was the invention of the mass, the doctrine
of transubstantiation, additional sacraments, priestly
absolution, the confessional.

   With the Reformation the true idea of a call to the
ministry was restored. We hear Luther, commenting
on Jer. 23 : 31, after this fashion : " Await God's call.
Meantime be satisfied. Yea, though thou wast wiser
than Solomon and Daniel, yet, unless thou art called,
avoid preaching as thou wouldest hell itself."   Calvin
held the same view.   The Reformers of the Church of
England, in arranging the formula for ordination,
compelled each candidate to express his belief that he
was " inwardly moved by the Holy Ghost " to take
upon himself the holy office.   And Bishop Burnet (last
of seventeenth century) writing of this says : " Our
Church must be construed to intend by this that it is
only Christ that sends, and that the bishops are only
His ministers to pronounce His mission."   Further, if
any candidate says, " ' I trust so,' that yet knows nothing of any such motion and can give no account of it,
he lies to the Holy Ghost, and makes his first approach
to the altar with a lie in his mouth, and that not to
men but to God."   If such a view of the call to the
ministry had been always cherished by the Church of
England, Leigh Richmond would never have been
obliged to utter the sad lament, " The national
Church groans and bleeds from the crown of its head
to the sole of its feet for the daily intrusion of unworthy men into its ministry."   The Wesleyan Reformation brought to prominence again the doctrine of a

personal divine call.   Whitefield held that any minister, before he undertakes to preach, should be able
to say, " The Spirit of the Lord is upon me, because
He hath anointed me to preach the Gospel."   The
Methodist Episcopal Church requires every man entering her ministry to say he is moved by the Holy
Ghost.   Vinet, of the French Protestant Church,
says :   " We must be called of God.   A call to a ministry which is exercised in the name of God, can
emanate only from Him. . . .   Whether external
or internal the call ought to be divine."   And the
Presbyterian churches, holding to the Westminster
Confession of Faith, all declare that the Word of
God is to be preached only by such as are duly " approved and called to that office" (*Larger Catechism*,
Ques. 158, with Scrip. proof).   It is thus seen that,
just as the Church has risen from impurities and cor-
ruptions in all her periods of restoration in all ages,
has she emphasized the idea of a spiritual call to the
ministry.

History thus shows that the Church holding faithfully to this doctrine has had the purest and god-
liest ministry ; that just as this idea has been lost
sight of has corruption crept in, leading either to the
extreme of sacerdotalism or to that of naturalism.

By this threefold argument, therefore,—by the
argument from Scripture, the argument from history,
and the argument from the nature of the case,—it is
made clear that he who enters the ministry should
have a divine commission behind him, as he is sent of
God ; a divine summons before him, as he is called of
God ; and a divine conviction within him, wrought of
God.   Ought any man to take upon himself the vows

of ordination who cannot reverently make the very
words of the Master his own, and by the grace of
God trustfully say, " The Spirit of the Lord is upon
me, because He hath anointed me to preach the Gospel " ?

The second great question now claims our attention.
If there is this special call of God to the ministry, *how
is this call certified to the individual ?*

The first element in the certification is *the conviction that one ought to preach the Gospel.*

This sense of duty or prevailing feeling of obligation
is vital.   And it is not simply negative—the absence
of any conviction of obligation to engage in some other
pursuit.   It is the grip of a " Thus saith the Lord."
At the outset, the conviction may not be very strong,
or deep, but it should come at last to amount to a " Woe
is me if I do not preach," seizing the mind with an imperiousness amounting to something like an inner compelling violence.   No man should dare be guilty of
stepping towards the Christian ministry whose mind
is a blank concerning this matter, so far as a sense of
obligation goes.   In any case, and for any occasion,
the conviction should be lodged more or less clearly
in the consciousness.   The direct and efficient *cause*
of the conviction is the Holy Ghost.   The occasions,
coincident with the conviction and leading to it, may
be various, as used by the Spirit.   Favouring circumstances, sense of adaptation, considerations of usefulness, providential indications—these may be *incidents*
and *attendants instrumental.*   But these are not the
call, nor are they the efficient *cause of the conviction.*
If they were, then every gifted young man in college
with scarcely an exception should feel himself called

to the ministry, and we should have no eminent Christian lawyers and statesmen and jurists. Why should not every Christian young man of good parts and powers be reasonably sure of greater usefulness in directly preaching the Gospel than in any other way, provided always he had the gifts? And the gifts that would make him a good lawyer are the very gifts needed for the ministry—viz., facility of speech, aptness to teach, discrimination and administration. It was not Paul's fitness, or taste, or circumstances, or any consideration of greater usefulness, that based his "Woe is me." It was *God's call*—I *must* preach.

A *second* element certifying to the divine call is the *desire* to preach the Gospel. This may antedate conviction, or it may follow. The desire may be present when there is great doubt as to fitness, or when circumstances may seem to hedge up the way. When it exists and *continues, without* any *conviction*, and the man enters the ministry with no profound feeling of duty, then it befits the candidate to consider whether the desire is not born of selfishness and the devil, instead of love to God. The man whose preference stands alone, without anything to bind him to his path but the inclination of his own heart, ought to ask himself if he is not treading on holy ground with sandalled feet.

Two questions, asked and answered, will *test* desire and go far to determine its genuineness and worth.

1. Is it a desire for the ministry itself? or for something in the ministry that suits the taste? The ministry furnishes splendid opportunity for the exercise of oratorical gifts. The ministry is favourable to the indulgence of a taste for literature. The min-

istry assures of social standing and of association with
the most intelligent and refined.   But these are things
in the ministry, incident to the ministry.   They are
not the ministry.   The ministry is the *divine business
of rescuing souls and building them up in Christ to
the glory of God.*   It is this that we should desire, to
have our desire any authentication of the divine call.

2.   Is the desire to preach to others unaccompanied
by any longings for personal holiness and nearness to
God?   If so, this of itself should cast serious doubt
upon the motive prompting it.   True desire for the
ministry will grow fervent as the spirit grows fervent.
And as the time draws near for the desire to be
realized the heart should be found hungering for
deeper spiritual experiences of divine grace, and leap-
ing to enter upon the ministry as these experiences
are had.

A third element certifying to the divine call is *the
possession of the natural physical and mental qualifications.*   Any serious defect of voice, unfitting for
effective public speaking, any serious bodily infirmity,
any looseness of mental machinery, constituting a
radical and incurable defect, should be evidence that
the following of some other pursuit would be more
likely to honour God and to be in the line of His
purpose.

A *fourth* element, certifying to the divine call, is
the *approving judgment of the Church.*   This publicly
corroborates and authenticates individual conviction.
It is certainly an element of considerable importance
in defining and settling one's duty.   For the personal
judgment may be blind and partial.   There may be a
sense of conviction and an honest, earnest desire, along

with real unfitness, because of mental defect or idio-
syncrasy. And this defect may not be patent to the
candidate, though very plain to others. Duty in such
case is imperative. The Church should deal kindly
but frankly with the candidate, and make known the
adverse judgment.

This adverse judgment should suggest *a doubt of fitness*, beyond all question; and lead to a careful *reexam-
ination of the grounds of the conviction that one ought
to preach, and of the motives prompting* the desire to
preach. If the conviction remains and the desire too,
then the candidate may go on, in spite of even the
judgment of his best friends. If the *ought* in his
bosom take on an imperiousness, and be of God, the
man will get into the ministry and God will vindicate
his right to be there by the power he shall wield with
God and man.

The bearing of this discussion of "the call" to the
gospel ministry, on ministerial character and efficiency,
is at once apparent. Thoroughly possess a man with
the conviction that he has been summoned to preach
the Gospel by a direct divine agency, moved by the
Holy Ghost to take upon himself the office of a bishop,
and it cannot fail of spiritualizing all his activities and
uplifting his whole life. If he feels that *God* has
called him into the ministry in a way in which men
are called to no other pursuit, then at once and forever it is to him a peculiarly sacred, a divine work,
not to be undertaken and prosecuted, save with an
active and absolute consecration, and to be secularized
or made subservient to selfish interests or ambitions
at the peril of his soul.

But if he is where he is, prompted by considerations

of ease, or literary indulgence or oratorical ambition,
or social possibilities; or if he is where he is, the mere
child of circumstances, drifted into the ministry without any profound conviction or burning desire to
glorify God in holding up to dying men a crucified
Christ, and in beseeching them, with a great yearning,
enfolding tenderness and love, to be reconciled to
God—O the pity of it all! And the shame! And
the sin! He may still preach in a perfunctory, mechanical way, the letter of the Gospel. But his real
nature will surely find a voice. And inevitably from
one and another of his hearers will come the words,
"What you are speaks so loud that I cannot hear
what you say." And what patience, what courage,
what steadfastness, what power must be born of the
conviction of being *called of God!* He who can say,
"Lord, I heard Thy call. It was Thou that didst
send me"—what can he fear to do or dare or suffer![1]

[1] See "Yale Lectures," by Burton, on "resounding" and "unre-
sounding" calls, p. 33.

X

THE STUDENT IN THE MINISTRY

SYLLABUS

Introductory.—Spirituality is the vital trait of ministerial character, but truth is for the *mind*. Ministers are to handle this truth ; to be apt to teach.

1. The basic elements for an ideal student in the ministry.
2. The quality of intellectual character.
    (*a*) Profundity rather than brilliancy.
    (*b*) Intensity rather than versatility.
3. Certain powers of mind will mark the ideal student.
    (*a*) He will be receptive.
    (*b*) He will be attentive.
    (*c*) He will be concentrative.
    (*d*) He will be assimilative.
    (*e*) He will be many-sided.
4. Certain habits of mind will mark the ideal student.
    (*a*) The habit of diligence.
    (*b*) The habit of thoroughness.
    (*c*) The habit of method.
5. Yet in all this he will not know one secret of the Almighty, unless *led in all his studies by the Holy Spirit.*

X

THE STUDENT IN THE MINISTRY

SPIRITUALITY is the vital trait of ministerial character, and should be conspicuously manifest in the whole realm of thought, feeling and life. Without it the biggest brain, the tenderest sensibility, and the intensest activity are as withes of tow in smiting sin or resisting the devil, or making Christ's kingdom come. No mere intellectual grasp of the things of God can give spiritual discernment or spiritual power.

But God's truth is for the *mind*. God's ministers are to handle this truth. They are " to *reason* of righteousness, temperance and judgment." They are to be "apt to teach," to be " thoroughly furnished," " handling the word of truth," and they are " to give diligence to present themselves approved unto God " in this business.

How then shall we characterize the ideal student in this gospel ministry ? Are there some definite things that we can take hold of and group together, and fix in our minds as distinctly of value in helping us to an ideal standard ?

1. The basic elements for an ideal student in the ministry. Let us say at the very outset that intellectual *eminence*, however desirable, is *not essential*. The ministry furnishes ample room for the most distinguished mental gifts, but they are not indispensable

to an ideal ministry. Given, however, *a mind to which truth can easily be made intelligible, a mind capable of improvement, a mind with nothing radically wanting in its working machinery, and a mind competent to make truth intelligible to others,* and we have the *basic elements* for an ideal student in the ministry of the Word. But defect at this point is radical defect, and the inevitable result would be pulpit impotency, except as God worked perpetual or frequent miracle. No young man thus handicapped should be allowed to enter the ministry, whatever his impressions of a " divine call."

2. As to the *quality* of intellectual character possessed by the ideal student in the ministry : (*a*) it should be *profound* rather than *brilliant.*

The brilliant gifts lie more at the surface. And the best qualities of mind—its truest, fullest capacity—cannot be developed by the cultivation of the measurably superficial. The minister should seek a mental development likely to ensure permanence of influence rather than present popular impression. He is to stand conspicuously before the same community for years—three, five, ten, twenty, thirty and possibly fifty years. What a record of fidelity ! And how impossible of realization except as he establishes himself as a power over others, not only by his godly walk and conversation, but by laying the foundations of his intellectual character *broad and deep !* Is not the lack of this one of the secrets of the frequent changes and disgraceful " short-stops " in the pastorate ?

While therefore the play of fancy, the sparkle of wit, the charm of vivacity, and all the ready and nimble mental parts and powers, are by no means to be ignored, the student's chief and distinguishing concern in an ideal ministry will be the development of the profounder parts of intellectual character that give depth and breadth.

(*b*) Another quality of intellectual character to be coveted and cultivated is *intensity* rather than *versatility*. A big receiving capacity that takes things in without doing much thinking about them, is incomparably inferior to a narrow æsophagus, admitting only what can be thoroughly digested. The ideal student will dare to be ignorant of some current popular knowledge, that the best things may be thoroughly mastered. Let the intellectual character be marked by choiceness and intensity, even at the expense of variety. Avoid the foible of omniscience!

And now having laid the foundations and issued the cautions, let us look at the ideal student, whether on his way to the ministry or in the ministry, whether at the door of college or seminary, or just entering upon, or in the full prosecution of, his life-work as a preacher of righteousness and servant of the most high God.

3. Certain powers of mind will mark the ideal student.

(*a*) He will be *receptive*.

Eagerness to know, thirst for knowledge, is his first and vital quality. He is open-eyed, open-minded, open-hearted, ready to be taught. All the avenues to his mind are unimpeded, inviting approach. No self-sufficiency, no "big-head." When a man is swollen with vanity, little else can find room. To be smitten with an immense conceit, is to be as impervious to ideas as a peacock is to the song of the lark. The bubble must somehow be pricked and the self-assurance abated.

An old Scotch clergyman of great learning and great common sense, had a young sprig in theology preach for him one Sabbath. The sermon was ambitious, soaring, inflated, blown full with oratorical wind; and when, after the sermon, the old Scotch minister rose to pray, he said: " O Lord, bless Thy young servant, and prick him with the Holy Ghost, and let the gas out." To be emptied is the road to fullness.

For national illustration of this truth see Japan. Some fifty years ago she determined to make room for whatever she could find among the nations that was better than she herself possessed. She flung wide her gates and nailed them open. She welcomed missionaries. Auburn Seminary sent missionary Verbeck through that open door. He, with others, was admitted to the counsels of the nations. He helped shape her new convictions and laws. To-day Japan is working out the best ideas of the leading civilizations, and is the surprise of the world.

Look at China by contrast. For centuries she was shut in by a conceit and self-sufficiency that mounted to heaven—stagnant, lethargic, unprogressive, her gates nailed shut.

But under Japan's inspiring example, even China is opening her eyes. Her great national wall of exclusion and prejudice is breaking down. She is becoming receptive to modern ideas. She is entering into the parliament of the world, and ere long she may be the foremost of powers in determining the currents of history.

As the nation, so the man. Not the least of the fruits of those social jubilees of mental victory which

we call our " World's Fairs," is the opportunity they
furnish for open, teachable minds. The man that
visits them, eager to know, is the man that leaves them
greatly enriched in stock. The ideal student anywhere is the receptive student.

(*b*)   The ideal student will be *attentive*.

He not only takes things in but knows them as they
enter. He is observant, detailed, definite, and therefore intelligent : not careless, hurried, superficial, and
therefore still ignorant. Whether the study be by
text-book, lecture, sermon, or original research, the
profit of it will be as the attention given to it.

If eye and mind are held to whatever is in hand ; if
the will commands eye and mind as its servants, and
compels them to be at their posts, wide awake, attent,
discerning—the unfailing result will be knowledge.
And not only knowledge, but self-mastery and power.
A student knows what he has seen or read or studied
who knows it after this fashion.

Charles Dickens says it is a truth holding equally
good of his own life, and of the life of every eminent
man he ever knew, that " the only safe, serviceable, certain, remunerative, attainable quality, in every study
and in every purpose, is the quality of attention."
"My own invention or imagination," he adds, " such
as it is, would never have served me as it has, but for
this commonplace, humble, patient, daily-labouring,
drudging attention." Here, in part at least, is the
secret of that power which made Charles Dickens so
remarkable as a delineator of character. Wherever
he went, this quality was at its post. It gave him
points of insight into character. It discovered little
idiosyncrasies. Where other men would see nothing

and go away empty, he would often see a wealth of things, and pass on laden with great spoil.

Why do some students know so much more than others ? Why are some students able to tell what they know so much more accurately than others ? Attention—lack of attention; that's the chief secret. There will be differences in native brain power, of course. But this "commonplace, humble, patient, daily-labouring attention," as Dickens calls it, accounts for the most of the contrast. And this is possible of attainment by every mind fit to be in the gospel ministry.

"But the lecture is dull." What of it ? "And the lecturer is uninteresting." What of it ? Attention ! That's the divine order. Say to the wandering mind, disposed to go wool-gathering, "See here ! Listen ! The business of this hour is to listen. That's your business. Do your business." It is wonderful what mastery this will at last give the student over his own faculties. But it is more wonderful what discoveries it will make of unguessed worth in the book or the subject or the man studied.

Professor Dwight of our college days stopped his lecture one day because he saw one of the class busy with a strange device on the blackboard by which the student sat ; and the professor made that incident the occasion of a talk on the value of attention. It impressed us profoundly. The next Sabbath some of us put the talk to the test. We applied it to the supposedly dull, prosy preacher down in the old stone church. We listened. We compelled ourselves to listen. It was a revelation. That preacher grew helpful, suggestive. And he became a formative force to us through the rest of our college life.

(*c*) The ideal student will be *concentrative.*

This quality is akin to the last ; but it means something more. It is *the faculty of using one's faculties,* focusing them, commanding their combined service for a specific result. It is also the *faculty of using one's materials*—massing these materials, having them at command through the law of association and relative suggestion, and arranging and ordering them in the interests of climax. It is that which gives *intensity* to thought and speech. Some men are walking libraries of digested information, but they do not know how to focus their learning. Some men have great vehemence of speech, but their vehemence has no solid backing to give it the concentrated essence of power. It is the concentration of materials, and the concentration of mental powers in the use of these materials, that give to speech intensity and that spell power and victory.

(*d*) But again: the ideal student will be *assimilative.*

The true student is not a passive receiver. Truths and facts are not taken into his mind as coffee into a bag. The coffee comes out of the bag just as it went in. And whether the coffee goes in or comes out, the bag remains the same old bag. But ideas with the ideal student are compared, studied, digested, assimilated, and so taken up into the chyle and blood and fibre of the mental and moral man. And the man is another, a richer, a more fruitful man for each day's study.

It is this kind of studying that has increased efficiency, widened capacity, multiplied agency. It has found " tongues in trees, books in the running brooks, sermons in stones." It has peopled seeming solitudes, and drawn nourishment from the arid breast of rocks. It is the kind of study that makes what a man studies his own. And out of the assimilating process is born that which blossoms at last into poem, or song, or picture, or law, or invention in art, or help to industry, or truth of reformation, or soul-searching sermon that finds the lost and brings him home to God.

(e) But again: the ideal student will be *many-sided*, seeking the development of every part of his nature.

The life-work to which a student for the ministry is looking forward, is many-sided, and he must be many-sided. The vast and varied need he is to face every Sabbath and study every week can only be met by a well-rounded man. Some of his flock will want the rigid steps of logic; some the airy flights of rhetoric; some will want imagery; some, plain matter of fact; some, simplicity; some, profundity; some, illustration; some, demonstration; some, poetry; some, history; some, the minutest details; some, only broad generalizations.

Therefore proportion, symmetry, balance, and not bulge, will mark the ideal student. He will aim to be well rounded. He will compel his dislikes to become likes, his prejudices to become preferences, if the dislikes and prejudices keep him from fields where he can get discipline or stock.

Hence an ideal student in the ministry *cannot be a specialist*. The very word suggests limitation, narrowness. It is contraction in order to concentration indeed; but contraction nevertheless. Of course specialists are desirable and useful—yes, absolutely indispensable. But they are not the best material for the Christian ministry. It is too wide and varied for a specialist. All humanity's needs are to be met by this ministry. The man of God is to be all things to all men that he may win some.

Can you by any possibility think of Jesus as a specialist? Is not the very idea incongruous? If you say, Jesus is outside human limitations, and not to be cited in this connection, take Paul, and judge if by any possibility he could have been a specialist, and at the same time have kept his many-sidedness and rare adaptability. He was always and everywhere anything to anybody that he might bring somebody to Jesus Christ. He could and did preach both to the Athenian philosophers and the rudest barbarians. His imagination was as lofty as his reason, and he used each with rare adaptation and power. His heart was as big as his head. His prayers were as mighty as his arguments. His love wrapped poor sinners about with an almost infinite tenderness; yet he was a very Jupiter in the searching and scorching vehemence of his righteous indignation. Think of his handing over the shepherding of the Ephesian flock and the care of their souls to some young parish assistant like Timothy, while he gave himself exclusively to thundering from his Ephesian pulpit! How impossible!

Hear his own strong, conclusive word on this matter: "To the Jews I became as a Jew, that I might gain Jews. . . . To the weak I became weak that I might gain the weak. I am become all things to all men that I may by all means save some" (1 Cor. 9 : 20-22).

Surely sub-division of labour may be carried too far.

Admit that pin-heads are a necessity. We can't well get on without them. But think of a man's giving his whole life to the making of pin-heads! Now we do not need to be told that there are makers of intellectual pin-heads, and that they sometimes get into the theological seminary and even into a professor's chair. But these are no patterns for men who have given themselves to the varied and manifold work of the ministry. No! The *ideal* student *in the ministry* will be full-orbed. The specialist may be a good, helpful and instructive preacher. He never can be an *ideal* preacher. The very exactions of his specialty make this impossible.

4. The ideal student will also be marked by certain *habits* of mind as distinguished from certain *powers* of mind.

(*a*) The habit of *diligence*.

This word, as the etymology denotes, means not only industry, but industry inspired and sustained by love. "The only secret of true industry in our work," says Trench, "is our love of that work." It is not the compelled service of a man constrained to duty by a sense of obligation or the lashes of conscience. And it is a far remove from the industry of the galley slave. Toil with delight, work with the heart in it, *cheery* industry ; this is diligence.

And this glad assiduity should be fixed and marked. It should begin in "the secret place," when one is alone with God. It should make its presence felt in the hours of study. It should accompany the preacher to the pulpit, and go with him out in the parish.

Indolence in the secret place of devotion is the death of effectual prayer. The men who have been mighty with God, used all diligence in the devotion of "the still hour." They toiled at their praying, and loved the toil.

Indolence in the study arrests mental growth, and leads finally to intellectual apathy if not atrophy. No amount of natural gift can be a substitute for persistent mental activity.

Indolence in the pulpit leads to easy, good-natured, lazy, perfunctory preaching. Indolence in the parish leads to a sauntering, superficial, social indulging, fitful pastoral visitation.

Genius is a good thing. But the habit of diligence is a far better thing. Spurts and bursts and spasmodic exhibition of natural brilliancy may temporarily dazzle, and may temporarily succeed; but the faithful, earnest and affectionate discharge of all duty will secure the most enduring results and bring most honour to God. A loitering, lazy minister is one of the saddest of anomalies; and his wasted hours and opportunities will make a terrible arraignment when accounts come to be settled.

(*b*) The habit of *thoroughness*, will also mark the ideal student.

The temptation is urgent and constant with the minister to spread his reading and study over a wide field, in view of its manifest desirableness and often its seeming necessity. But quantity at the expense of quality has little value in it. Better far less work with the fullest justice, than more work indifferently accomplished. A mill may be stopped by too much water as well as by not enough. To have a limited field and to be an authority in it, is better than to have a wide field and be an authority for nothing.

Thoroughness! *Throughness!* It will make a man stand before kings.

(*c*)   *Method* will also characterize the ideal student.

One can carry twice more weight when it is compact and well-arranged.   One can do twofold more work where method rules, than where disorder reigns.   It is *systematic* toil that has changed the face of the world. Months of precious time are wasted in precious minutes.   And a life without a plan will inevitably be crowded with wasted minutes.

One half hour saved each working day of the year, seems a comparative trifle rescued from loss.   And many a minister, heedless of these half hours, is wondering where his time goes, and is sighing for more.   But these half hours slipping from him every day, as if of small account, make up a total in ten years amounting to *five hours of study each day for one entire year*.   In other words, a *year* of study has been lost in ten years of daily wasted half-hours.

Method has a season for everything, and hence there is no loss of time by confusion.

Method prevents waste by indecision and hesitation as to what ought to be done next.

Method prevents waste by aimlessness.

Method makes every stroke tell, and go to the furtherance of some predetermined plan.

Yet method *should not be inflexible*. No plan of life, no distribution of time, no methodical arrangement of work should be so rigid as to dispense with judgment and make a man a machine.

> "The man that never breaks a rule
> Is little better than a fool."

5. And now let it be said with all possible emphasis that a student in the ministry may be all that has been named—receptive, attentive, concentrative, assimilative, many-sided—and he may have the habit of diligence and thoroughness and method ; and yet be totally unfit for conveying God's truth to dying men. There are secrets of truth he can never know unless he is taught, and led of the Holy Spirit. Filled of the Spirit, illuminated by the Spirit, he must be, or be a blind leader of the blind : the truths he daily faces and handles proving mere cold intellectual notions, gotten into his head ; and never, never the faintest approach to spiritual dynamics vitalizing his speech and life. He may have been glib in the recitation room, rattling off the letter of the doctrines of God ; he may have been the banner man of his class, and won a fellowship, and gone to Europe for post-graduate scholarly work ; and he may be now a perfect storehouse of Greek and Hebrew roots, and loaded to the full with the fruits of original research, and yet not know one secret of the Almighty, unless day by day he has found his way to God and prayed, " Open Thou mine eyes, that I may behold wondrous things out of Thy law," and has *gotten that prayer answered.*

The deep necessity, the everlasting condition, the crowning glory of the ideal student is this—that he be led in all his studies by the Holy Spirit.

XI

THE MINISTER'S STUDY

SYLLABUS

Introductory.—Local conditions may put limitations on choice; nevertheless common ground may be found for basis of judgment.

I. As to locality or place where.
    (*a*) The study should be easily accessible, yet free from ordinary intrusion.
    (*b*) Needs no outlook, but should have good exposure.

II. As to size.
    Thinking does not want much space; brain cells are not big, but they are roomy enough for the widest and deepest thinking. The very words we apply to "the study" such as "den," "workshop," "retreat," indicate its limitations.

III. The books in an ideal study.
    (*a*) Books that will open up the varied mines of truth are desirable.
    (*b*) Books that will help in seeking and finding the great spoil of Scripture are *indispensable*.

IV. Books that should grow in the ideal study.
    A scrap-book; a commonplace book; a text-book; a lecture-room-talk book; and a record book.

V. Buying books.
    (*a*) Buy first the essential helps in critical study, and the recognized standards.
    (*b*) Buy no book because it is cheap.
    (*c*) Buy no book merely on a publisher's notice.

VI. Reading books.
    (*a*) Read with pencil in hand; mark striking passages; make marginal notations.
    (*b*) "Abandon as early as possible the childish dream of reading everything."
    (*c*) Object of reading should determine manner of reading.

(1) For general drift, read rapidly; (2) For style, read carefully; (3) For suggestion, read thoughtfully; (4) For exact information, weigh every word; (5) For devotional purposes, yield to the current of religious emotion ; (6) For relaxation, read according to mood.

VII. Studying books.

    (*a*) Read first of all preface, table of contents, and introduction.

    (*b*) Be sure to understand the author as reading proceeds.

    (*c*) If author fails to convince the judgment, reader should pause and find out at what points he and author differ and *why*.

    (*d*) Compare author with other authors on same subject.

VIII. It is in the spiritual realm the ideal study comes to its crown and glory as the minister's "Mount of Vision."

IX. Value of revolving bookcase and hanging shelf.

XI

THE MINISTER'S STUDY

THE ideal student is naturally suggestive of the ideal study. But they do not necessarily go together. Conditions make strange bedfellows. Stress of finance, lack of room, parish adjustments put limitations on choice, and make absolute ideals sometimes impossible, even in so seemingly limited a matter as a ministerial workshop. And an ideal study for one man might be far from ideal for another man.[1]

Nevertheless, it must surely be possible to find common ground for a basis of judgment on this important matter, and where at least common agreement may be reached, as to much that shall go to make up an ideal study.

I. ITS LOCALITY.

The *place where* is a matter of no little importance. Shall it be in the church? or in the home? In determining locality two things are to be kept in view: that the study must be *easily accessible* and yet must

---

[1] "Dr. Storrs had three studies. His home study was a small room, with a few books, at the end of the parlour hall, in the quiet, red-brick house in Pierrepont Street, Brooklyn. In the Long Island Historical Society, of which he was founder, president, and constant inspiration, he had his private room up-stairs, with attendance upon his needs and with thousands of books at his hand. But the favourite study was in his beloved church in Remsen Street, in the rear, up one flight of broad steps, where the great trees shaded the windows softly. There he would be nearly every day, reading, thinking, deep in study."

be *free from ordinary intrusion*. Emergent occasions
will, now and then, and sometimes frequently, arise
in the parish, making an immediate interview with
the pastor almost a necessity. If he is perched in a
steeple-loft or tower, with the door below locked, he
may miss meeting a real necessity or a golden opportunity. Moreover, a study outside of, and at a
distance from, the home, necessitates many incon-
veniences to the home and the family. On the whole,
the preponderance of reasons seems in favour of the
home, as the place for the ideal study.

But while thus easily accessible, it should be absolutely free from ordinary intrusion. Never should
it be an open family highway. And never a place for
a romp of the children, except by special appointment
or permission. For some holy intimacies, in connection with the child-life, it should be kept especially
sacred. It would grow hallowed in memory, and unspeakably precious, in the progress of years, if known
as the place for the family altar.

As to an *outlook*, it needs none. It is the room of
all others for *inlook*. It is a *study*. And what does
a study want of scenery, whether of mountain or
river, landscape or sea? Intellectual and spiritual
insight, the man of God is there for. Vision—vision
of God and of God's truth. He enters his study to
delve in books, to commune with the great minds of
the past and the present, and to look long and lovingly
into the glass of the Word to discover some new revelation of his Lord there. He is not after flowers and
fields, and stretches of beautiful landscape. His face
is heavenward, Godward. He would see "the King
in His beauty."

But the ideal study will have a good *exposure*, that two things may get into it which are absolutely vital to its ideality; viz., *sunshine* and *pure air*. Let it be flooded some time in the day, whether morning or evening, with God's blessed sunbeams, and let it be flooded all the day with God's pure air. A gloomy study is not conducive to a hopeful spirit. And a close atmosphere is the occasion of many a dyspeptic sermon.

II. The Size of the Ideal Study

The very word, "study," suggests retirement, quiet, concentration, absorption. Thinking does not want much space. The immense sweeps of thought do not feel the confinement of four walls. Brain cells are not big, but they are roomy enough for the highest, widest, deepest thinking. The very terms we apply to "the study" suggest this same idea. It is the minister's "den"—his "workshop"—his "retreat." Think of a "den" taking up the biggest space of any room in the house. Think of a "workshop" with auditorium proportions. Think of a minister's "retreating" to a great council chamber. But does not a growing library demand more and more room? Certainly. But not by expanding the "study." Let the books find more shelf-room out in the adjacent hall, in the reception room, anywhere for convenient use. A great *library* needs large spaces, and must have them. An ideal *study* is a *den*.

III. The Books in an Ideal Study

A study is nothing worth without *books*. Every minister of the Gospel expects, in the course of time, to surround himself with books. And he purposes, by the grace of God, to grow more and more familiar with the Book of books. Every minister should therefore have a study that will help him to be something of a bibliographer, and *very much of a biblicist.*

To be a bibliographer, versed in the general knowledge of books, is well. To be a biblicist, versed in the knowledge of the Book of books, is indispensable. To delve in the various mines of truth is desirable. To seek and find the great spoil of Scripture is vital. Therefore, while seeking to be a scholar, the preacher should be, by eminence, a biblical scholar. In this department, his knowledge of books should be exceptional. He should make it a specialty. It is the *sine qua non* of an ideal ministry. Weakness here, is weakness at the foundation. Ignorance here, is inexcusable folly. The Bible is not only the preacher's daily manual of devotion, but his great and only book of subjects; his authoritative letter of instructions ; his one exclusive treasury of spiritual truths. Everything that can throw light on this should be at his command. Necessity may compel him to let other departments go. But for neglect of this department, there can be no necessity.

First of all, therefore, the books vital to an "ideal study" will be critical apparatus, biblical helps, the literature that directly conduces to biblical learning— the books that tend to make the minister a devout, able, scholarly student and preacher of the mysteries of God. These should be known and, as far as possible, possessed by every minister of the Gospel.

After these, in importance, will be books of philosophy, history, science and art, of general literature, of poetry and fiction, of social and civic life, of commerce and industry, of labour and capital.

But all these, and all other acquisitions in the ideal study, will be for the one purpose of making the student a more effective preacher of God's Word. All culture will be subordinated to professional efficiency. The ideal student in the ideal study will sink the man of learning in the preacher. He will determine that no charms of secular erudition, no alluring paths of classical literature, no popular "ologies" or "isms," shall tempt him to their pursuit, if from them he may not, in some way, learn how better to declare God's truth to dying men; that if they cannot help him to that, they shall not have either his time or thought. And he will test all study by this question, Will it contribute to the efficiency of my ministry? He will arrest the reading or the investigation that absorbs his time, without correspondingly fitting him for his chosen work. He will resolutely put under foot all desire for the fame of secular authorship. In everything undertaken with books, he will keep the one sacred object in view—better preparation for the great, unspeakable work of preaching the Gospel and saving the lost. No pursuit of science, history or literature for its own sake; no reading of any book, no grappling with any social, civic, or religious problems, save for some good reason connected with his ministry.

IV. Books that should *grow* in the ideal study— a scrap-book, a commonplace book, a text-book, a lecture-room-talk book, and a record book. These five books cannot be found at the bookstore. No money can buy them. They are products of expe-

rience; records of work done and to be done; in a
sense, personal histories and prophecies. They cannot be made to order. They are growths. They are
blank-books when a minister begins with them. They
will become bank-books, before he is through with
them, with ever-increasing balance to his credit upon
which he can draw at will, if they have been kept
with any kind of discriminating care.

The scrap-book[1] should be the receptacle of every
chance newspaper article deemed for any reason
worth preserving. The article or paragraph should
be cut out as soon as read, and placed loosely in some
drawer or pigeonhole; otherwise, it is likely to be
forgotten or lost. The pasting may be deferred for
an accumulation of articles, and some leisure half-hour.

This book may be a sort of hodge-podge. But classification is better, even of scissorings—as for example: (1) Incidents; (2) Illustrations; (3) Statistical items—(*a*) Of crime; (*b*) Of charities; (*c*) Of
intemperance, etc.; (4) Scientific items; (5) Ecclesiastical items; (6) Poetry.

A great many things to point a moral, or to fortify
a possible position, or to give vividness to a desired
impression, may be laid away in a scrap-book. If he
who picks up a pin is sure to find some use for it, he
who seizes and lodges for safe-keeping a floating, but
significant, fact or figure, will be sure to find some use
for that.

If, in addition to the general scrap-book, a *personal*

---

[1] The *envelope system* may be thought a better scrap-preserver, and
it has its advantages. But for ease of reference and security of preservation the scrap-book is perhaps preferable. Either, if rightly used,
will do the business.

scrap-book[1] is kept, it will be found to be frequently and happily serviceable. Personal participations in public functions, discussions, controversial and otherwise, travels, vacationings, comments on public events, criticisms of one's self, public appearances, exchanges, etc.—all these, with *their dates*, will be of very considerable value in the coming years ; correcting many a memory, confirming many an impression, even sometimes settling what might otherwise have proved a very serious controversy ; and above all, perhaps, renewing some hallowed, tender associations that left their deep impress without perpetuating their details.

The commonplace book should be for the minister's own miscellaneous and fleeting thoughts, suggested by reading and observation, or the fruit of chance meditation. Many a good thought is " born to blush unseen," because it is neglected and forgotten almost with the hour of its birth. If it were given verbal dress, and put away in a commonplace book, it might not grow, but it would *keep*, and some day it would be of service. Into this book should also go the striking thoughts and terse sayings of others, heard in public speech or gotten from books only temporarily at one's command.

The text-book should be paged and indexed, and should have a classification of topics ; appropriate space being

[1] If the author may be permitted a personal note, he would say that he has five such personal scrap-books in possession, compiled chiefly by her who has shared all the duties and delights of his ministerial life, and that these personal scrap-books have been not only valuable helps to memory, where accuracy of statement was valuable, but illuminating in reminiscence, sacred in many an association, and profitable both for their commendation and rebuke.

assigned to each topic. Then, whenever in reading, hearing or meditating, a text of Scripture stirs the mind with fresh and special interest, it should immediately be transferred to the text-book under the appropriate topic, *together with whatever theme or thought or plans of treatment* have been suggested with it. In this way, varied and valuable materials will, in time, be gathered for future sermons.

The lecture-room-talk book. This should contain the salient points of every talk made in the mid-week service, or on miscellaneous occasions. Any talk of this kind worth making is worth preserving. It may be subsequently elaborated, and made the foundation and substance of a sermon. It would certainly prevent the often dangerous tendency of running in a groove, or harping on one string. The book might well have at least three divisions : mid-week prayer-meeting talks ; Sabbath-school talks ; miscellaneous talks.

The record book. This should be aside from the church records, and for the minister's own use and possession. It should contain a record of sermons by texts and topics, numbered in the order preached, a record of marriages performed, of baptisms, and, above all, a record of the names of those received into the church on profession of faith, as having been born to God under his ministry ; this last being one of the most sacred associations of life.

These are the books that should *grow* in every ideal study.

V. Buying Books

In *buying* books for the ideal study, no extended list can be authoritatively given. Tastes differ—fields differ. The *personal* equation is an important matter.

The *immediate* needs and the *permanent* needs are to be considered.

In general, it may be said the essential helps in critical study, and the recognized standards, are of the first importance. Books that bear directly upon the study of the Scriptures, and that make up the minister's critical apparatus and helps in exegesis, are the *sine qua non* of an ideal study.

No book is to be bought simply because it is cheap. A book for which is seen no special use, is dear at any price. Haste to have a large library makes lots of waste. You cannot get an ideal library *by the yard*. Standard books of reference should be bought as far and as fast as possible. They are always needed.

But a few books for which there is seen immediate need will be worth a thousandfold more to the preacher than many books hurriedly got together, and often under real financial stress, prompted by the foolish ambition of *starting* with a fine library. The ambition is born of parade and show. What are books to a man, if he does not get inside them?

The books of an ideal library, it may be further said, will not be bought *merely on a publisher's notice*, no matter with what flourish of trumpets heralded. This is by no means an implication that publishers are dishonest; but they are not always the best judges of their own wares.

The approving judgment of time is the best judgment. But this cannot always be waited for. Reliable book notices—scholarly, thorough, impartial— are a great help in book-buying. And some publishing houses, some periodicals, and some papers, both secular and religious, have an established reputation

in this department.   At least two such authorities in
book-reviewing should be subscribed for, and will have
warm welcome to every *ideal* study, and they will not
need to knock in order to get in.

Charles Wentworth Dilke, the founder of *The
Athenæum*, and an important influence in the development of modern English literature, once said, "A
library is nothing unless the owner be a living cata-
logue to it."   And, illustrative of this, is the story of
what his son's wife once wrote to him: "There are
all your old Juniuses, looking so smart you will not
know them; bound according to your own instructions; no two alike.   What a dandy you are without
knowing it! a real dandy at heart!"   To which he
answered, "Half-truth, half-error.   I am a dandy, but
quite conscious of it. . . .   You have drawn right
conclusions from wrong premises.   My Junius volumes
are bound, 'no two alike,' that I may know each one
at a glance.   But I admit I have a sort of social life
in my books.   They stand to me in degrees of rela-
tionship.   I feel to some of them as towards old
friends. . . .   I have a heartful acquaintance with
some of them. . . .   They were once weighed
against gold. . . .   Many and many a day have I
tramped the same streets to get a glimpse of the same
treasure, turned and returned, and at last with desperate resolution carried it off with triumph."   This
suggests a reported *mot* of Rufus Choate's, that "the
greatest pleasure in life is buying a book you cannot
afford."

VI. READING BOOKS

(*a*) In reading books, read with pencil in hand.
Mark striking passages.   If important, repeat the

reading. Make *marginal notations* that will readily strike the eye when the leaves are turned again. And pay all heed to the wise words of Broadus : (*b*) "Abandon as early as possible the childish dream of reading everything." [1]

(*c*) The *object*, in reading books, should determine the *manner* of reading. If reading for the general drift, read rapidly. If for style, read carefully, with an eye to the structure of the sentence as connected with the impression produced. If for suggestion, read thoughtfully, pausing to allow the mind play. If for exact information, weigh every word, stamping it upon the memory by a fixed and undivided attention. If for devotional purposes, drop all criticism and yield to the current of religious emotion. If for relaxation, read as the mood inclines ; only be sure to guard against an overdose. "Excessive recreation is destruction."

In the matter of *studying* books, certain things seem to deserve emphasis as connected with the ideal study.

Suppose a book is selected for special study : What steps shall be taken to secure thoroughness ? In any ideal study, will not these following points have place ?

(*a*) Read first of all and very carefully the preface, the table of contents and the introduction. These will give at once the reasons for the work, the plan of it, and the approach to it—three things that ought to be of real service in any proper understanding of a book worth studying.

(*b*) Let the student be sure he understands the author as he proceeds. He who bolts books as some

---

[1] "Preparation and Delivery of Sermons," Broadus, p. 124.

men bolt food will ruin mental digestion. And he who passes a point or a page of an author without knowing just what he means, will be likely to be in a fog, or something worse, through the entire remaining discussion. Pause, therefore, and review till the meaning is perfectly apprehended. Frederick W. Robertson so studied Plato, Aristotle, Thucydides, Butler, Jonathan Edwards, that he could say they had passed, like the iron atoms of the blood, into his mental constitution. He once wrote: "I have got a small, popular book on chemistry, which I am reading now, of one hundred and sixty pages. I have read little else for a fortnight: but then I could bear an examination on every law and principle it lays down."

A distinguished English barrister, Sir Edward Sugden, gave the following as the secret of his professional success: "I resolved, when beginning to read law, to make everything I acquired perfectly my own; and never to go to a second thing till I had entirely accomplished the first." Such a man never skims; never flits over the surface; thoroughly understands as he proceeds.

(c) If the author does not carry the student's judgment, let the student find out exactly at what point he and the author differ, and why. This will be likely to reveal either the author's fallacy, or his own.

(d) Compare the author studied with other authors on the same subject. Light from various sources cannot fail of illuminating the field of discussion. And this comparison of author with author will familiarize the reader with diverse and conflicting views, and lead to a broader and more comprehensive judgment.

But it is in the *spiritual* realm, in *the possibilities*

of *devotional uplift* and *spiritual vision and power,*
that the ideal study comes to its *crown and glory!*
It should be oftenest the minister's mount of vision,
his inner secret room, where he keeps tryst with his
Lord, his ford-Jabbok wrestling-place, his laboratory,
his holy of holies. Here he will meet God—here, or
nowhere. Here he will grow familiar with the sword
of the Spirit, that he may go out and use it to cleave
souls asunder. Here he is to commune with the great
minds of the past, so that, in the intellectual and spiritual fellowship thus furnished, he may be the more
enriched for his work. Here he is to get upliftings
and inspirations, sometimes making it seem as if he
were caught up to the third heaven. Here he is to
bring to God the great needs of his people—their
hungerings, battlings, defeats, heartaches, and personal
histories. Here he is to think for them, plan for them,
pray for them, with strong crying and tears, and
when away from all human presence, face to face with
God and eternity. Here he is to kneel with the burden of still unsaved souls, and cast his burden on the
Lord, to find the Lord mighty to save. Here he is to
prepare his bow and select his arrow from the quiver,
and get it winged of the invisible God, that it may go
straight home to some sinner's heart.

O what throes of labour, what toil of brain, what
struggle and anguish of spirit, what joys unutterable,
what visions of God, what victories of faith, have toiling, praying, wrestling ministers of Jesus Christ experienced in their studies! There they have climbed
the heights and got into the secret place of the
Most High, and taken Jacob-like hold of God, saying,
"I will not let Thee go, except Thou bless me."

So what the study is to every pastor, he will be likely to be to his people. If the study bring revelation to him, he will bring revelation to his hearers. If there he gets power, in the pulpit he will have power. If he finds nothing in the study, the people will, ere long, find nothing in the pulpit.

Hence, the " ideal study " will have a shelf or section given up wholly to books designed for, and adapted to, spiritual nurture and the life of the soul. Of course, a Bible will be in this section—preferably a *particular* Bible, kept always on its own shelf, and kept solely for spiritual nurture, thumbed more often than any other book of devotion, and margined everywhere with pointers to its treasury of devotional expression, and holding supreme and unchallengeable place in any cluster of "helps " to devout and reverent speech in talks with God. How the "delicatessen " things that are "got up" and "made to order," as "forms" of prayer for weekly public worship, suffer by comparison with the prayers that are born of heart-hunger and yearning and sense of present need. Even the prayer given us by our Lord, and most often on our lips, was prefaced by these significant words : " After this *manner*, therefore, pray ye." As if even He, in the most comprehensive yet most specific prayer ever offered in the same number of words, would not tie us to the letter of worship, lest we, in our proneness to outward form, should lose the spirit of worship.

The book we call " The Psalms "—what a treasurestore of devotion ! A great number of these psalms are prayers—prayers of trust, of longing, of penitence, of refuge, of triumph. What a cry of the contrite sinner for pardon is the Fifty-first Psalm : " Have

mercy upon me, O Lord, according to Thy loving kind-
ness." What a shout of confidence is the Forty-sixth
Psalm: "God is our refuge and strength." How the
soul in the Ninety-first Psalm goes to hiding in the
secret place of the Most High, and gets covered with
His pinions, and makes Jehovah its "refuge" and
"fortress." How the Twenty-third Psalm has helped
many a believer to "walk through the valley of the
shadow of death," fearing no evil! What marvels of
trust and devotion are the prayers of the Master!
How His prayer for His disciples that "they may be
one," has hushed strife! How His prayer in Gethsem-
ane, "If it be possible—If it be possible—let this
cup pass; nevertheless not as I will, but as Thou wilt,"
has taught the Church that intense desire before God
is consistent with perfect submission to the will of
God.

And Paul, the peerless reasoner, the deep-toned
thunderer, the preacher of the strong doctrines of God
—how he prayed![1] With what intensity and fervour
and sweep of petition! So that his prayers seem
even mightier than his arguments.

[1] For this cause I bow my knees unto the Father of our Lord Jesus
Christ, of whom the whole family in heaven and earth is named, that
He would grant you, according to the riches of His glory, to be strength-
ened with might by His Spirit in the inner man; that Christ may
dwell in your hearts by faith; that ye, being rooted and grounded in
love, may be able to comprehend with all saints what is the breadth,
and length, and depth, and height; and to know the love of Christ,
which passeth knowledge, that ye might be filled with all the fullness
of God.—*Eph.* 3: 14–19.

For God is my record, how greatly I long after you all in the bowels
of Jesus Christ. And this I pray, that your love may abound yet
more and more in knowledge and in all judgment; that ye may ap-
prove things that are excellent; that ye may be sincere and without

But while the Bible is the book of books for devotional expression, there are other and blessed helps to the language and spirit of devotion in the literature of worshipping hearts.

The "Confessions of Augustine"; Thomas à Kempis' "Imitation of Christ"; Taylor's "Holy Living and Dying"; Baxter's "Reformed Pastor," and "Saints' Rest"; Bunyan's immortal "Pilgrim's Progress"; and the book of which it was born, and without which it could not have been written, viz., "Grace Abounding to the Chief of Sinners,"—a great heart-study; Rutherford's "Letters," rich, quaint, juicy, precious; Phelps' "The Still Hour," a very *multum in parvo* on prayer; Bowen's "Daily Meditations"; deeply spiritual, yet marked by great sanity as well as sanctity; Dickson's "All About Jesus," on a section of Canticles; Shedd's "Sermons to the Spiritual Man"; McClure's "Growing Pastor"; Speer's "Remember Jesus Christ"; Gibson's "The Devotional Use of the Holy Scriptures"; Horton's "The Open Secret."

These and many more may well find their way to the ideal study, and take their place in the section devoted to the literature of spiritual nurture; and this section will ere long be filled with the choicest devotional products inside and outside the Word of God; and while the ideal study will grow to be a very garden of spices in the care and culture of the years, this particular section or alcove will come to be to the ideal student the *dearest spot in the garden.* He will saturate his

offense till the day of Christ; being filled with the fruits of righteousness, which are by Jesus Christ, unto the glory and praise of God.— *Phil.* 1 : 8–11.

mind and heart with these outpourings of spiritual fervour, as they shall have been gathered for his meditation and use. And to such a student of the communings and devotional rapture of God's saints with their God, a set form and order of prayer will be a bondage. It will not meet his varying needs nor answer to his varying moods. Much less will it fit in to the ever-changing needs and moods of his people. Fixed grooves are not the channels of a free spirit.

One word more as to the ideal study must suffice. Imagine the student at his study table. What should he have within easy reach?

A revolving bookcase should be at his right hand. And in this bookcase should be the most commonly needed helps for daily use: his lexicons, English, Latin, Greek, and Hebrew; a concordance; a Bible dictionary; and a thesaurus of English words. Here also he should have a volume of some one or more of his favourite authors—Browning, Mrs. Browning, Tennyson, Carlyle, Emerson, Whittier, Mark Twain, Wordsworth—to turn to when the mood is on. And the new book just out and making a stir, he should have that within easy reach that he may dip into it in any unexpected leisure half hour. Here also should be put week by week the exegetical critical helps, the commentaries, and such other books as are likely to be needed for reference in the preparation of the week's sermon, to be returned to their respective shelves every Monday, and replaced by others suited to the next week's work. And not far away from his study chair should be a *hanging shelf* that could be swung out when needed; and so made as to require neither nail nor screw nor hammer to fasten it to its place; thus serving as a table where he may *stand* to do his work: a great relief from the protracted *sitting* posture. On this inclined shelf one or two of the big dictionaries might be open for convenient use.[1]

With an ideal student such as we have already described—receptive, attentive, assimilative, concentrative, many-sided, and listening with the ear of his soul for the Holy Spirit's communications, and having the habit of *diligence* (toil in the love of it), *thoroughness* (throughness) and *method* (everything in its time and place) with such a student, and with anything like a near approach to the *ideal study* herein set forth, we have all the conditions favourable to the ideal sermon : *i. e.*, to the sermon *perfectly adapted* to do the work of God. Nearer and nearer approaches to this ideal will be the sermons born in that study— begotten in the throes of that toiling and praying student.

---

[1] Any carpenter with a board and four hinges (two for the shelf, and two for the swinging legs underneath) and a couple of sockets or supports to hold the legs in place, could make this shelf at a trifling cost ; and it could be put up or taken down by any one in two minutes.

In the Albert Barnes study of the old First Church of Philadelphia, a high *fixed desk, built in with the bookcases,* ran along one entire side of the room, and there this beloved man of God paced back and forth for many years, doing that *pioneer* popular commentary work which gave him a name throughout the Christian world. He was in his study at four o'clock in the morning occupied with his commentary. But precisely at the stroke of the old clock on Independence Hall for the hour of nine, he dropped his commentary pen, and went to his study desk for his sermonic work.

XII

THE LAW OF ADAPTATION

SYLLABUS

Introductory.—If the Gospel is the power of God, the preacher's chief concern is with the *application* of this power. Hence it is of vital importance that regard be had to the *law of adaptation*.

I. Comprehensively, adaptation in preaching is saying the right thing at the right time in the right way.

        The objection that the minister's one concern is to preach the truth, and that only the Holy Spirit can make the truth effective, makes effects in the kingdom of God purely arbitrary, and is contradicted (1) by reason ; (2) by experience; (3) by the Scriptures.

II. Adaptation requires that the sermon should always answer some definite end.

III. Adaptation has respect to men as they are, not as they should be.

IV. Adaptation has respect to differing minds and temperaments.

    (*a*) Some need heroic treatment.

    (*b*) Some are of an excitable temperament.

    (*c*) Some are naturally belligerent.

    (*d*) Some are warmly emotional.

V. Adaptation has respect to differing conditions.

    1. General.

        (*a*) The spirit of the times.

        (*b*) Ignorance.

        (*c*) Doctrinal error.

    2. Special.

        (*a*) Inactivity.

        (*b*) Sorrow.

        (*c*) Alienation and estrangement as between Christians.

        (*d*) Impenitency.

        (*e*) Honest doubt.

        (*f*) Wandering.

        (*g*) Honest inquiry.

VI. Adaptation compels variety, and makes the preacher many-sided.

XII

THE LAW OF ADAPTATION

IF the Gospel is the power of God, the preacher's chief concern is with the application of this power. How may the Gospel be best applied? In what way can it be best presented, so as most effectively to reach men's consciences and hearts? It is of vital importance here, as in every other work of life, that regard should be had to *the law of adaptation*. There are conditions to be noted, circumstances to be considered, times and temperaments and places and prejudices to be taken into account in the public presentation of gospel truth, which may, and which should, make a marked difference in the kind of truth presented, and in the manner of presenting it.

First and comprehensively, adaptation in preaching is *saying the right thing at the right time in the right way*. It is fitness of matter, fitness of moment and fitness of method, in pulpit discourse. It is the apostolic ability and willingness to become all things to all men, so as by all means to save some.

To this it is objected that gospel truth is gospel truth, however presented; and it must be left to the sovereignty of the Holy Spirit's operations for any effect it may produce.

But the objection makes effects in the kingdom of God purely arbitrary. Results have no connection with appropriate means. Everything is without order

and without law. One form of truth is just as likely
to be effective as another, without regard to time or
place or condition of heart. This is contradicted
alike by reason, by experience, and by the Word of
God. Reason contradicts it: for reason demands an
adaptation of means to ends in the spiritual world as
everywhere else. Experience contradicts it: for experience makes it clear that such adaptation has always been connected with the best results. The most
effective preachers of the Gospel have been those who
knew the art of applying its power by skillfully adapting its varied truths to the varied needs and moods of
men.

And the Word of God contradicts it: for it commands *wisdom* in winning souls, and wisdom is impossible where results are arbitrary and lawless. And
Paul was a fool to make himself a servant unto all,
and to become as weak to the weak, as a Jew to the
Jews, as without law to them that are without law,
and "as all things to all men, that he might by all
means save some."

If adaptation is of no moment in the presentation of
gospel truth, then let us have human parrots or skillfully constructed talking machines in our pulpits, and
put living and thinking men to a business that requires
the use of judgment and reason for its prosecution.

If adaptation in preaching is an admitted necessity,
then it is a prime necessity, and should have every
preacher's thoughtful study. Here should be exhibited the skill of a workman who needeth not to be
ashamed. Here should be practiced the consummate
art of a wise master-builder, carrying up the walls of
God's spiritual temple with living masonry. He is

dealing with souls, and what range and compass, what infinite variety, what prejudices and passions and tastes and temperaments, what resistances and preferences and lying refuges, what shut and open doors, what wills—active, sluggish, pliant, defiant—what inroads of doubt and of fear, joy and sorrow, of hope and disappointment and even dark despair! Surely to meet all this requires rare facility of adaptation. And herein is the chief wisdom of winning souls and building them up in Christ. It is a business demanding utmost tact and good judgment and knowledge of human nature and familiarity with the Word of God. After years of preaching, the preacher will only reach an approximate knowledge and observance of this law of adaptation; involving the fit application of the infinitely varied truths of God to the infinitely varied needs of the souls of men.

II. *Adaptation in preaching requires that the sermon should always answer some end.* Never should it be written for the mere sake of writing. Never should it be written because the drudgery of weekly toil opens each week with the question : How am I to get ready for Sunday ? and because the process of grinding out one or two sermons must be gone through with in answer to that question. Preaching like this is mechanical and burdensome—not the work of a freeman in Christ. It begets bondage, and is likely to be smitten with barrenness.

Nor should the sermon be written in the mere purpose of expanding a passage or developing a theme, leaving it to the sovereignty of God to produce this effect or that.

There should be a reason for selecting one theme

rather than another, and for treating it one way rather than another. Hence the question to be asked and answered is, Why expound such a passage, or develop such a theme ? or, What " call " is there from " the body of the house " for next Sabbath's sermon ?

A vast and varied need is before the preacher week by week, and it will be a reproach to him—it will seriously mar the effectiveness and the fidelity of his ministry—if he does not see to it that that need is in some way met. To get through the week's inevitable work will not be his chief concern, nor will it be any concern. But he will be pressed to his study and to the inner sanctuary of prayer with the cry, What shall I do to help and heal, to reach and save my people— to stimulate to a duty undone ; to safeguard some tempted and imperilled soul; to give hope to a despondent heart that may have had blow on blow, until it seems to that heart as if God had forgotten to be gracious ; or to warn some reckless despiser of God's mercy that the hour that seems big with mercy may be big with doom, if he do not repent ?

So, the theme will be chosen, and the sermon written *to suit some present condition*. The true gunner in pursuit of game does not swing his gun at a flock of birds flying by, and *fire as he swings ;* he takes aim at some single bird in the flock and fires. So the adaptive preacher will have his eye open to some immediate definite need, either of the congregation or of a class, or of an individual in the congregation ; and he will be on his knees before God, and in diligent search through the Scriptures, *for his message ;* and he will be at his study table with toil of brain and heart, to unfold and enforce that message.

Even the crudest workman in ordinary handicraft pays some heed to the law of adaptation. He selects from his tools the one best fitted to the peculiarities of the task he has in hand. Now, of all work in the world, the preacher's is the transcendently important work. His *sermons* are his tools. Each one should be made and used for the peculiar effects it is both designed and adapted to produce, either on the spiritually alive or the spiritually dead of the people committed to his care. Mark the skilled dentist, even in so slight a matter as the treatment of a tooth. How thorough his examination! And then with what painstaking care he makes selection from the kit of tools, so as to get the instrument most perfectly adapted to do the needed work. Note the eminent surgeon! Examination before amputation, always. Note the distinguished physician! Diagnosis before prescription, always.

And yet in this God-given trust of ministry to souls, is it not undeniably true that preaching too often contents itself with an exhibition of truth, either by a process of logic, or a flight of imagination, or a shower of rhetorical brilliants, without any specific or determined purpose whatever on the part of the preacher, beyond the discharge of his own thoughts!

III. *Adaptation has respect to men as they are, not as they ought to be.* Men ought unquestionably to be willing to hear and heed the Gospel, no matter in what manner presented or by whom. They ought to be willing to pay regard to its truths whatever the verbal dress of those truths, or the offensiveness of the manner of their presentation, or whatever their inherent unpalatableness. But men are not so

willing.   The preacher must take men as he finds
them, as it has pleased God to place them before
him.   And he must lift them out of their weakness,
charm them away from their kennels of prejudice
and folly, find the available avenues to their hearts ;
and, while making no compromises with their sins,
manifest the wisdom of the serpent and the harmless-
ness of the dove.   To attack at once their prejudices
would be to arouse in them every element of opposition, and to make it impossible to secure favourable attention to whatever else the preacher might have to
say.   If it is God's truth that has aroused opposition,
the preacher should not be content with simply saying, "Well, it is the truth of God I have preached,
and men ought to hear it and heed it."   Of course they
ought.   But is it not the business of the preacher,
whenever his message has stirred to angry protest or
sullen silence, to challenge himself with questions like
these : Has not my method been at fault ?   Might I
not have got a favourable hearing for this same
truth if I had paid heed to what men are in their
present condition and circumstances, and had approached them in a somewhat different way, yet without abating one whit the claims of God's imperial
Word ?

IV.   *Adaptation has also respect to differing minds
and temperaments.*   Men take in truth in different
forms, and by different avenues or sides of their
minds.

(*a*)   There are some who need heroic treatment,
whom to reach and move you must hit boldly and
hard, whacking with the severest cudgels of logic and
denunciation.   It is the only way to rouse them.

They are sluggish in temperament, phlegmatic, lethargic, with sensibilities largely beneath the surface. They will bear the thunderings of a young Sinai.

(*b*) Some, on the other hand, are of excitable temperament. To deal with these, as with the class just named, would be either to rouse a fearful tempest in them, or to crush all heart and hope out of them.

(*c*) Again, some are naturally belligerent, smelling the battle afar off, eager for the fray, delighting in nothing so much as controversy. Will you conciliate such souls, and disarm them of opposition by coming into their presence bristling all over with offensive weapons, flaunting aloft your battle-flag, and shouting aloud your battle-cry ?

Some are unemotional, and have little of the pathetic or sympathetic in their nature. They don't like tears, and are unmoved by them. Appeals to the feelings fall like snowflakes on the pavements in the warm springtime. They want truth in logical forms —hard, close, clear reasoning. The nakeder the argument, and the less accompanied with illustrations, the better. To attempt to give such hearers the truth by tropes and metaphors and all poetic forms, or by illustrations and touching appeals, would not meet their need at all. They must be fed through their reason. They can best be reached and influenced in that way, and not very well in any other way.

(*d*) Again, some are warmly emotional. They are dominated by the feelings. They like the sermons that are full of gush and glow. They are fed by them; for they knock at the side of their nature at

which truth enters. It is only in emotional forms
that they apprehend truth. Truth is floated in to
their souls on the watercourses of their tears.

Others have æsthetic tastes, delighting in the play
of the imagination, in the beautiful forms given to
thought and feeling by the artistic touch of fancy.
Truth in plain and homely garb is not attractive to
them. Now to insist on feeding such minds with bare
syllogism, with the exactest statements and definitions,
as one would set a system of theological truth before
an examining committee, would be like reducing
" Paradise Lost " to a series of propositions in Euclid,
for the purpose of exhibiting its beauties to the lover of
æsthetic and poetic forms.

Still others have plain natures, with no imagination
and little culture. These must have truth in a plain
way. In short, preaching should have constant regard to the differing minds and temperaments in the
congregation, if the preacher would feed the whole
flock of God. It should not be purely intellectual,
nor purely emotional, nor purely to the imagination,
nor purely in the plain garb of every-day life. Hence
every hearer should expect to like some sermons better
than others. If the law of adaptation is observed by
the preacher, this varying preference of the hearer
will be inevitable. Hence also every preacher should
expect to get a different judgment from his people as
to the work and fitness of particular sermons. *The
man the sermon finds* is likely to be the man heard
from the next time he and the preacher meet. And the
varying proof of appreciation should be the best of
evidence to the preacher that he is meeting the varied
need of his flock.

V. *Adaptation has respect to differing conditions.*

1.   These conditions are *general* and *special.*

(*a*)   *The spirit of the times.*   Difficult as it may be to define this spirit or to analyze it, nevertheless there is such a spirit; and it is constantly changing in the advancing years.   It is subtle, pervasive, wide-reaching, influential.   The men of most influence in any department of activity are the men who most truly represent this spirit, and who adapt their methods to its changing phases.   The preacher is no exception. He holds fast to the old and everlasting truths; but he will change the means and methods and forms of their presentation, by an adaptation to the spirit of the times in which he lives.

If Paul were living now with his noble sinuosity and rare adjustableness, fitting himself to the need of the time, he would not preach as he did in the first century.   Many of the mighty sermons of even only fifty years ago would lose their effect if repeated now, unless recast in a mould suited to the hour.

(*b*)   Another general condition may be that of *ignorance.*   Amongst a people unfamiliar with the Gospel, untrained in the Sabbath-school, unused to the instruction of the sanctuary, and generally uneducated, the law of adaptation would surely require the simplest forms of speech, and a presentation of the very rudiments and elementary principles of the Gospel of Christ.   The whole tone and tenor of preaching, its forms and even subject-matter, should be adjusted to this state of things.   And the preacher should remember that, even in the most favoured community, there will always be a considerable class who need to be fed with the "milk of the Word," rather than "the strong meat." Better far will it be for the preacher to take the risk of being thought no great reasoner and no mighty intellectual athlete, than to fail of *adapting* truth to that large number in every congregation who are utterly unable to appreciate the subtle refinements of close reasoning, and the ingenious connections of logical processes. Probably the most prevalent fault of the ministry of our day is the taking, in things spiritual, too much for granted as already known by the congregation.

(*c*) Still another general condition may be that of *doctrinal error*. A preacher may be called, in the providence of God, to a community where some mischievous error of doctrine has taken wide and deep root.

Shall he directly and openly attack it?

The temptation will undoubtedly be to rush with hot haste and consuming zeal to the demolition of the pernicious heresy. But the zeal, after all, is not likely to be according to knowledge.

If the error is limited in its influence, and not immediately ruinous to souls, ordinarily it would seem to be the better plan to have the error supplanted by the persistent, bold, faithful presentation of *truth*, with *little or no reference to the error in question*.

But if the error is wide-spread and influential, a marked, notorious thing, then to the question: "Shall error be directly and openly attacked from the pulpit?" the answer should be: Yes, *provided one is sure of his guns;* that they are of sufficient range and calibre to knock the thing all to pieces.

But possibly the better way even here would be to pour truth into the conscience; to aim directly at souls. And if the guns are given range by the Lord Almighty, and the shot strike, and the cry come from men, What shall I do to be saved?—*error will slink away*. It can't stand before the mighty moving of God's Spirit. The best antidote for heresy is a revival of religion.

2. There are also *special* conditions, as well as general, to which adaptation has reference :

(*a*) *Inactivity*. Some souls have gone to sleep or are smitten with supineness and sloth. The preacher would bring them abreast of the workers and watchers who are at their posts, bearing the burdens and heat of the day. Preaching adapted to arouse these inactive souls will not so much smite their inactivity, as it will show them the vast interests imperilled by their idleness; or as it will dwell with loving and glowing enthusiasm on the rewards of active obedience; or, better still, perhaps, as it will show them their grieved Lord—grieved because of alienated and estranged disciples who have grown forgetful of their vows and promises, and before whom He stands pleading, as in the days of His flesh, He pleaded, saying with tenderness and tears, "Could ye not watch with Me one hour?" "Will ye also go away?"

Far better this than the chronic pulpit scold. Now and then, a flashing rebuke for supineness and inactivity, given with Christlike tenderness and fidelity, would be the preacher's justification, and exhibit the very mind of the Master. But so-called "scolding sermons" are of questionable value either to pulpit or parish.

(*b*) *Sorrow* is another special condition calling for wise and tender adaptation. The preacher will study to meet this condition. And he will vary the truth so that it will always answer to the special and peculiar need.

At one time he will come with the Gospel's rare and sweet consolations. At another he will dwell on the rich fruits of sorrow. And, again, he will press the lofty thought of God's sign and seal in sorrow. And still again, he will stimulate to a great duty in which once engaged the soul will *forget* its sorrow.

(*c*) *Alienation and estrangement as between Christians.* Preaching adapted to this will let it alone so far as dealing with it directly and openly from the pulpit is concerned. But the preacher now and then will make his sermons so exhibitive of the Christly qualities of forgiveness and patience and gentleness and loving sufferance, that he will weigh down that side of the scale in alienated hearts, and make hate and bitterness and all uncharitableness "kick the beam."

(*d*) *Impenitency.* This condition is always special and varied, and requires rare delicacy of treatment. Each soul should be studied as to its defenses and approaches, its dispositions and prejudices, its shut and open doors. In the course of time, down through one's ministry, the pastor should aim to have each soul's need met by truth prepared specifically for that soul's case.

There are at least two urgent reasons why there should be far more of this aiming directly and adaptedly at individual souls.

First. *The preacher never knows when he is face to face with his last opportunity.* The soul may not be there another Sabbath to aim at.

Second. *An ounce of instruction to a soul in Christ, is worth a ton of instruction to a soul out of Christ.*

Still other and greatly varied special conditions will suggest themselves.

(*e*) A condition of *honest doubt.* There is doubt and doubt—the doubt of cavil and the doubt of love. There is a vast difference between fearing a thing may be false and *wishing* it false. The recorded interview between Christ and Thomas is here in point. When the other disciples reported that they had seen the risen Lord, Thomas said, "Except I shall see in His hands the print of the nails, and put my finger in the print of the nails, and put my hand into His side, I will not believe." When next the disciples met, Christ was with them. How did Christ treat this honest doubter? He said to Thomas, "Reach hither thy finger, and see My hands ; and reach hither thy hand and put it into My side ; and be not faithless but believing." To honest doubt Christ *furnished the evidence.* To the Pharisaic doubt of cavil and hate, Christ sometimes gave silence, sometimes intense and scathing rebuke.

(*f*) Another special condition is that of *wandering and worldly-mindedness.* What a picture we have of Christ's approach to such a church or heart, in the words: "Behold I stand at the door and knock." Christ waiting ; waiting just outside ; waiting to come in, if only the sinner will open the door. Have *we* been after heart or church in that patient, waiting, pleading, adaptive way?

(*g*) And still another special condition is that of *honest and earnest inquiry as to the way of salvation.* Blessed is the ministry that frequently faces this con-

dition, and that often hears the cry, "What shall I do
to be saved?" In order to anything like a proper
answer to this transcendent question, adaptation requires a knowledge of at least two things—*human
nature* and *the Word of God*. The minister may be
acquainted with a lot of people, yet not know human
nature. He may have a perfectly orthodox system of
theology, yet not know his Bible.

The surgeon does not venture to use his tools
on a living body, without knowledge of the complicated physical framework. Surely that complex and
subtle mixture of will and affection, of intellect and
passion, of reason and conscience, constituting human
nature, must be known by the preacher, before truth
can be adapted to its need. And for the most perfect
adaptation, he must know the actual human nature
before him, Sabbath after Sabbath—the temperaments,
tastes, prejudices, and conditions of his people.

And this varied and varying need necessitates
knowledge of the Word of God to meet it. The
claims of the law of adaptation will send the preacher
on diligent and prayerful search through the Scriptures for the truth adapted to each special case. He
will light on some sweet promise with which to buoy
up the despondent. He will dig deep till he finds the
ore with which to enrich some other labourer for God
striving to lay up treasure in heaven. He will get
honey from some spiritual rock of God's Word with
which to fill the mouth of one hungering for the
sweets of Christian discipleship. Yea, he will look
long and lovingly into the glass of the Word, and get
so familiar with the face of his Beloved, beholding
His glory, that he will be able to show Him to many

an inquiring soul, who "would see Jesus"; and thus be the blessed instrument of transforming them into the same image from glory to glory.

VI. As a kind of conclusion from this somewhat extended discussion of the law of adaptation, it is manifest that adaptation *compels variety and makes the preacher many-sided.*

The reaction on the preacher is not the least of the advantages of an observance of this great law. When he comes to make it the controlling, unwavering purpose of his ministry to meet both the specific and general need of his field of labour, he will find his sermons taking on an endless variety. It cannot be otherwise. Ruts deeply worn will be impossible. Adaptation will free the preacher from monotonous repetition. It is a perpetual "declaration of independence" of any arbitrary sermonic rule, as if every sermon were to be squared and hewn to that. The preacher with a bulge will not be found in this company. Many-sidedness is its crown and glory. As a fisher of men he will bait his hook to suit all tastes. Now he will put a truth in the groove of syllogism. Now he will give it æsthetic or emotional form. Now he will spread his wings and fly, in the joy of a vigorous imagination and take some of his hearers with him to get new visions of God through revelations of His grace and glory. Now he will take the pedestrian style and go afoot and show his lowly hearers how the commonest paths of service bloom with God's best, and how the lowliest flowers, scarce daring to look up in the face of one of God's beautiful days on earth, seem to catch a great deal of sunshine and to reflect the very azure of heaven.

And if he seem to preach only half so well to the intellect as to the heart he will now and then *preach to the intellect*, if there are minds before him craving that form of Truth's presentation.   If some dear parishioner says of a certain style of sermonizing, " That's the preaching for me; stick to that, and you cannot fail of doing good," the wise preacher will not " stick."   But he will remember the well-meant counsel, and put it away in his private note-book, and once in a while he will recall the sermon that helped and comforted and proved manna of heaven to that believing heart, and he *will try to preach another like it* for that same believing heart.

But the ideal preacher will keep out of a rut in his preaching.   He is dealing with souls.   And no two of them are ever alike.   And therefore he will be kept in no form of public presentation of truth that will make him a one-sided preacher—a preacher with a bulge: leaving half his people unhelped, unmoved, undeveloped, while ministering with acceptance and spiritual profit to the other half.

XIII

PREACHING OLD DOCTRINES IN NEW TIMES

SYLLABUS

I. What are the old doctrines?

II. What are the new times?

III. How shall the old doctrines be preached in the new times?

    (*a*) In their totality—the new times must hide no truth.

    (*b*) In their Scriptural fullness. Hell is not a mere euphemism. The Atonement is something more and deeper than a moral influence.

    (*c*) With constant regard to the law of adaptation.

        (1) Bows are not to be drawn at a venture.

        (2) Adaptation will have reference to men as they are, not as they ought to be.

        (3) The perspective, and therefore the proportion and the emphasis of truth, will change with the changing years.

XIII

PREACHING OLD DOCTRINES IN NEW TIMES

WHAT do we mean by the old doctrines? And what do we mean by the new times? Definite knowledge of what these things are is in order before we undertake to fit the one to the other. Let us have a roll-call of the old doctrines, and then let us have a characterization of the new times. With these fairly in mind, we may be well on the road to their best adjustment.

I. The old doctrines are the doctrines of God, of Christ, of the Holy Spirit, of sin and its punishment, of God's love in the divine incarnation, of the life, death, resurrection, ascension, and intercession of Jesus Christ, of His atoning expiatory sacrifice, of everlasting reward and punishment, of justification by faith, of spiritual regeneration, repentance for sin and growth in grace, of death and the resurrection and the judgment—these, and doctrines like them, the profoundest truths ever grasped by the human mind, and that make the Book that contains them the completest and the all-sufficient revelation of God to man —these are the old doctrines; old, yet ever new, that may change their form but not their substance; whose order of succession, whose method of illustration, and whose proportionate expression may vary with the successive centuries, but whose inner and eternal realities are like Him in whom they inhere, and from whom they came, "the same yesterday, to-day, and forever."

"Heredity" and "environment" and "the stream of tendency" and "the survival of the fittest" and "the law of selection" have not done away with sin. "Atrophy by disuse" is only a partial answer to the Scriptural doom of death. The fires of intense physical tortures as the penalty of sin may have burned out, but the fierce flames of a wrathful conscience have not burned out; and the human bosom is still wrung with the cry of Satan, "Which way I fly is hell; myself am hell." Evolution still leaves us bridgeless gulfs that only the divine interposition involved in the incarnation and the resurrection of Jesus Christ, and in the regeneration of a human soul, can help us over. Personal responsibility is not yet resolved into a "brain-track." The "I" of personality is still the tremendous factor in human existence. The word "ought" is in all dictionaries. The "reign of law" makes more room for God.

II. What now of the "new times"? Is this a mere phrase, the coinage of the hour? Or does it stand for a recognizable and indisputable fact? The times are new, beyond a doubt. They are ever new. There is no long dead-level either of excellence or stupidity. New conditions prevail. New forces are let loose. New social order is established. There's a new world next door. The nations have entered into such near relation to each other that at any hour they may hold a conversational club meeting. Society is complex, yet so knit together that ideas spread like a contagion. The stir is prodigious. A heart-beat is felt around the world. If a man who "fell on sleep" a hundred years ago should wake up now, he would rub his eyes and say : " Old things have passed away. Behold, all things have become new." New men, new measures, new thinking, new agencies, new processes, new relations. New ideas come trooping in at new sides of the mind. New forces are at play, changing mental attitudes, suggesting mental challenges, threatening to play havoc, or playing havoc, with mental convictions. Warfare is not waged as it was. Business is not done as it was. News is not heralded as it was. Out of what struggle and push and whirl and weariness men come into Sunday ! The pulpit has now a harder task than it ever had in this world. As Ruskin once put it, " Thirty minutes to raise the dead in ! "

III. How, now, shall the old doctrines be preached in these new times ?

(a) *In their totality.* The " times " cannot change the truths or the facts. Man's need as a sinner, Christ's power unto salvation, and everlasting life and death, remain persistent factors in all social relations, and in spite of all scientific discoveries. When we get to putting great doctrines of God on the shelf because they are not suitable or palatable, we are guilty of Saul's sin of substituting sacrifice for obedience ; and however sweet-smelling the savour of some other truth we bring, it will no more find favour with God than Saul's best sheep and oxen. The new times must hide no truth. It would be strange, indeed, to further God's cause and kingdom of truth by proving infidel to God-ordained truth !

(b) Again, the old doctrines must be preached in *their Scriptural fullness.*

Just what they mean in God's Word, they must mean in the modern pulpit. To preach the old truths, and yet so preach them that they are emptied of their deep and essential significance, is as great recreancy to truth as not to preach them at all. Hell is hell, and Christ made it dreadful by every possible figure of speech. And to hide its terrible features by a euphemism, to interpret all the dread imagery that is used in Scripture for setting hell forth as if it indicated mere atrophy of powers, or the mere searing of conscience, or the mere shrivelling of the soul at last into nothingness, is to preach a hell that many a man would welcome as he left this world, counting entrance into it a positive joy.

And to preach Christ crucified as a marvellous "governmental expedient," or a mighty "moral influence," or a matchless "vicarious sacrifice," would be to preach the truth of the Atonement indeed, but not all the truth. To set forth that marvel and miracle of grace in its Scriptural fullness is to put into the doctrine of the Atonement *expiation for sin.* The world is full of vicarious sacrifice, but there never was but one exhibition of it that affected sin, and made it possible for God to forgive the sinner. A mother may suffer cheerfully, and to the point of death, in her child's behalf and stead, but no anguish of her soul can take her child's sin away. The absolutely unique and transcendent thing in Christ's sacrifice is this, that it is expiatory. And to preach the doctrine of the atonement with this left out is to preach the doctrine with its heart left out.

So, too, with all the old great truths. Love and law go hand-in-hand. Mercy and truth meet and kiss

each other. Millions of free wills act and interact
in the midst of sovereign and eternal purpose. We
shall find the harmonies if we go deep enough. All
seeming antagonisms melt into friendships in the
divine reciprocity of the kingdom of God. Each old
doctrine holds in its fullness, and must be preached in
its fullness, in old times and new times.

(c) But, again, the old doctrines are to be preached
in the new times *with constant regard to the law of
adaptation.*

"Study to show thyself approved unto God, a workman unshamed by his work," is the perpetual divine
injunction. (1) Bows are not to be "drawn at a
venture." Haphazard shots, simply because the arrow
is drawn from the quiver of God's Word, can have no
justification. Adaptation is the magic thing that will
fit the old doctrine to the new times. Not adaptation
that looks to change of fundamental truth, that would
cut and hew and chip away at doctrine until it was so
disfigured and marred as no longer to reflect the
divine image, or to be radiant with the glory of God
upon it ; but adaptation that looks to change in the
method of handling doctrine, and of fitting it into
present living need, this is the necessity. Not elimina-
tion, nor modification, but adjustment.

(2) This adaptation will have respect to men as they
are ; not as they were fifty years ago ; not as they will
be fifty years hence ; not as they ought to be to-day,
but as they are to-day. The actual human nature in
the pew before the preacher Sabbath by Sabbath—
this is the study of the man of God, next to his Bible,
and equally with his Bible. Coordinate with Scripture
exegesis will be *this exegesis of human nature,* this

reading of heart histories, this investigation of methods
of approach, this purpose to know what his hearers are
thinking about, what defenses they are building, what
subterfuges they are resorting to, what the secret,
subtle, insidious, and sometimes unconscious reason is,
for their indifference, or their antagonism, or their
active opposition.   He must get at them, get alongside
of them, inside of them, lovingly, sympathetically,
practically, sinuously.   A burglar will make a study
of a bank-vault for weeks and months that he may get
at its elaborately locked-up and triple-bolted and barred
treasures.   Too many preachers spend much time in
studying the deep things of God, but no time at all in
studying how to get these deep things of God into the
deeps of a human heart.

Some belligerent preachers come with a battering-
ram every Sabbath, as if every hearer's heart were a
fortress, walled up at every avenue of approach, and
encased in steel, and to be entered only by sheer force.
Some are forever making a downy pillow of the Gospel, and shying it at people week by week, week by
week, as if those making up the whirl of the world,
whether in Millionaire Avenue or Little Hell, were
aching and sighing for the touch of the Gospel's
feathery softness, and wanting nothing on earth but a
gospel lullaby!

Adaptation!   Adaptation!   It is the magic wand
that will make an old doctrine fit in to any time, and
seem like a birth of yesterday in its sweetness and
light.

(3)   Of course the perspective, and therefore the *proportion* and the *emphasis* of truth, will change with the
changing years and customs and habits of thought and

needs and antagonisms of men.   The burning question is not always the same question.   The theory of a process of God is not always the process.   Inspiration is far more than any theory of inspiration.   That *an old theory* has been exploded is no proof that *the doctrine* has been exploded.   The crude old notions of creation are exploded; but "in the beginning God created the heaven and the earth," opens the record of Scripture to-day with all the authority of a thousand years ago.   Punishment may not be literal fire any more, but to correct the crude conception of the doctrine of retribution that made hell a bed of hot coals is not to cease to preach the doctrine of *retribution for sin*.   Dives, the rich man, begging for a drop of water to cool his tongue, may not mean physical torment of flame, but it *means something unspeakable*.   And science joins hand with Scripture in the contention that as a man sows he shall surely reap.

XIV

THE METHOD OF ANSWERING
QUESTIONS

SYLLABUS

A preacher worth anything will start questions. A study of Christ's method of answering questions should help us in making wise reply.

I.   Christ often wrapped His answer in a parable; He replied by a story.

II. His answer often embodied a principle, rather than a rule.

III. He made much of the *Word of God ;* and often sent the inquirer to the Scriptures.

IV. He looked at the spirit of the questioner, rather than at the letter of the question.

V.   He often answered one question by asking another.

VI. He sometimes met a questioner with silence, and answered "not a word."

VII. The question of questions, *What shall I do to be saved ?* How did Christ answer that? He made His answer to *suit the case.* Sometimes His reply was, "*Believe.*" Sometimes, "*Repent.*" Again it was, "Sell all that thou hast and give to the poor." And again His answer was, "Choose ;" the answer being determined in each case *by the particular attitude of the inquirer's mind.*

Three things mark Christ's answer to this question of questions : " What shall I do to be saved ? "

1. They make it clear that the door is *open to every honest inquirer.*

2. They make it clear that the door is *Christ.*

3. They set the inquirer to doing nothing but what, *in the doing,* would *give salvation.*

Clearly, any answer that does not send the inquirer straight to Jesus Christ, is big with possibilities of false guidance and disaster.

" *The heart of the righteous studieth to answer.*"—*Prov.* 15 : 28.

XIV

THE METHOD OF ANSWERING QUESTIONS

THE art of questioning is of acknowledged importance. It has had wide attention and study. The art of answering questions is hardly less important. But comparatively little thought has been given to it. It has not had the attention it deserves. The Word of God tells us " a soft answer turneth away wrath." It also commands us to "answer a fool according to his folly." And yet " not to answer a fool according to his folly." Evidently there is need of wide and wise judgment in the replies we make to questioners. " The heart of the wise studieth to answer ; " but caught with a question, there is often no room for study. And hence the word spoken in reply is not " right " or " in due season." The wise man says : " A man hath joy by the answer of his mouth ; " but every minister knows that that is a way of sorrow as well.

A preacher, worth anything, will start questions. A live parish will fairly bristle with interrogation points. There are mental challenges in every pew, and these often find a voice. Honest doubt has its inquiring mood. And dishonest doubt puts on one. Ignorance leans expectantly for knowledge ; and captious, cavilling self-conceit wants to know, you know. Questions speculative, doctrinal, practical—questions

187

of Christian casuistry, of religion, politics, future life
—these crowd to the door of the lips and press for
answer.   We are all concerned to know how to make
reply.

Manifestly the replies Christ made to those who
came to Him with one or another word of inquiry
should prove an interesting and illuminating study.
The thorough consideration of the nexus of the questions asked Him, of the spirit or incident that gave birth
to them, of their grouping or classification, and of the
reach and profound significance of Christ's answers,
ought to yield a large profit.

For the pastor in the frequent and inevitable ques-
tionings of his parish ; for the parent brought often
face to face with the difficulties raised by an inquiring
child ; for the teacher before his class where the spirit
of inquiry has been stimulated by his guidance as he
has led them into the mysteries of Scripture ; for the
Christian before gainsayers seeking to entrap him, and
shame or silence him by their cunning interrogatives
—this field of study ought to have special and peculiar
interest.

In looking over the principal occasions when Christ
was approached by an inquirer, we shall find rich and
abundant material, to help us in determining how to
make reply when we are face to face with a questioner,
whether his inquiry be a cavil, a challenge, an honest
desire to know, or a helpless cry.

I.   It is quite apparent that Christ often wrapped
His answer in a parable.   He replied by a story.   In
this respect (I say it reverently) our martyred Lincoln
was greatly like Him.   How Lincoln sometimes shot
a man through with an anecdote !   How he laughed

another out of his absurdity by a story! This silent, sad man, with his marvellous intuition, parried many a dagger of interrogation thrust at him, by this method of reply. His stories were often rough and crude; they smacked of the farm, and the frontier, and the county court-house; but there was always an irresistible point to them, and now and then an almost infinite pathos. Men went away from him rebuked, confounded, captured. Men who could batter down argument with argument, men who could listen to and resist his logic, who could fling back challenging questions and keep up a running fire of hot discussion, could not stand before one of his irresistible stories. Into these were often crowded argument, illustration, tenderness, appeal; and they frequently silenced where they did not convince. What Lincoln's method was in a crude, crass, but often effective way, Christ's method was in a finely fibered and flawless way. "Who is my neighbour?" asked a lawyer. Jesus did not pick him out. He told the parable of the Good Samaritan. He did not define the limits of neighbourhood. But His story made each one of us kin to any one in need, and showed that the question savoured of narrowness and ought never to be asked. Men have known ever since that if they found anywhere a man with the blood of the human race in his veins and in need of help, no matter of what race or sect or caste or colour, they were to be a *neighbour* to him after the deed and the spirit of the Good Samaritan. All the moral dissertations of the centuries have not put that lesson in the world's heart like this gospel story.

Again, the question of Peter, "Lo, we have left all and followed Thee; what, then, shall we have?"

brought out the story of the labourers, all hired for a penny a day, though at different hours, and each getting simply his penny ; thus teaching that it is *acceptance of a condition and not amount of toil* that secures us heaven.

"Is it lawful to heal on the Sabbath ? " they asked Him. And seizing a common incident of Eastern life, He answered : "Is it lawful to help an ass out of the pit on the Sabbath, and wicked to help a man out ? "

Incidents, anecdotes, word-scenes,—they are better than arguments. They illuminate, they translate truth into life, they take abstractions and put flesh and blood on them. They do not antagonize. They never fight. They *win* their way. Logic cudgels. Parables exhibit. We ought to have more of them, and have them handy, and learn to grow facile in their use. Many a question can best be answered by a story.

II. Another feature in Christ's method of answering questions was this : His answer embodied a *principle* rather than a *rule*. The letter was nothing much to Him ; the spirit was everything. Tithing of mint He by no means condemned ; but upon the weightier matters He threw the infinite emphasis. Men came to Him asking questions in arithmetic. And their figures seemed impertinences in the spirit and sweep of His answers. They asked for some technical and formal rule. He gave them a great principle.

One of the scribes inquired, " Master, which is the first commandment of all ? " Christ did not begin to weigh the commandments, one by one, to see which was greatest. He did not pick out the first, or the third, or the tenth, and say, " For reasons this is the greatest." He said : " The first commandment is,

Thou shalt love the Lord thy God with all thy heart. And the second is like unto it, Thou shalt love thy neighbour as thyself." That is, the second is also first. And there is no first, no second. *Love is all!* Love is the fulfillment of the whole law. Be not concerned about which commandment is greatest, lest you thereby miss the spirit that alone makes it possible to obey at all.

So when Peter asks the Lord, " How oft shall my brother sin against me, and I forgive him ?   Till seven times ? " Jesus replies, " Not until seven times, but until seventy times seven "; that is, an unlimited number of times; that is, make no count of forgivenesses in the possession of the spirit of forgiveness. Forgiveness is not a sum in addition or multiplication. " How many times ! "   When a man begins to count the times he has pardoned, the true spirit of forgiveness is dead in him.

"Who is my neighbour ? "   Does Christ answer this question by describing a neighbour, pointing him out and naming his characteristic ?   No.   That is mechanical, artificial, arithmetic again.   He exhibits and illustrates the neighbourly spirit.   And the Good Samaritan makes the whole world kin.

Have we not here a very wholesome lesson as to the method of dealing with a very large class of inquirers ? A good deal of fog in the field of Christian casuistry would be dissipated if we answered inquirers with an illuminating principle rather than a formal rule. None the less, but rather the more, would there be abstention from matters of doubtful expediency, if questions concerning them were answered after this method of the Master.

III.   Another feature of Christ's method of meeting inquiry was this :   *He made much of the Word of God.* He sent the questioner to the Scriptures.   One would think He might have drawn upon His own resources. He had unsearchable riches of wisdom and knowledge. And the use of these would have helped to establish His claims, and could certainly have been made over- whelming in every case of inquiry.   But He met ques- tion of friend and foe, of wavering faith and cavilling unbelief, with the Scriptures.   "To the law and the testimony," was His constant word.

You ask for my credentials, He said to the unbe- lieving Jews.   "Search the Scriptures ; they testify of Me."   And to answer the wondering query of doubting disciples, "beginning from Moses, He inter- preted to them in all the Scriptures the things con- cerning Himself."

"Whose wife shall she be ? " asked the skeptical Sadducees.   And Christ's reply was : "Ye do err, *not knowing the Scriptures.*   Have ye not read that which was spoken unto you by God ? "

"What shall I do to inherit eternal life ? " said the lawyer, tempting Him.   "What is written *in the law ?* " was the prompt reply.   "How readest thou ? " And when the lawyer read the law, Jesus said, "This do, and thou shalt live."

"Why do the disciples that which is not lawful on the Sabbath ? " was the challenging question of the Jews, as the disciples plucked ears of corn.   "Have ye never read what David did ? " was the ready an- swer ; and back they were sent to the oracles.   "Is it lawful for a man to put away his wife for any cause ? " asked His enemies, tempting Him.   And He answered,

" Have ye not read ? " To the Scriptures ! What is written ? Did ye never read ? How commonly did He thus reply. Not much reasoning ; little theological discussion ; and no philosophy. *What saith the Word ?*

Here, as often elsewhere, Moody was right. In this respect at least he followed Christ's method. The positively best answer to any question is an " It is written." In our replies to inquirers let us have less of human opinion and speculation and more of " Thus saith the Lord." Let us open the Book and find the page and read the words !

IV. A study of Christ's method of answering questions discloses another feature : that *He looked at the spirit of the questioner* even more than at *the letter of the question.*

He could. Often we cannot. His omniscient eye swept the field of motive. He knew all that was in every man that came to Him. How little we know. But how desirable that we *should* know—know something, at least, of the posture of the questioner's mind. Hence the need of turning inquirer and ascertaining the occasion of the question, the motive behind it, the attitude towards truth, whether doubt is born of fear that a thing may be false, or of a *wish* that it were false, before we make answer. Diagnosis before prescription is as good in casuistry as in therapeutics.

See, now, how Christ devoted His answer to the spirit of the man who asked Him a question, meeting the real need of the inquirer first, and making the letter of the inquiry second and subordinate.

Some came to Him with idle curiosity. " Are there few that be saved ? " asked one. Did Christ go into a calculation, counting up infants and covering centuries? No! The inquirer seemed more interested in a matter of arithmetic than of conscience. And to loose him of his folly, Jesus said, in substance, in answer to the question, Are there few that be saved? *See that you are.* "Strive to enter in at the strait gate," is His searching, solemn word; "for many, I say unto you, shall seek to enter in and shall not be able." Which was as if He had said: It is amazing folly to be paltering and pothering with a question of statistics in connection with salvation, when so many miss the way, and *you may be among them!* And yet Christ meets the letter of the inquiry before He gets through, and clearly implies that a great multitude shall be saved when He says: "They shall come from the east and from the west, and from the north and from the south, and shall sit down in the kingdom of God."

Again they question Him, and now it is the disciples who are the inquirers, saying, "Who is the greatest in the kingdom of heaven?" Did He speak of Moses, or Elijah, or John the Baptist? He takes a little child, sets him in the midst of them, and makes answer: "Except ye become as little children ye shall in no wise enter into the kingdom of heaven." And they were shot through with the shame and sin of their pride. And yet the letter of their inquiry gets answer; for Christ's reply is as if He had said, "The humblest; he is the greatest."

"When shall these things be?" asked the disciples, as they heard Christ speak of the coming of the Son of Man, and of the end of the world. And Christ's answer substantially is, "Dates, times, seasons, the

day and the hour—what are these? *Be ye ready.*
That is the vital matter."

"What shall this man do?" is another question of
idle curiosity that is met with "What is that to thee?
Follow thou Me."

"Lo, we have left all. What shall we have?"
Still it is speculation and surmise as to matters of no
eternal moment. And while Christ answers that they
shall have a hundredfold, He adds, "*But* many that
are first shall be last, and the last first"—that is,
"Have a care! Be not too eager about what ye shall
have. The heavenly riches are not for those who are
thinking more of what they have given up and what
they are to get, than of what they were, and are, and
ought to be."

So the Master always sought to meet the deeper
need *betrayed in the spirit of the questioner rather
than the surface need indicated by the question.* This
should be our way.

V. Still further, in considering Christ's method of
reply, it will be found that He often answered one
question by asking another. But almost invariably
this was when the question was in the line of challenge or rebuke.

"Why do Thy disciples transgress the traditions of
the elders?" they loftily asked. And the answer
came, "Why do ye transgress the commandment of
God by your tradition?" They had assumed there
was something wrong in Christ's deed or speech. His
reply showed them that they were guilty of a deeper
wrong. "Is it lawful to give tribute to Cæsar?" they
questioned. Jesus perceived their wickedness and
said: "Why tempt ye Me, ye hypocrites?" And

holding up a penny, He asked, " Whose is this image
and superscription ? " And, compelled to answer,
" Cæsar's " ; Christ's swift reply was, " Then render
unto Cæsar the things that are Cæsar's, and unto God
the things that are God's." And seeking to entangle
Him, they themselves got enmeshed.

VI. Still another method of Christ's reply to
questioners was by silence. He sometimes answered
nothing.

" Hearest Thou not how many things they witness
against Thee ? " asked Pilate. " And He gave him no
answer, not even to one word." " What! Carest
Thou not what is said of Thee ? Hast Thou no defense ? " And the lips that could blast those perjurers
were still.

Again, at the cross, they rail on Him, wagging their
heads, saying, " He saved others ; Himself He cannot
save." And amidst that questioning and challenging
Babel of hell the Son of God is silent ; He answers
nothing.

The disciple is not above his Master. There may
be times in *our* lives when a challenging question will
best be met by silence. We may suffer thereby. The
unspoken answer, if uttered, might free from suspicion,
rid us of calumny, vindicate us before an onlooking
crowd, save us from the shame of seeming to be weak
and false ; yet it may be better that the word be left
unspoken. Doubtless this is one of the bitterest acids
that can be applied to the coin of Christian integrity.
It may cut to the quick to be thus questioned and answer not a word ; but the spirit of glory and of God
is on us then. So the Master walked on silently,
when they thrust their sneering, jeering questions at

Him. But it was the way to His crown and kingdom!

VII. And now, the question of questions, What
shall I do to be saved? How did Christ answer that?
Certainly not by laboured reasoning; nor by some
specific and unchanging formula. He had no set answer of any kind as a reply to an inquiring soul, seeking to know how to get rid of sin, and to obtain eternal life. He knew the exact posture of every inquirer's mind that came to Him, and His answer was exactly adapted to *that particular attitude of mind.* It
suited the case. It met the questioner's difficulty, and
answered to his need. So far as possible we should
see to it that our answer is like Christ's in its adaptation to the inquirer's need.

But how can this be? We are not diviners of
hearts as Christ was. Well, what does the physician
for the body do, when called to a case? He makes a
diagnosis, before he makes a prescription. To tell
one, who comes asking what he must do to be saved,
to believe on the Lord Jesus Christ, might not touch
the secret of the difficulty *with him;* for it might not
be the point of the Spirit's striving. Paul told the
Philippian jailer to believe on the Lord Jesus Christ.
That answer suited the case. But Peter told the Jews
at Pentecost, in answer to the very same question, *to
repent.* And Jesus told the rich young man who came
asking what he should do to inherit eternal life, " Go
and sell all that thou hast and give to the poor." And
to the people at Mt. Carmel who came " halting between two opinions" ("limping between the two
sides") Elijah said, " If the Lord be God, follow Him.
If Baal, then follow him." In other words, *choose.*

Make up your minds.   When an inquirer is " halting
between two opinions," hesitating, wavering, it is not a
question of repentance or of faith, but of *decision*, of
choice.   The mere act of choice carries everything
with it.

Three things thus mark Christ's answer to the question, What shall I do to be saved ?

1.   They put it past all shadow of doubt, that the
door is open to every honest inquirer.

2.   They put it past all doubt that *the door is
Christ*.

3.   They put it past all doubt that no inquirer is
to be set to doing anything which *in the doing* will
not give salvation.

Clearly any answer that does not send the inquirer
straight to Jesus Christ, is big with possibilities of
false guidance and disaster.

" *The heart of the righteous studieth to answer* "
(Prov. 15 : 28).

XV

METHODS OF PREACHING

SYLLABUS

Comprehensively, three methods : Extempore, Manuscript, and Memoriter.

Extempore.

I. Exact definition.

II. Nothing inherent in mental structure to forbid this.

III. Reasons for beginning one's ministry with its practice : (*a*) it is the ideal delivery ; (*b*) occasions sometimes make it necessary ; (*c*) saves time for study.

IV. Direct advantages over other methods : (*a*) mind is stimulated by reproduction ; (*b*) greater animation in delivery ; (*c*) face to face contact with audience; (*d*) greater power of riveting attention ; (*e*) reaction from the audience ; (*f*) freedom to follow leadings of the Holy Spirit.

V. Essentials to success : (*a*) thorough premeditation ; (*b*) self-possession ; (*c*) persistent practice.

VI. Helps to facility : (*a*) a full and careful syllabus or brief ; (*b*) be satisfied at first with simplicity and accuracy ; (*c*) let trifling mistakes in language go ; (*d*) be diligent in the general study of words : (1) by frequent reference to a good book of synonyms ; (2) by careful speech in ordinary conversation ; (3) by careful writing ; (*e*) guard against mistaking mere fluency of speech for extemporaneous ability ; (*f*) begin extemporizing at the outset, and let the practice be uniform once every Sabbath ; (*g*) do not as a rule use prepared paragraphs ; (*h*) get an uplifted soul.

VII. Objections to extempore preaching : (*a*) apt to be rambling and desultory ; (*b*) apt to be superficial ; (*c*) apt to lack *balanced* treatment ; (*d*) great tendency to neglect thorough preparation.

Four safe-guards : (1) Thorough mental discipline. (2) Wide resources of knowledge. (3) Facility in using these resources. (4) Diligence in adding to them.

Manuscript.

I. Use of manuscript does not make the user any the less a preacher.

II.   Reasons in favour : (*a*) writing improves style ; (*b*) tends to give clearness to thought ; (*c*) gives greater compactness ; (*d*) gives relief to the mind in delivery ; (*e*) likelihood of securing well-balanced treatment ; (*f*) allows more undivided attention to devotional parts of service.

III.   Objection to manuscript preaching : (*a*) liable to lack direct address ; (*b*) mechanical delivery ; (*c*) lessened probability of riveting attention.

Memoriter.

I.   Favourite method of the ancients, owing to marvellous cultivation of memory.

II.   Advantages : (*a*) Looking and speaking directly to audience ; (*b*) language already prepared ; (*c*) giving one's self wholly to delivery.

But, an indispensable proviso : that the memory recall without conscious effort.

III.   Disadvantages : (*a*) the labour required to write and commit ; (*b*) the tendency to mechanical delivery ; (*c*) the fear of possible failure ; (*d*) the bondage to an already prescribed course ; the claimed freedom, only an apparent freedom ; the *introverted look* betrays the bondage.

Indispensable to ideal memoriter preaching is a memory swift to act ; and that never slips.

Indispensable to ideal manuscript preaching is complete mastery of the subject-matter, and complete familiarity with its verbal form.

Indispensable to ideal extempore preaching is just as complete mastery of the subject-matter, but no slavery whatever to any verbal form.   All the advantage of the pull from without which the audience gives, is joined to all the advantage of the push from within which meditation and study and prayer have given, making extempore preaching *the ideal of the ideals.*

A consensus of opinion, as to choice of method.

Helps in determining method.

XV

METHODS OF PREACHING

THERE are, comprehensively, three methods of preaching: The extemporaneous method, the manuscript method, and the memoriter method. And each of these methods has its distinct and definite ideal. Other methods are simply combinations or modifications of these, and may be classed under some one of these three broad generic divisions.

EXTEMPORANEOUS PREACHING

I. First of all, let us have clearly in mind the exact meaning of the phrase, extemporaneous preaching.

Negatively: (*a*) It is not meant that such preaching is wholly impromptu, off-hand, the birth of the hour. It is indeed extempore—for the time; but not from the time, as if the sermon were the product of the particular instant of delivery. Such utterly unpremeditated discourse could only be made effective on rare occasions, and after long and severe mental discipline; unless, indeed, it came by direct inspiration of God. Preaching without preparation has led to a great deal of superficial, rambling talk in the pulpit, without ideas and without power. And it has brought this whole matter of extemporaneous pulpit discourse into disrepute.

(*b*) Nor is extemporaneous preaching *extempore* in the sense of being " from *all* the time," as Dr. Shedd

suggests:[1] the result of the whole life and culture of
the preacher. It does undoubtedly embody, and is a
resultant of, all his past labour and discipline and accumulation. But this is just as true of the other methods
of preaching. It is equally the case with the written
and the memoriter discourse; and, therefore, it does
not define, or distinctly characterize, the extempore
method. What is true of all three methods cannot be
the differentiating feature of any single method.

Positively : Extemporaneous preaching, in its best
accepted sense, is ex-tem-po-re, from the time, *as to the
language alone.* It gets its clothing of *words* on the
instant of delivery ; and commonly it gets nothing
more. The theme, the plan of treatment, the order of
the thought, the arguments and illustrations, the entire subject-matter of the discourse, may have been,
and should have been, premeditated and prearranged.
But *the language is the birth of the hour,* born in the
very process of delivery ; ex-tem-po-re.

This, therefore, is the difference, and it should be
the only difference, between written and extemporaneous discourse. They have the same antecedents of
discipline, study, reflection, experience. Produced by
the same mind, in like conditions, the same logical
order, the same mastery of the subject, and the same
breadth and depth and clearness of thought, may prevail in the extempore as in the written discourse.

II.   There is nothing inherent in mental structure
to forbid an extempore oral expression of premeditated
thought, *when such an expression is possible by the
pen.* The varied powers of the mind are not shut up
to the written symbol. The form the thought shall

[1] " Homiletics," p. 219.

take is so secondary a matter that discipline and
practice may make a reasonably good form possible in
extempore speech to any one thinking that thought.
The difficulty is certainly not in the constitution of
the human mind. It is in the circumstances—the things
outside the mind, " standing around " ; such as the presence of critical and cultured hearers, the importance
of the occasion, past mistakes, and partial failures—of
which any man may measurably be the master.

III.   The reasons for beginning and continuing
one's ministry with the practice of extempore
preaching.

Negatively :   (*a*)   Not because our Lord and His
apostles thus preached.   Christ spake as never man
spake.   He knew men ; could read their hearts.   He
knew God, He was God, and, therefore, He could be
no model or precedent for us in this matter of extempore speech.   He did not need to make preparation in order to preach the sermon on the mount.
Dr. Storrs speaks of the extempore as the apostolic
method.   But we must beware of quoting apostolic
example in this matter lest we get Balaam's ass in the
pulpit without the ass's inspiration.

(*b*)   Not because all preachers can become preeminent extemporizers.   It is only given to the few
to rise to the full height of effectiveness and pulpit
power possible by this method.

But, on the positive side, the reasons for the frequent
and persistent practice of extemporaneous preaching
are clear and unmistakable.

(*a*)   It is the *ideal* delivery—the perfection of
oratory.   It is the most direct way of speaking to
men.   It is a living man pouring out his heart to

living men, in the mode which nature prompts—a
free, flowing, animated utterance, a lifting up of the
soul into the eyes, a tingling of passion to the very
finger-tips, a glow in the whole mien and the whole
man, such as is impossible by any other method.
Hence the best extempore preaching is not only the
best of its kind, but it is better than the best of any
other kind.

(b) Again: Occasions are frequently arising in
the ministry where extemporaneous speech is greatly
desirable, and sometimes even imperative. Grave
questions in ecclesiastical bodies are not infrequently
decided by a single speech, elicited in the heat of
debate, and precluding the possibility of written discourse. And facility in extemporaneous effort may
make just the difference between victory and defeat
in such a case.

Unexpected emergencies also, startling providences,
a great calamity, may make it desirable to speak upon
a topic for which there is absolutely no time for
written preparation, and upon which, nevertheless, it
may be to the last degree important that the man of
God should speak. Opportunities of great usefulness
will thus be lost to a minister who does not trust himself to pulpit discourse without a manuscript.[1]

[1] Spurgeon of London had agreed to preach in his father's pulpit one
Sabbath morning. But as the hour for service approached, and the
substitute did not put in an appearance, the father felt that he himself would have to do the preaching. So he hurriedly looked up a
text, and lighted upon this: "By grace have ye been saved through
faith; and that not of yourselves; it is the gift of God" (Eph. 2:8).
When he had concluded the discussion of the first head, "By grace
have ye been saved," he saw his son enter the church door, and he
said, "Ah, there he is; he will come up and *finish the sermon*." And

But with facility in extemporaneous effort once acquired he may improve all such occasions without personal mortification, and to the sure profit of his hearers. We may even go further than this, and say there will be occasions he is bound to improve, places and times in which there may be a sacred obligation to preach the Gospel, with no possibility of written preparation, and no use for it if it were possible ; yet where silence would be recreancy to duty, and would surely bring loss of influence. Never should a preacher of Christ's Gospel be so bound and trammelled by the necessity of a manuscript as to suffer "the mortification of being silent when he ought to speak, is expected to speak, and would do good by speaking." It is exposing Christian ambassadorship to the charge of imbecility, and is a dishonour to God. It furnishes ground for the stinging interrogative of Fénelon : "Shall the preacher not venture to speak of God to his people, without having arranged all his words, and learned like a schoolboy his lesson by heart ?"

(c) Still again : The habit of extemporaneous preaching saves time for *study*. The man of God must be a *student*, thoroughly furnished. Amidst the pressure of engagements in connection with his work he will more and more feel the need of redeeming the hours which he can devote to profitable study and re- search. He who *writes* his sermons must ordinarily take the working hours of at least two or three days in the mere manual labour. The time of writing at

Charles went to the pulpit, got from his father the exact situation, and finished the sermon on that text, taking the clause, "through faith," as the second head of the unfinished discourse.

least one sermon should be saved to him by the extemporaneous method. That much can then be spared to devote to mental discipline and accumulation. And in the course of years the gain in intellectual equipment and power would be simply incalculable.

Of course, it is not meant by this that there is to be the least abatement of the toil of preparation for extempore discourse. No lessened labour and time is to be thought of or tolerated, save as it is involved in the mere writing out of the premeditated discourse.

(d) Another reason favouring extempore effort is this: When creditable and efficient it is held in high public esteem. Facility of speech is attractive to men. It commands attention. It awakens interest. It gives influence and power, because it is supposed to indicate ability and power. Doubtless the public judgment is often at fault in this matter. Beyond all question, fluency of utterance is often mistaken for depth and capacity and wealth of resource. It is an erroneous standard of judgment. But in spite of all that may be said by way of exception, the extemporaneous effort is nearest to nature's method, and gifts in this direction will be highly esteemed by the mass of hearers. It is therefore a clear consideration, urging to the faithful and persistent cultivation of these gifts by every preacher of the Gospel of Christ.

IV. The direct advantages over other methods.

(a) One capital advantage is, the mind must repeat the process of production, and "re-present to itself in a living form the whole thought and emotion of the discourse." It must summon up and clothe with flesh and blood, and set before men, that which has had existence only in the mind of the preacher. It is therefore a kind of *second birth* that is given to a discourse, in the act of extemporaneous delivery. This very effort of invention is necessarily stimulative. The mind is roused and vivified in the process. There is no such action called for in preaching from the manuscript, and hence there is less likelihood of spiritual infection and of summoning into play all the activities and sympathies of the preacher's soul. Feeling is born of mental action; and intense mental action will produce corresponding increase of feeling; and intensest action and emotion project the most into the minds and hearts of an audience.

(*b*) Greater animation and earnestness in delivery is another advantage of the extempore method over other methods.

As the thoughts rise fresh in the mind and quicken the sensibilities, the effort to give them expression in speech engenders warmth of utterance. Excited sensibilities will make a more fitting mould for the thoughts, give naturalness to gesture by giving it freedom and meaning, and the whole action and speech will be surcharged with energy and vigour.

(*c*) The consciousness of speaking face to face with the audience is another advantage.

Extemporaneous preaching tends inevitably to more direct address. Style is less involved, less abstract. The speaker is in immediate contact with his audience, and the contact is undisturbed by frequent reference to a manuscript, thrust as it were between himself and his hearers. And this speaking directly to an audience gives:

(*d*) The greater power of riveting attention and arousing sympathy.

He can best get another's attention, and secure heed to what he has to say, who looks his listener in the face. The Germans have an expressive way of saying that if a man has anything of importance to tell, and would have another disposed to listen to him, he must say his say "between four eyes." Surely to take a paper out of the pocket and read it to him would be a piece of gross stupidity, pardonable only where exactness in the very words was needed as a matter of record.

(e) The reaction of the attention and sympathy of the audience on the speaker, is a further advantage of the extemporaneous method.

Living contact with aroused and sympathizing minds will stir to an action of intellect and an eloquence of expression impossible in the quiet of the study. If the discourse is written, this reaction can be of little service to the preacher, for his thought has already received a fixed form, from which he is not likely to break away. But in extemporaneous discourse, this reaction has full play to quicken, purify, and elevate the speaker's mind, to flood his heart more fully with the emotions he sees kindled in his hearers; and therefore to give his glowing thought a better, intenser expression. There is a mighty "pull from without" as well as a "push from within." Sometimes preachers are almost lifted off their feet by this inspiration. And it is then they lift their audiences to heights of feeling and spiritual power otherwise unattainable.

(f) Freedom to follow the unanticipated suggestions and leadings of the Spirit of God, is a still further advantage of the extemporaneous method.

The Holy Spirit's assistance should always be sought

and expected in the delivery of pulpit discourse, whether it be written or unwritten. That the Spirit does sometimes give such aid, illuminations, elevations, enlargements, will not be questioned. That all such experiences are traceable to the Holy Spirit, it is not claimed. That they *may* be His work, who will dare deny. Now he who has his manuscript before him is liable to restrict himself to what he has written. He is in greater peril, therefore, of ignoring or disregarding the Spirit's leadings in actual delivery. The extemporaneous preacher, with no restraint of already written discourse upon him, is free to accept the slightest suggestion, and to profit by the invoked assistance of the Spirit of God, whose liberty in sacred discourse, Calvin impressively says: "no possible danger must be permitted to abridge." "In general," says John Newton, "the best and most useful parts of my sermon occur *de novo* while I am preaching." [1]

V. The essentials to success in extemporaneous preaching.

(*a*) The first essential to success is *thorough premeditation :* subject-matter for mastery, and the mastery of the subject-matter. Let this be made sure, before and above all else. "Abundance of matter begets abundance of words," says Cicero. But it does not always contain, as Tyndall says non-living matter does, "the promise and potency of life." All else in a sermon is secondary to its contents. And the preparation of the matter should be more thorough in unwritten than in written discourse, for it is commonly the all in all in extemporaneous preaching. The preparatory work of the written sermon may be revised

[1] "Letters to a Student,"

in the process of writing. But the preparatory work of the extemporaneous sermon cannot possibly be revised in the process of actual delivery. And the extemporized product will be as the premeditated matter. If the preparation has been faulty, hurried, superficial, illogical, these faults will inevitably appear in the sermon. Therefore, no abatement of honest, earnest, hard labour is to be by any possibility allowed, in preparing the matter of extempore discourse. Self-indulgence here will inevitably prevent efficiency. Neglect at this point will ensure and perpetuate failure. Hence the preacher should make it a matter of principle and conscience to allow no readiness or fluency of speech, no temptation to self-confidence, no pressure of other work, nothing whatever save absolute necessity, to keep him from the most thorough and painstaking fidelity in premeditation.

This premeditation involves, just as in written discourse before the act of writing, (1) a distinct conception of the subject to be treated, and of the object to be accomplished, a logical and orderly plan of treatment, and the full collection and arrangement of materials for explanation, proof, and illustration.

It also involves, (2) a personal active interest in, and sympathy with, the theme, the occasion, and the hearers.

This, too, belongs to the written discourse, but it is preeminently requisite in extempore effort, and is to be secured by the same means; namely, by meditation on the occasion for which preparation is made, on the object in view, on the theme to be treated, and by prayer. The Athenian Pericles could not ascend the bema without an earnest invocation to the immortal gods for their assistance. Surely, for an aroused interest and sympathy in ascending a pulpit to handle the deep things of the Gospel, there can be nothing so effectual as earnest prayer to the God of the Gospel.

(*b*) Another essential to success in extemporaneous preaching is *self-possession*.

Not the self-possession of inordinate vanity and self-conceit. Men have this and mount the pulpit, and never trip in extemporaneous discourse; but they are "as sounding brass or a tinkling cymbal." They may captivate some ears, may impose for a time on some judgments, but neither in them nor in their speech does power lie. Self-observation, the thinking how one is doing it, is utterly incompatible with true eloquence. The self-possession born of conceited assurance is unspiritual, and not only not to be coveted, but to be cast out and trodden under foot.

The self-possession or confidence of the pulpit should be born of confidence in the promised assistance of God. Proficiency in this direction is the child of piety and grace. To be lifted above hampering and unnerving fear as in the sight of men, one needs to be filled with holy fear as in the sight of God. This is the only foundation for true self-possession. [1]

And this is entirely compatible with two things: (1) A tremor and agitation more or less manifest to consciousness, and even to the observation of others, just prior to and at the outset of extemporaneous effort. Cicero "grew pale at the beginning of a speech and felt a tremor in every part of his frame." "I am

[1] "Thou therefore gird up thy loins and arise and speak unto them all that I command thee: be not dismayed at their faces, lest I confound thee before them" (Jer. 1:17).

now an old man," said Luther, "and have been a long
time occupied in preaching, but I never ascend the
pulpit without a tremor."[1]   Let one realize what the
work is to which he is set, the sacredness and responsibility and possible consequence of each act of
delivery of pulpit discourse, and he can hardly be unmoved in its anticipation and performance.   But this
agitation will disappear as the preacher is lifted, by
absorption in his theme and by the fullness of the
Spirit, above all regard to self and the fear of man.

(2) But the self-possession born of confidence in
God is also compatible with the conceded influence of
a timid, shrinking temperament, of already achieved
success, of thorough preparation, and of natural and
acquired gifts.   Grace does not dispense with reason.
Piety is not a substitute for common sense.   Piety
does not materially change one's mental and physical
conditions and temperament.   Confidence in God does
not dispense with the use of means.   The point is, not
that natural timidity and past success and thorough
preparation and gifts, both natural and acquired, have
no influence on self-possession, but that these things
should be made to *contribute* to self-possession.   Hence
natural timidity should be early overcome by
conscientious and careful practice ; hence we should
secure the earliest possible success ; hence we should
make the most diligent and exhaustive preparation ;
and hence the gifts in which we are deficient should
be assiduously acquired.   But it still remains true

---

[1] Rev. John McNeil says that " he is just tingling in every nerve before going into the pulpit till he gets under way with his subject." He
does not think a man will make a good preacher without this nervous
susceptibility (Personal interview, 1893).

that faith in God is the chief, the basic, element in the confidence, or self-possession, of extemporaneous discourse. "Believe," says Monod, "that He who sends you will not have you speak in vain. Seek the salvation of those who hear you as you do your own. Forget yourselves so as to behold nothing but the glory of God and the salvation of your hearers. You will then tremble more before God, but you will tremble less before men."

(*c*) The third essential to success in extemporaneous preaching is *persistent practice.*

Resolution is much. But unyielding, steady, persistent practice is much more. The unwontedness of the effort, the presence of critical minds in the audience, literary sensitiveness with respect to style, mistakes and partial failures, will all plead against continuance. Resolutely let the ears be shut, and the heart steeled, against all such counsel. Hold the mind determinedly to this one thing, and be inflexibly fixed in the purpose, even through much mortification, to enter into this kingdom of power. With perseverance will come ability, a growing familiarity, a disregard of the possible posture of some hearer, a fervid, direct style of speech, and, ere long, the impossibility of failure. And let it be remembered for encouragement always, that the great apostle preached in weakness and in fear and in much trembling; that Thomas Scott sat down from an extempore effort in a kind of despair, saying, "It does not signify, it is impossible that I should ever be able to preach extempore;" yet he came ultimately to preach in no other way; that Leigh Richmond's first effort was a total failure, and he was so ashamed of it that he declared he would not repeat the attempt; yet, induced to repeat it, he came at last to have no difficulty; that Robert Hall, twice at least in his very earliest experiments, failed utterly, and in a way that was really painful to witness, and still more grievous to bear; yet he became a prince and a power in extemporaneous discourse; that Dr. Tyng who in his day was one of the best extemporizers in the Episcopal Church, so failed at the outset that his mortified wife said to him on the way home, " I trust that's the last ; " that Dr. Storrs was driven back to his manuscript with great mortification after a serious failure in extemporizing. Success by this road may be painful, and sometimes to the last degree humiliating, but with persistence it is absolutely sure.

VI. Helps to facility in extemporaneous preaching.

(*a*) A complete analysis of the discourse to be delivered—a full and careful syllabus or brief.

It will be well to write out the plan—the divisions and sub-divisions, and to use mnemonic catch-words to indicate the order of thought and illustration under each head.

This brief should not be too minute, too comprehensive of details: for then it may become a burden to the memory, and the preaching take on the character of a memoriter effort. Dr. Storrs' first effort at Brooklyn, after his installation, was a personal mortification, and he attributed it to too much preparation in detail. He was all the time looking backward, not forward, in preaching. Afterwards he wrote brief outlines, covering only one or two sheets of common note paper. The outline should be like a blazed path through the woods, so that the mind can pass naturally

and easily from point to point through the entire
sermon.

Then, this brief should be thoroughly studied, mastered—gone over again and again—so that no effort
will be required to recall it.   Let it be written out in
a plain, bold hand and learned completely by heart.
A German witness once said when asked if he couldn't
change an opinion which he declared he had formed,
" No," said he, " I can't.   It's *all mixed up mit my
mind.*"   Let the preacher get his outline all mixed up
with his mind.   Then, whether he takes the written
outline in the pulpit or not, will be of little consequence.   The absolutely best way is to have no notes
whatever.[1]   Face the audience without a scrap of
paper between speaker and hearer.   But if the speaker
is not in perfect possession of the brief, let it be taken
to the pulpit, and referred to as infrequently as possible.

(*b*)   Let the preacher be satisfied at first with saying simply and accurately just what he has to say,
without elaboration or illustration or ambitious oratorical display.   He should not attempt fine things
till he has learned to do well the ordinary, the plain,
the direct, the simple.   The chaste diction, the drapery
and grace of elegant speech, may come afterwards.
Try the wings with low flights, before seeking to
career aloft and to go soaring and gyrating in the
upper air.

(*c*)   Let trifling mistakes in language go.   Sweep
on with the thought.   Do not stop and return to
make corrections.   It was Whitefield's course " never

---

[1] So Dr. Storrs, Spurgeon, Talmage, and many others unite in testifying.

to take back anything unless it was wicked." Pausing
to reconstruct will be likely to prove fatal to that
ready flow so essential to success in extempore effort.
It will turn the thought to the style and away from
the subject, and so lead to hesitation, repetition, and
possible confusion. And why advertise a blunder to
the entire audience that may not have been noticed
by a single hearer. Push right on with the discourse.
The speaker may be sure the mistake is magnified
more to his own consciousness than to the mind of any
one listening to him.

(*d*) Be diligent in the study of words: and so become the master of an ever-enriching vocabulary.

(1) The frequent reference to a good book of
synonyms [1]—Crabbe's or Smith's [2]—and familiarity
with a Thesaurus of English words, will very soon
increase greatly one's ready and discriminating command of good English.

(2) Careful speech in ordinary conversation will be
helpful. One who is accustomed to a careless and slov-
enly use of words all the week can hardly expect a
rich vocabulary from which to draw supplies for extemporaneous discourse on the Sabbath.

(3) Careful writing also—writing with constant
regard to correct and chaste expression—will tend to
give a command of richer and fitter words in unpremeditated speech.

(*e*) Guard against mistaking mere fluency of speech
for good extemporaneous ability. Study, hard study,

[1] In the English language, as used by the masters, there is really no
such thing as a synonym.

[2] A recent work is "English Synonyms, Antonyms and Preposi-
tions," by J. C. Fernald (Funk & Wagnalls Company, New York).

makes the difference between mere flow of words and
real power in extempore speech. And it is recreancy
to the sacred calling of the ministry, and an offense
against God, to indulge in idleness and neglect of
study, because endowed with natural fluency.[1] Volu-
ble loquacity may be superficial rant, mere wordy
emptiness seeking to "supply the place of thought"—
a ready flow of sound, twaddle and platitude. It
costs the speaker nothing, for it is nothing. "It is a
hideous gift," says Spurgeon, "to say nothing at extreme length."

(f) Begin the extemporaneous method of preaching at the very threshold of the ministry, and let the
practice be uniform, once every Sabbath. If already
in the ministry and accustomed to the manuscript exclusively, break the usage once every week. And we
are such slaves to usage, not only as to method, but
as to time and place, that complete deliverance from
bondage can be had only by preaching extempore,
now and then in the morning and now and then in the
evening.

Dr. Alexander tells of a friend of his once asking
a celebrated painter how young persons should be
taught to paint. The reply was: "Just as puppies
are taught to swim—chuck them in." It is so with
this kind of preaching. Dare to plunge in at once, if
you would be a good extemporizer. The worst floun-

---

[1] When Thiers was president of the French Republic he was about
to issue some important manifesto, and submitted the draft to a
critical friend. "Yes," said the critic, " the matter is clearly expressed, but I miss the ease and fluency of your usual style." "Ah!"
replied Thiers, "I have not worked those in yet. The ease will cost
me much labour, and the fluency I shall have to drag in by the hair
of its head."

derings and splutterings will ere long give way to ease and exactness and buoyant movement in these waters.

(*g*) Do not as a rule use prepared paragraphs carefully written out. The passage from these to the unpremeditated portions of the discourse cannot be easily and naturally made, save where great excellence in extempore effort has been already attained. Dr. Storrs characterizes the use of such prepared paragraphs as the poorest possible plan for himself. To use his own striking phrase, "The whole sermon became a series of jerks."

Yet the rule has its exceptions. Robert Hall often paid minute attention to the verbal structure of those portions of his sermons where the force of an argument or the probable success of an application depended mainly on the language. Dr. N. S. S. Beman [1] usually wrote out with care his introduction, and the first few sentences under each head, as if he would thus get up steam and gather momentum, to push on through each division ; or as if he would thus feel his way to confidence, boldness, and liberty.

(*h*) Get an uplifted soul. *Pray.* Open the sluices of the heart. Beseech God to flood them. The preacher is to come into most intimate and vital fellowship with living men. He is to lay his hands on their heart-strings. He is to look into their faces and pour passion along the mysterious channels of sympathy into their souls. To attempt all this with a perfunctory preparation is to make a mock of the holy work. The rather, with a mental equipment perfected

[1] A very able extemporizer and mighty man of God in the first half of the last century; and who with Barnes and Breckenbridge constituted the three B's that made such a buzzing in the Presbyterian hive in those stormy days.

at every point, let the man of God fail not to pray, earnestly and wrestlingly, that he may speak *amidst the illuminations and sanctities of the Eternal Spirit.*

VII.   Objections to extemporaneous preaching.

(*a*)   It is apt to be rambling and desultory.   This is impossible, unless the premeditated plan is rambling. If the preacher has distinctly conceived what he is to say and what object he is to aim at in saying it, and the successive steps by which that object is to be reached; if he has surveyed the whole ground and marked out the whole track of thought, and thus blazed his way through—all of which is essential *prior* to each extemporaneous effort—rambling and disconnection are simply out of the question.

(*b*)   Extempore effort is apt to be superficial.   This is also impossible, unless the premeditated thought has been superficial.   There is nothing to prevent as deep and profound thought in preparing for the pulpit this way, as any other way.   The thought should be just the same—just as vigorous, protracted, and thorough. It is only the *language* that is the offspring of the instant of delivery.

(*c*)   Extempore preaching is apt to lead to the undue enlargement of one point, and hence to a want of balance and symmetry in the treatment of the subject. This is unquestionably true, and can never be wholly guarded against.   Discipline and persistent practice will do much, however, to correct this evil.

(*d*)   But the chief objection to extemporaneous preaching is the great and dangerous tendency to neglect thorough preparation. (1) This tendency comes in part from facility of speech.   Nothing is so dangerous as facility.   It tends to intellectual carelessness and indolence, and has often proved destructive of habits of diligent study. It is questionable whether natural facility is any great boon. "It is often mistaken for genius, but it generally ends in mediocrity," says the sculptor, W. W. Story, in a lecture on art. Gerome, the eminent French artist, writing of his own experience, declares: "I watched myself closely in my work, and one day having made a study rather easily I scraped it entirely from the canvas, although it was well done—so much did I fear to slip on the smooth plane of facility."[1]

That smooth plane of facility! Many a young minister has slipped there to his sore and grievous hurt, and sometimes to the permanent impairment of his pulpit power—so that he has come to be known as a man " whose linguistic fluency is unembarrassed by intellectual activity ; " and his patient, wise parishioners find it in their hearts to pray that the Lord would baptize their young pastor with a rich experience of this blessed embarrassment.

(2) But the tendency to neglect thorough preparation for the pulpit has often a more honourable source. It frequently comes from the pressure of other and important ministerial work. This work sometimes presses its claims with imperial urgency. And certain as the fluent extemporizer is of his ability to furnish a discourse to his hearers that will be reasonably acceptable, trusting to the occasion to inspire him, remembering that often some of his best thoughts have come to him in the very hour of delivery, he yields to the pressure of other work, and neglects the protracted and thorough study of his theme. This

[1] *Century Magazine*, February, 1889.

inevitably ends, if continued, in repetitions and commonplaces, and the utter dearth and death of all freshness and originality.

One safeguard against this evil is an inflexible determination, by the grace of God and as a matter of conscience, to keep certain hours or days sacred to this one thing—studious and thoughtful preparation for the pulpit.

Another safeguard is the fixed habit of writing, as well as of extemporizing sermons, perfecting each manuscript with the utmost care. It is a good deal of an assumption for a young man to lay aside the habit of writing sermons. Surely the purpose is born of ignorance or conceit. For to an extemporaneous preacher, if he is to have anything more than mere temporary success, the four following things are indispensable.

(1) The most thorough mental discipline, leading to exact habits of thinking.

(2) Wide resources of knowledge.

(3) Facility in using these resources.

(4) Diligence in adding to them.

If he have not these, his sermons will inevitably come to show that he spins out " the thread of his verbosity " long after he is done with " the staple of his argument," and like the argument of Gratiano, they will have " two grains of wheat hid in two bushels of chaff."

PREACHING FROM A MANUSCRIPT

I. Let it be said, first of all, and with emphasis, that the use of a manuscript in the pulpit does not make the user any the less a preacher.

It is often objected that *reading* is not *preaching*. " I object to being read at when I go to hear the Gospel," is Parker's way of putting it. " Be a preacher, and not a reader of the Gospel," he further says. Bishop Simpson, in his " Yale Lectures on Preaching " (p. 178) quotes from Potter's " Sacred Eloquence," to this effect : " In no sense of the word can reading be called preaching. . . . The sermon which is merely read from a paper never has been, and never will be, anything more than a piece of reading."

And Sydney Smith waxes merry with the subject after this fashion : " Pulpit discourses have insensibly dwindled from speaking to reading—a practice of itself sufficient to stifle every germ of eloquence. . . . What can be more ludicrous than an orator delivering stale indignation and fervour of a week old, turning over whole pages of violent passions— reading the tropes and apostrophes into which he is hurried by the ardour of his mind, and so affected at a preconcerted line and page that he is unable to proceed any further."

But all this pungent and vehement objection to preaching from a manuscript, is more witty than wise, and fuller of sound than sense. What is " preaching " ? It is the public exposition and application of God's truth. The use of the manuscript is one method of doing this, just as extemporizing is another method, and memorizing another. It might as well be urged that the extemporizer extemporizes the Gospel, or the memorizer memorizes the Gospel, as that the user of a manuscript reads the Gospel. Each preaches, and one equally with the other, but each after a distinct method. Therefore, to Parker's say-

ing, " I object to being read at, when I go to hear
the Gospel," the sufficient reply is, " I object to being
extemporized at or being memorized at, when I go to
hear the Gospel; " and there is no sense in either.

As to Sydney Smith's satirical pleasantry, in his
tirade against preaching from a manuscript, one or
the other of two things is the inevitable conclusion
from his premise: either *no preparation whatever* is
to be made for the Sabbath, or some kind of *thoughtful* preparation is to be made that does not involve
writing. In the former case it is true that the
preacher will avoid all possibility of "delivering
stale indignation and fervour of a week old." But he
will be likely to go floundering in a sea of extemporized juvenilities and pious platitudes.

In the latter case, if the preacher is a man and his
thinking worth anything, there, in the quiet of his
study, where he thinks and prays, preparing for the
Sabbath, his soul will be stirred with " indignation
and fervour." But that " indignation and fervour "
will be just as " old " and " stale " when he comes to
his pulpit with it on Sunday, as if he had it in black
and white in a manuscript. And again, if feeling is
born of thought in the study, why should not that
same thought produce even intenser feeling in the
kindling presence of a sympathetic audience!

II. The reasons in favor of manuscript preaching.

(*a*) Writing chastens and purifies the style. Of
course, there is a kind of hurried, unstudied, extemporaneous writing that does nothing of the sort.
It is neither preceded nor accompanied by thought.
And the preacher goes dashing over the pages of his
sermon paper, with no effort at exact expression.

This is even worse than unstudied, extemporaneous *speaking*. For the latter has some helpful adjunct in an occasion and an audience. And a manuscript is not the least assurance against intellectual vacuity. Even after the most thoughtful and thorough preparation for the sermon, if it be " written with fury," it should be "revised with phlegm." If the writing has been with constant regard to exact verbal expression, of course this critical revision will not be necessary. But, in either case, expression is carefully studied as a means of greater distinctness of thought, of lopping off redundant words, of giving directness and plainness to involved sentences, of strengthening a weak expression, of making every sentence and every word tell towards the furtherance of the one object of the discourse. And this must inevitably chasten and purify and invigourate the style.

(*b*) *Writing tends to give clearness and vividness to thought*. The very effort to put a conception in words often discloses the vagueness of the conception. We are not sure of the exact possession of a thought until we have sought to give it verbal form. Writing favours precision of thought as well as purity of speech. Channing doubts "whether a man ever brings his faculties to bear with their whole force on a subject until he writes upon it." [1] When Robert Hall constructed the language of any part of his sermons the sentences were formed with minute attention to their verbal structure. Buffon says: " To write well is to think well, to feel well, to render well." Cicero is credited with saying, "The pen is the best and most excellent informer and director of

[1] Vol. 1, p. 263.

the tongue." And the brilliant Dr. Richard S. Storrs, so long the eminent and scholarly leader of the Brooklyn pulpit, voiced his conviction after this manner: "The pen gives march to the mind."[1] "Better give up half your library than let the pen fall into disuse."[2] "Nothing but the pen can break up books for us, and transmute them into knowledge and thought."[3]

Surely the style of the pulpit cannot afford to dispense with this aid to chasteness, dignity, and force. Blemishes in diction need the correction of the pen.

(c) Greater compactness with greater variety of material may be secured by writing. The discourse is surer to be rid of superfluities, and to move in straighter lines. It will be likely to contain more varied and multiplied shades of thought and illustration than would appear in extempore effort.

(d) The manuscript gives a certain relief to the mind in the actual process of delivery. There is no effort of memory such as is often, and sometimes painfully, apparent in memoriter speaking. There is no labour of invention and style, together with the apprehensions by such labour, as in extempore speaking. The prepared discourse—prepared both in thought and language—enables the preacher to enlist all his powers in the actual work of public utterance. If now he has become thoroughly familiar with his manuscript, so that his eye is not held unbrokenly to it in the process of delivery, this method of preaching ought to be greatly effective. It may approach to something of the freedom of the extempore effort. Into his delivery the preacher may put his whole soul,

[1] "Preaching Without Notes," p. 49.   [2] *Ibid.*, p. 50.
[3] *Ibid.*, p. 52.

possessed with his theme and concerned to possess his hearer with it. Chalmers and Robertson and Alexander Maclaren, Howard Crosby and R. D. Hitchcock and William Taylor and Cuyler and a great and goodly host besides, so preached, and their preaching was with living fire. Such preaching is not "reading," and should not be so-called. It is widely different from, and immeasurably above, that which holds the eye fettered to the manuscript and keeps the mind occupied in taking in the sense.

(e) Another reason favouring manuscript preaching is the likelihood of securing well-balanced, and hence more thorough, treatment.

In writing, the undue elaboration of any one point may be noted and checked. But in extempore effort, the excitement of delivery, when the rush is on, the stir and fervour of aroused interest in the point under discussion, may lead to enlargement and amplification that will leave little or no room for the discussion of other and equally important points. Fit proportion, and therefore greater thoroughness of treatment, are likely to be secured by writing.

(f) The written sermon also favours more undivided attention to the *devotional* parts of the service.

The secret of many a barren prayer in the pulpit may be just here. The mind has been busy with the coming sermon, which is to be extemporized. Concern about that, the consciousness of inadequate preparation, and apprehension of failure, may easily prove the death of a true spirit of devotion.

III. The objections to preaching from the manuscript.

(a) The written sermon is liable to be too studied

in expression, too literary and scholastic, so as to lack naturalness and that vital feature of all oratorical effort—*direct address*. There is a tendency in writing to write for the eye, to pay too great heed to the rare niceties and delicate colourings of expression, and too little heed to the direct end in view, the supreme object to be accomplished. It is difficult to write as an orator would speak, and few perfectly succeed in composing in solitude as if the audience were before them. But eloquence in the pulpit demands an oratorical style. It tends to move straight on men's hearts. It is not by involved and highly-finished sentences that it secures its ends. Quintilian says it is "regardless of the nicety of paring the nails and adjusting the hair."

(*b*) With the written sermon there is also the liability to mechanical delivery.

Just in proportion as the mind is occupied in picking up the thought from the written page, is restraint put upon posture and gesture, and the mind is taken away from the object in view, from the desire to accomplish it, and from sympathy with the audience—*three of the chief sources of power in delivery.*

To avoid this, the sermon should be written in a bold, legible hand, the beginning of sentences should be distinctly marked, the body of the writing should be broken up into paragraphs, the lower right hand corner of each leaf should be lightly folded over so that the leaf may be easily turned in delivery, and the manuscript should be given two or three careful readings before it is taken to the pulpit. Otherwise it is likely to put restraint upon look, gesture and posture, and to lessen the flexibility and quench the fire of oratorical action.

(*c*) The lessened probability of riveting attention, of profiting by the reaction of the sympathy of the audience, and of using the unanticipated suggestions of the Holy Spirit, may also be used as objections to this method of preaching, though they have been named as advantages in extempore effort. *Eye must meet eye, thought must not be bound by fixed forms*, and the leadings of the Holy Spirit must have *instant and constant heed*, in order to the best oratorical success. Nothing but a burning heart, aflame with devotion and swept as with a passion for souls, will meet the difficulties presented by a manuscript. But a burning heart will make the hearer forget the preacher has a manuscript before he has gone over a half dozen pages. "How would you heat a cold church?" was one of the questions sent up to Moody, in one of his big tabernacle gatherings in New York City. Back came the answer, swift as lightning, "Build a big fire in the pulpit." Away will go all thought or suggestion of a manuscript and all objection to it, in that same kind of conflagration.[1]

The Memoriter Method of Preaching

I. This was the favourite method with the ancients, and in it they attained success. The orators of succeeding ages have never surpassed them.

[1] I have asked scores of people, fresh from the public service, and commenting enthusiastically upon the sermon, if the preacher used a manuscript, though I knew he never preached without one, and they could not tell whether the preacher had preached from notes or not, so wholly had they been absorbed in the spirit and power of his message. Surely, as weighed against the message and the man, method kicks the beam.

But the secret of their success was their almost incredible and inconceivable cultivation of memory. Crassus, we are told by Cicero, would sometimes dictate as many as six different parts of the same argument to six clerks, at the same time, and then go immediately into Court and deliver the whole without once looking at his papers. But such marvellous feats of memory are rare, and seldom possible even with laborious culture and the most severe discipline.[1]

II. The advantages of the memoriter method.

(*a*) Looking and speaking directly to the audience, as against the manuscript method.

[1] William H. Seward was probably one of the best representatives of this class of effective public speakers among our American statesmen. In the Lincoln campaign of 1859–60, I distinctly remember his stenographer testifying that the three or four speeches Seward made for the central West in that great campaign were dictated by Seward before he left Auburn, and then given, without a scrap of paper before him, to his eager and enthusiastic audiences. In one of these speeches occurred that memorable phrase, "the irrepressible conflict," which was quoted from one end of the land to the other and became historic.

But this remarkable feat of memory is a far remove from the memoriter exploits reported of Macaulay. That he knew "Paradise Lost" by heart was common report. One evening at Edinburgh there was a bet of a copy of "Paradise Lost" between Macaulay and Jeffrey as to a certain line of that poem. The next morning Macaulay came with a handsomely bound volume. "There," he said, "is your book; I have lost; but I have read it through once more, and I will now make you another bet that I can repeat the whole." Jeffrey took him at his word, and put him on in passage after passage without once finding him at fault. This Lord Jeffrey told to Mr. Hayward. It caps the story of Sir Robert Peel saying to Macaulay that he believed he had never forgotten anything he wanted to remember; to which Macaulay retorted that he had never forgotten anything. No process of strengthening the memory could give such prodigious power, without great natural retentiveness and readiness.

(*b*)   Language already carefully prepared as against the extempore method.   Hence :

(*c*)   Giving oneself wholly to the work of delivery; adapting force, pitch, time, articulation, emphasis, and gesture to the varying thought and sentiment.

But to these unquestionable advantages is attached an *indispensable proviso*.   The proviso is that the *memory must recall without conscious effort*.   If the effort to recall is a labour, so engrossing attention as to keep the mind from giving full swing to all the other powers of effective speech, then the supposed advantages disappear, and the *disadvantages* come to the front with an emphasis and a force quite unmistakable.

III.   The *disadvantages* of the memoriter method.

(*a*)   The labour and time required to write and commit.

(*b*)   The tendency to mechanical delivery, as indicated in the fatal, tell-tale, introverted look.

(*c*)   The fear of possible failure from unforeseen circumstances.

(*d*)   The bondage to an already prescribed course, sentence by sentence : for to switch off the appointed track would endanger subsequent connection.   So that the claimed *freedom* of this method is, after all, only an apparent freedom.

The *possession of an extraordinary verbal memory* would obviate the most of these difficulties, and is the indispensable condition to efficiency by this method.

The words *must seem to come of themselves*.   Any toil of remembering, or dread of forgetting, will vitiate delivery and make spoil of the deliverer.   When the speaker's eye is turned inward on the tablet of his brain, as if in search of thoughts and words that ought to be crowding to the tip of his tongue, how can that eye flash with enthusiasm, or be charged with electric fire? When that telltale betraying, and never-to-be-mistaken *introverted look,* shows that he *does not see his congregation,* he can neither be in close sympathetic touch with his hearers, nor responsive to their varied moods and needs.[1]

Here, then, are the three generic ideal methods of preaching. Any other methods are mere modifications or combinations of these.

For the ideal memoriter method of preaching, it is absolutely indispensable that the preacher have a memory ready and retentive, swift to act, and that never slips.

For the ideal method of preaching from a manuscript, it is absolutely indispensable that there should be both complete mastery of the subject-matter, and

---

[1] I have never heard a memoriter speaker who did not sooner or later show that he was memorizing, and thus betray his enslavement to a manuscript. Dr. John Hall, of blessed memory, so long the beloved and honoured pastor of one of New York's great churches, was one of the freest memoriter preachers, and apparently in familiar and sympathetic relation with his audience. His gestures were telling and abundant. He often leaned far forward from the pulpit as if to come in closer touch with his hearers, and to talk to them in the most companionable way. And his freedom from the manuscript was often occasion of remark. But I once happened to be seated immediately in front of him, not more than ten feet away, as I was to officiate in the installation service. The platform was low, and I could see distinctly every feature of his fine face. But there was that same telltale introverted look. He did not see his audience once, from start to finish. His eye *was on the manuscript,* or the copy of it that was stamped upon his memory; and as to who was in his audience, what they were doing, how affected, he seemingly was as blind as if he were sightless.

complete familiarity with its verbal form, so that bondage to the manuscript shall be lost sight of in the freedom and glory of utterance.

For the ideal method of preaching extemporaneously it is absolutely indispensable that there be just as complete command of the subject-matter of the sermon as in the other methods. But there must just as absolutely be no slavery to any verbal form. The verbal form must be got in the presence and under the inspiration of the audience. For this is the all-in-all of extempore speech. It is this pull from without which the audience gives, joined to the push from within which is given by meditation and prayer in the quiet of the study, that makes ideal extempore preaching, as has been already said, not only the best of its kind, but better than the best of any other kind. That is, *the ideal of the ideals!*

CHOICE OF METHOD

Here is a little consensus of opinion. It might well be labelled "a bundle of contradictions."

Dr. Richard S. Storrs: "If you find, after sufficient conscientious trial, that you can do more useful service with the pen, than without it, use the pen. . . . I have never believed it the best plan for all ministers to preach without notes" ("Preaching Without Notes," p. 67). A wise and weighty word.

What he means by "conscientious trial" let his own words tell us: "Make the failure a reason for more intense succeeding effort; a wing, not a weight; a spur to stimulate to fresh endeavour, and not a stiletto to stab out the life" (*Ibid.*, p. 66). Another wise and weighty word.

But his last counsel is, changing a word of Paul's,
" One man esteemeth one way above another : another
man esteemeth every way alike. Let every man be
fully persuaded in his own mind " (*Ibid.*, p. 68), which
seems to leave this vital matter of method in preaching absolutely to one's personal preference.

Dr. William Taylor : " *Memoriter* preaching is the
method that has the greatest advantages, with the
fewest disadvantages."

And yet, " Preaching from a manuscript is the
method in which if he choose to train himself in it,
the man of average ability will make, on the whole,
the best of his talents."

And yet, he says, " Abstractly there can be no
doubt that free speech is the *normal* method of the
pulpit."

" Make choice of the method which suits you best ! "
(" The Ministry of the Word," pages 150–152.)

Dr. Parker : " On the whole, . . . free speech
in the pulpit is infinitely preferable to the most finished written composition " (" Ad Clerum," p. 44).
But he *wrote*, and then laid aside his manuscript, and
this he called " free speech." In other words, he made
a verbal groove for his thought, and then got into it
or kept out of it according to the mood of the moment.
The probabilities are that he commonly got into the
ditch and stayed there.

At the risk of being regarded as over-bold and even
presumptuous in the presence of this galaxy of celebrated preachers and authorities in the field of
Homiletics, the author would submit the following
as proving suggestive and helpful in determining
method.

Helps in Determining Method

1. No method is to be *exclusively* used at the out-set of one's ministry.

2. On the whole, in view of all the considerations, pro and con, the memoriter method *seems the least desirable of the three*, save where there is a natural and very unusual gift of memory. And then it is not to be used to the exclusion of the *extempore*, but only of the *manuscript* method. When by writing a sermon, and reading it over once or twice, a preacher can so command the precise verbal expression that he need only open his mouth to reproduce it—reproduction being almost as spontaneous as his breathing—he may employ the memoriter method to advantage. But where recollection is a labour, either antecedent to delivery or in the process of delivery, the method is unadvisable. It consumes time, instead of saving time. But, whatever the power and the facility of remembering, this method should never be used exclusively.

3. As to the other two methods of preaching—preaching from the manuscript and preaching extempore—each tends to correct the faults of the other. The two methods are a balance and corrective, and should invariably go together, while habits of thought and style are forming. No preacher can at the outset reject either without impairing his efficiency. He will write better by extemporizing, and he will extemporize better by writing. Writing tends to correct the looseness and inexactness of verbal expression in extempore effort, tends to counteract undue amplification of one point, so common in extempore effort, and tends to thoroughness of preparation.

On the other hand, the extempore method tends to correct the scholastic and too studied and often involved style of the written sermon, tends to immediate contact with the audience, and hence to that freedom of delivery which has been the inspiration of waiting assemblies since the day of Pentecost.

4. Objections to combining these two methods by writing out the sermon in full, and then preaching without the manuscript :

(*a*) The time saved for study by the purely extempore method is thus lost altogether.

(*b*) The effort to write out carefully two sermons a week will either prove exhaustive to the preacher, or lead to careless superficial writing.

(*c*) The actual delivery, with most minds, would be likely to be a struggle between the memoriter and the extempore. The mind would naturally run in the groove of verbal expression already made in writing the sermon, and the reproduction would be embarrassed by the tendency.

(*d*) Hence, the want of *that perfect freedom of utterance* which is the glory of the best extempore speech.

5. The *proportion in which each should be used will* be determined somewhat by circumstances.

(*a*) Regard must be had to *occasions*. There are occasions when the most careful preparation, extending to the entire verbal expression and demanding exactness in every line and word, is essential. There are occasions, on the other hand, when a written discourse would be strangely out of place. The prayer-meeting address, a kind of sermonette, the familiar weekly talk of the pastor with his people, should be invariably without notes. At funerals, except on great public

occasions, the speaking should be extemporaneous. In
localities unused to the Gospel, in unlettered neighbour-
hoods, in gatherings at schoolhouses, in the midst of
an assembly caring little for the Gospel and knowing
less, the use of a manuscript would be a weakness and
a hindrance, making it almost impossible to hold attention.

(*b*) Regard must be had to *subject* also—some subjects requiring that exact didactic form of expression
to which writing is favourable. Some subjects also
compelling an entrance on unfamiliar lines of thought
and the use of unfamiliar modes of expression.

6. In view of all the points considered, the principles involved, and the historic facts in evidence, is not
the following a fair and adequate summary of the counsel concerning methods of preaching? For the first five
years in one's ministry, let one sermon each week be
written with great care. With equal care let the *plan*
or *outline* of another sermon be prepared each week ;
and so prepared that the preacher shall know what he
is going to talk about, and the track of his thought
from start to finish, without knowing the exact *verbal
form* his thought is to take, until he is in his pulpit in
the actual process of delivery.

Then let the preacher steadfastly and determinedly
see to two things : first, *that no natural fluency or sur-
passing facility of utterance shall keep him from the
constant habit of careful writing ;* second, *that no
natural timidity, no stumbling and halting at first
ventures, shall keep him from the constant habit of
preaching extempore.*

If five years of persistent practice do not give ease
and readiness and measurable success in extempo-

raneous effort, then either the foundations that are the basis of all effective discourse are worthless, or the preacher will have disclosed some radical defect in temperament or mental structure unfitting him for this ideal method of telling men of Jesus Christ, through the public proclamation of His Holy Word.

XVI

KINDS OF DISCUSSION

SYLLABUS

Discussion—its place in sermonic structure. Three generic kinds: explanatory, observational, propositional.

I. Explanatory discussion embraces narration, description, exemplification. Its chief business is exposition—but exposition always in *order to persuasion*. It is exhibitive, not demonstrative. But it is not mere *commentary*. It is dominated by a [purpose to *move the will Godward*. Some suggestions that should have heed in explanatory discussion.

II. *Observational* discussion. Its nature. Not demonstrative. But the observations should be clearly suggested by the text, strictly germane to the subject, aimed at some definite object, and pervaded by unity.

Advantages : it tends to variety, freshness, vivacity and originality.

Dangers : that the observations will be rambling, disconnected, and more or less wanting in direct Scripturalness.

Examples of observational discussion.

III. *Propositional* discussion. Its nature and aim ; demonstrative ; step by step ; appeals to the reason.

The ideal explanatory discussion not only makes the meaning perfectly clear, but aims to reach the will.

The ideal observational discussion not only has Scripture for the basis of each observation, but so arranges them as to make the sermon a climax.

The ideal propositional discussion is that which proves its case and leaves "no hinge or loop to hang a doubt on."

Of these three ideal kinds of discussion the greatest is explanatory ; for

1. Its limitless variety furnishes adaptation to the most varied need.

2. It makes a more intelligent and stable body of believers.

3. It was the way of the Master.

XVI

KINDS OF DISCUSSION

DISCUSSION is that part of discourse which unfolds the theme. The plan of the sermon is the skeleton. The discussion is this skeleton, clothed with flesh and blood and put to a living use, for the purpose of securing some object. Here the instruction is furnished, or the proof displayed, that is to inform the understanding of the hearer, and lodge conviction, and lay a foundation for excitation and persuasion.

There are three general kinds of discussion—explanatory, observational and propositional, and each has its own distinct ideal.

I. *Explanatory discussion.*

This looks towards informing or instructing. It aims to set forth in a clear light that which is obscure ; to give directness and vividness to a subject not clearly apprehended or understood.

(*a*) What it embraces : Explanatory discussion embraces *narration*, or the setting forth of events in their chronological or causal order, and as centrally connected with some specific theme, as, for example, the circumstances attending the denial of Christ by Peter.

(*b*) Explanatory discussion embraces *description*. A character, an attribute, a duty, a doctrine, may be more distinctly apprehended as it is vividly set forth by fit and forceful speech. Getting a subject fairly and fully before an audience, by perfectly accurate but vivid word colouring, may make just the difference between its acceptance and rejection.

(c) Explanatory discussion embraces *exemplification*—or the setting forth a theme by *examples;* as national or individual, from history or from fiction; *e. g.*, Christian heroism,—illustrated by the martyrs at the stake; " Virtue its own reward "—set forth by particular instances of comfort and peace in the practice of self-denial; " The pain of the present swallowed up in the joy of the future "—illustrated by Christ Himself," who for the joy that was set before Him, endured the cross, despising the shame." [1]

(d) But explanatory discussion has its chief crown and glory in what is technically known as *expository preaching*. This preaching is based upon a somewhat extended section of Scripture. But while the chief business of expository preaching is *explanation*, it is always explanation in order to *persuasion*. It is not mere commentary. Commentary is simply for information, may stop here or there without regard to completeness of thought, explains with equal care and fidelity every part of Scripture text, runs on from

---

[1] Fine material is furnished in Heb. 11, for a series of sermons illustrating explanatory discussion by *exemplification*. Taking the first verse of the chapter as the basis of the series, what a roll-call of heroes follows in exemplification of the *power* of faith !—"By faith, Enoch" —" By faith, Noah "—" By faith, Abraham "—" By faith, Moses "— and others of the goodly and godly group who, through faith, "subdued kingdoms," "wrought righteousness," "obtained promises," " stopped the mouths of lions," " quenched the power of fire," " waxed mighty in war," and " turned to flight " whole armies. How easy to imagine an entire church transformed by such a series of sermons, and led to say in the joy of invincible persuasion, "*We can do anything through faith,*"

verse to verse and chapter to chapter, and is utterly indifferent to oratorical arrangement. On the other hand, the expository sermon has what Vinet calls "a mother idea" running through it from beginning to end, as in a parable. And hence, while there is predominance of analysis in the expository sermon, it is not analysis that cuts the subject into infinitesimal bits, and leaves the sermon a mere bundle of chips.

(e) Explanatory discussion must therefore forever respect the oratorical form and spirit of the sermon, so that all the particulars brought out in the processes of exegesis and analysis shall be made to flow in one strong current, and in increasing volume towards a definite end. Exegesis must not be so detailed as to halt movement. It should show results rather than processes. For a sermon is first and last and always an address, a speech; and its animating genius is climax; and minute critical exegetical details are absolutely hostile to oratorical form and flow.

(f) Explanatory discussion is *exhibitive,* and not demonstrative. It never reasons. It unfolds. It does not come with the cudgels of logic. It tells a story. As was seen in our discussion of the ideal method of answering questions, Christ frequently met both honest inquiry and challenging unbelief by a story. Again and again in the gospel record it is said of Him : "He spake a parable unto them." And in every case His purpose is made clear. It was not to entertain His hearers, nor to arrest or fix attention; but to drive home some vital truth embosomed in the heart of His story. "Behold a sower went forth to sow "—and the different sorts tell us in a matchless way one of the secrets of rich and poor harvesting in the kingdom of

God. And how the parable of the prodigal son has brought many a wandering boy back to his father's house. And how the story of the Syrophenician woman and her daughter has made many a mother feel she too may have power with God and prevail.

1. Explanatory discussion must therefore be dominated from start to finish by *a purpose*. And that purpose must determine the *relative emphasis to be put upon the successive points in the discussion*. For example: Paul in his second letter to the church at Corinth is making, as we would say in the usage of to-day, an appeal for a church collection. In the midst of his appeal he urges this marvellous plea for Christian liberality: "For ye know the grace of our Lord Jesus Christ, though He was rich, yet for your sakes He became poor, that ye through His poverty might be rich" (2 Cor. 8 : 9). Here all the infinite riches of grace and glory in Christ Jesus before the world was, and all the poverty and shame and sorrow the life He lived here and the death He suffered, are brought to bear upon a mere matter of self-denying Christian liberality. And it is simply tremendous in its appeal. It embraces all the exceeding and eternal weight of glory that Christ had with the Father before the world was, all the poverty and desolation and doom of death involved in the incarnation and crucifixion, and all the eternal riches of grace and glory won for us by the amazing sacrifice. To go into explanatory and unfolding details of all this would require a volume of divinity. Even a dozen or more sermons on the riches from which Christ came and the poverty to which He came, that He might infinitely enrich our poverty, would scarcely touch the hem of the garments of these

mighty themes. Explanatory discussion could not and
should not undertake detailed and minute explanation
of these vast reaches of thought, including, as they do,
many of the great doctrines of God, such as the eternal
Trinity of the Godhead, the eternal glory which Christ
had with the Father, the divine incarnation in the
flesh, the humiliation, poverty and shame of Christ's
incarnation, the crucifixion, and the great doctrine of
the atonement for sin it represents, the resurrection,
the ascension, and the divine, perpetual and effectual
intercession. In expository preaching on this Corinthian chapter, these vast themes should be used as
motives to Christian liberality, and nothing more.
They should be marshalled in brief, and pressed to the
accomplishment of this distinct and specific object.
But in each clause of this wonderful section of Paul's
first letter to the Corinthian church, lies a great truth
of God. And if one wished to enrich his flock with
the full unfolding of these respective truths, so that
their great glory would be a perpetual inspiration to
Christian loyalty and service and sacrifice in any field
of labour and for any call of God, he would, after a
while, turn back to this signal passage, take up the
several clauses one by one, and *make a sermon on each
clause,* and each of these sermons either observational
or demonstrative. In other words, having used them
collectively in explanatory discussion, he could afterwards take them up singly, and find rich and abundant
material in each for observational or propositional discussion.

2. Suggestive helps that may well have heed in explanatory discussion, where the preaching is purely
expository :

(*a*) The exposition should begin with some brief and detached portion of Scripture that has already had the preacher's study and heart, and which he has found particularly fruitful and suggestive. The exposition will then be no task to him, and will have the warmth and glow of personal interest.

(*b*) If the exposition is to be *in course*, before beginning the series, it would be well, (1) To make a general survey of the field to be traversed. . Read the entire epistle, or the biography, or the historic record again and again, and in the translation, if the Greek or Hebrew is not familiar. This will give the flow, the current, the continuous movement so vital to a comprehensive view—the general facts and their relation to each other; or the successive points in the argument, and their relative force and application. (2) Lay out a definite plan of procedure. Determine at least these three things: the limit of each section to be expounded ; the leading idea to be developed and enforced in connection with each section; and the practical uses to which each section may be put. With this work mapped out beforehand, one thing will certainly be secured—the *general unity of the book*. And one thing will certainly be avoided—*all probability of repetition*.

(*c*) The limit of the passage for exposition should be predetermined by the leading thought. We cannot cut the text of an expository sermon at random from the body of Scripture. It must be a passage measurably complete in itself, having a natural beginning and ending, so that the sermon may be a rounded whole, having subject and object and oratorical structure, and pervaded throughout by essential unity.

(*d*) There should be predominance of analysis, but analysis always *in order to synthesis*. Analysis is not decomposition. It should respect the soul of the passage. Here is room and demand for the closest critical scholarly study.

II. *Observational Discussion.*

This is discussing a text or a theme by a series of observations, that shall bring out its salient leading points. The observations are not in the order of a demonstration : not successive steps in a logical process. But the observations should be clearly suggested by the text—strictly germane.

This kind of discussion is applicable chiefly to subjects where the different parts of the text furnish the basis for the observations ; and to Scriptural incidents whose respective details furnish a like basis. But it is possible, and may be made exceedingly profitable, with almost any portion of Scripture. F. W. Robertson is the conspicuous modern example of this method of discussion. He went through the two epistles to the Corinthians in the use of this method. And that this work is richly suggestive, with possibilities of rare variety, and charged to the full with applied theology, will hardly be gainsaid. His sermons on individual texts have the same stamp : illustrating both the dangers and advantages of this method of discussion.

The *advantages* are that this kind of discussion tends to variety, freshness, vivacity and originality in the preacher. The *dangers* are that the observations will be rambling, disconnected, and more or less wanting in direct Scripturalness, through temptation, to a fertile and suggestive mind, to display its own ingenuity. With these dangers scrupulously guarded against, there is no reason why this kind of discussion should not be frequently and profitably employed in sacred discourse.

EXAMPLES OF OBSERVATIONAL DISCUSSION

This example is given by Shedd,[1] as from Beddome, on the text: "Saul, Saul, why persecutest thou Me?" (Acts 9 : 4).

Observation 1. It is the general character of unconverted men to be of a persecuting spirit.

Observation 2. Christ has His eye on persecutors.

Observation 3. The injury done to Christ's people, Christ considers as done to Himself.

Observation 4. The calls of Christ are particular— "Saul, Saul."

The first observation might well be challenged. But the rest have a clear evidential value as to this method of discussion, and the Scriptures are full of such fine possibilities.

One of these fine possibilities is furnished by Galatians 6 : 10 : "So then as we have opportunity let us work that which is good towards all men, and especially towards them that are of the household of faith."

Theme: Opportunity.

Observation 1. Opportunity is the measure of duty.

Observation 2. Opportunity has swift wings. If we would see it before it gets by, we must have our eyes open.

Observation 3. Opportunity does not always come flying by; but sometimes it is so in our power to ar-

---

[1] Shedd's "Homiletics," p. 150.

range and order events that ere long opportunity will
be seen winging its way to our door.

Observation 4. Opportunity has no limit of sect or
caste or colour. " Let us work that which is good
towards *all* men."

Observation 5. Opportunity has special reference
to " the household of faith."

III. *Propositional Discussion.*

This kind of discussion involves logical proof. It
aims step by step to establish an affirmation or propo-
sition as true, and either to lodge conviction in the
mind of the hearer, or to confirm by fresh argument
the conviction already there. It appeals to the judgment and the reason of men. Out of the nature of the
theme grows the argument, a logical succession, a
process of demonstration. It is the highest philosophic
form of discourse. Trained minds delight in it, love
to see it built up. It should be the aim of every
preacher to discuss now and then some truth after
this fashion. But trained minds are few in most con-
gregations. They are few in almost every promiscuous assembly. Their need should be *proportionally*
met, as we have seen in our discussion of the law of
adaptation. But even such minds are often longing
for simplicity, directness, and spiritual illumination
rather than logical process.

Here, then, are the three leading, generic kinds of
pulpit discussion—Explanatory, Observational, Propositional. They virtually cover the entire field.

The ideal *explanatory* discussion is that which so
exhibits God's truth by narration, description, exemplification or exposition, that it not only makes the
meaning absolutely clear, but also shows a distinct

and dominating purpose to *reach the will and move it Godward.*

The ideal *observational* discussion is that which has a clear "Thus saith the Lord," for each of its observations, and that so focusses these observations as to make the sermon a climax, gathering power as it proceeds, and determinedly bent on accomplishing a specific object.

The ideal *propositional* discussion is that which has its theme in a logical rather than a rhetorical form. The rhetorical form is simply exhibitive, suggesting no particular kind of discussion. But the logical form is assertive, suggesting and demanding proof. "The sovereignty of God," for example, is a theme opening the door to almost any kind of discussion of God's sovereignty. "God is a sovereign" is a theme inviting and almost compelling its support by proof. Let the preacher announce for his theme, "The sovereignty of God," and we can imagine a hearer at once saying to himself, "Let us see what he has to say about it." But if he announce for his theme, "God is sovereign," that same hearer would almost inevitably be saying silently to the preacher, "You say, 'God is sovereign.' *Furnish the evidence.*" Well, the ideal propositional sermon *furnishes* the evidence. It is bent absolutely and exclusively on proving its case. Step by step it passes down the logical succession, with inexorable precision, leaving "no hinge or loop to hang a doubt on," until the end is reached and the victory won.

We have thus before us the three ideal kinds of discussion. Is there one of these that is not only the best of its kind, but better than the best of either of the other kinds? In other words, is there one that is the ideal of the ideals ?

We think this honour clearly belongs to ideal *explanatory* discussion, and for the following reasons :

1. It covers a broad field, allows an almost limitless variety, and therefore is adapted to a vastly varied need. It includes *doctrines,* where their lucid explanation is their vindication, dissipating prejudice and winning assent. Many a doctrine of God is rejected simply because it is not understood.

Explanatory discussion includes *duties.* A duty must be understood before any appeal for the discharge of the duty can be successfully pressed home. Many an exhortation has come from the pulpit for the doing of a certain duty, when the sufficient and satisfactory answer from the pew has been, " That is not my business." The hearer must be made to see that it *is* his business. Take the duty of Christian forgiveness. An explanatory discussion would bring out points like these: that the *spirit* of forgiveness is to be always cherished, but that actual forgiveness is dependent on the repentance of the wrong-doer : for forgiveness means restoration to the old place of trust and love, and penitence is the only open door to that good estate, and Christlike forgiveness is impossible when there is no repentance.

In fact, there is no part of God's Word that does not come within the scope of explanatory discussion. And this is one persuasive reason why this kind of discussion should take conspicuous place in the public preaching of the Gospel—it meets more varied need, fits into more social and civic conditions than either of the other kinds of discussion.

2.   A second reason for giving priority and supremacy to explanatory discussion is, that it makes a
more intelligent and stable body of believers.   All Scotland was once, and to a degree is still, proof of this
claim.   With the Bible in their hands, the people followed the reading and expounding of the Word of
God, and so their minds and hearts were saturated
with Bible truth.   It got into their prayers and made
them rich in devotional expression and fervid in devotional ardour.   It got wrought into their spirit and
made them mighty in faith, and fearless of man or
devil.   So that a Scotchman was known as a man who
could stand before kings, and face tyranny with his
argument, and "nail it wi' Scripture."

3.   But a third reason for claiming ideal explanatory
discussion to be not only the best of its kind, but better than the best of any other kind, is this : it was *the
way of the Master*.   He never preached a propositional
discourse.   He never once followed a line of reasoning
down through the successive steps of a logical process.
His premise was often an incident, a parable, a story—
and from it came a conclusion.   *That's all*.   The
premise was always unchallengeable ; the conclusion
was always irresistible.   He sometimes put a question
that compelled a certain answer, and then made that
answer the ground for a challenge that cavilling Pharisees could not meet, and dared not deny ; and that
timid, doubting, troubled, but believing and loving disciples accepted, and grew bold because of: "Two men
went up into the temple to pray, the one a Pharisee,
and the other a publican"; "Hear what the unjust
judge saith"; "What man is there of you, who, if his
son ask for a loaf, will give him a stone"; "If ye then,

being evil, give good gifts unto your children, how much more shall your Father which is in heaven give good things to them that ask Him?" Thus by parable and story, by incident and illustration, Christ taught us about all we know concerning prayer—its power, its tenderness, its persistence, its reasonableness. "Our Father which art in heaven," are the words that all around the world let lowly and loving hearts into the secret place of the Most High.

Thus always and everywhere He *exhibited* truth, He *illustrated* truth, He made truth *plain*. O man of God, put in trust of this Gospel, in imitation of your Master, make truth plain; dare to make truth plain. Give explanatory discussion the supreme place in your preaching that Christ gave it in His, though this should be at the expense of swelling periods, and long trains of reasoning, and the intricate processes of scientific research, and the details of higher or lower criticism. *Make God's truth plain.*

But do we not want defenders of the faith? Certainly, we want defenders of the faith. Let it be said with all positiveness: As error is championed by the ripest scholarship, truth must be alike championed, or leave the field. Therefore, let the Christian scholars that are set to this business confound the gainsayers. But people do not come to the house of God to be fed on the reputation of sceptics. In preaching, follow your Master. *Exhibit* truth, as He did. And *live* the truth as He did. Never let the man behind the sermon give the lie to the sermon. Exhibit truth. Illustrate truth. Explain truth. And make it so plain that a little child may take it in and walk in the path of it.

But was not Paul a mighty reasoner, distinctly

marked among the apostles as " reasoning of righteousness and self-control and the judgment to come "?
Yes, his eighth of Romans is an ascending way up the
mount of Christian confidence, and for every step of
the way of ascent he has a logical warrant. But when
we would see Paul at his best, we go to one of the
Corinthian chapters, where there is not a suggestion
or trace of logical process. But instead, in matchless
setting, the queen jewel in the diadem of Christian
graces is held up to view. Thousands go to that apostolic exhibit of love and linger there, where one follows the steps of Paul's logic. Just so with the Old
Testament singer of Israel and seer of Christ. Multitudes of believing hearts have gone with him up the
heights of Christian triumph, but far more have found
their comfort and their joy in the green pastures and
by the still waters of the Twenty-Third Psalm, where
Christ is simply exhibited as the Good Shepherd. A
good old saint in one of my parishes was wont to say:
" When things go wrong, and I am worn and weary,
and the burden is heavy, I like to go and lie down
awhile on the Twenty-Third Psalm." And how many
a lost wanderer from God has heard or read of the
tender, yearning, seeking and searching Father in the
parable of the Prodigal Son, and coming back to his
Father's house, has been met, while yet a great way
off, as the Father saw him and was moved with compassion and ran and fell on his neck and kissed him.
All the reasoning in the world has not brought so
many wanderers back to God as this gospel story of
the wandering and returning prodigal.

XVII

SERMON PLANS ILLUSTRATIVE OF DIFFERENT KINDS OF DISCUSSION

XVII

SERMON PLANS ILLUSTRATIVE OF DIFFERENT KINDS OF DISCUSSION

The first three plans are from the same text, and they show what possibilities of variety there are in the different kinds of discussion.

EXPLANATORY DISCUSSION

Text :—But grow in the grace . . . of our Lord and Saviour Jesus Christ (*2 Peter 3 : 18*).

Introduction :—The grace here spoken of is the grace of godliness; of Christlikeness; of which Christ is the Author. It is the heart of the Gospel; the very essence of all true religion. It is vital that we understand this matter.

Object :—To stimulate growing in grace by helping Christians to see what it is, and why and how they should grow.

Theme :—Growing in grace.
  I.   The thing itself—or what this growth is.
        (*a*) Increasing nearness to Jesus.
        (*b*) Increasing delight in His service.
        (*c*) Increasing love for His followers.
        (*d*) Increasing hatred of sin.
  II. The why of it—or the reason for growth.
        (*a*) It enriches the soul.
        (*b*) It glorifies Christ.
        (*c*) It is commanded of God.

III.   The how of it—or the method of growth.
  (*a*) By meditation—looking unto Jesus.
  (*b*) By self-denial—crucifying the flesh.
  (*c*) By outward activity—labouring for others.

Conclusion :—Christians, if you will daily ponder these reasons, and prayerfully use this method, you will exhibit, to the joy of your soul, to the good of men, and to the glory of God, what growth in grace means ; more nearness to Jesus, more delight in His service, more love for His fellows, more hatred of sin.

OBSERVATIONAL DISCUSSION

Text :—But grow in the grace . . . of our Lord and Saviour Jesus Christ (*2 Peter 3 : 18*).

Introduction :—The Christian life is no dead level— neither a macadamized road nor a stagnant canal. It is a progress and an ascent ; onward and upward, until the full-grown man is reached—the measure of the stature of the fullness of Christ.

Object :—To stimulate and shame Christians to growth in grace by their splendid possibilities and poor attainments.

Theme :—Growth in grace.
  Observation 1.—Grace is a matter of degrees— Peter, Paul, Moody.
  Observation 2.—Growth in grace is in our own power. We can have less of it or more of it ; a good deal of it or none at all.
  Observation 3.—There are some vital conditions of growth.

(*a*) Association.
(*b*) Appropriation.
(*c*) Assimilation.

Practical Lessons :—
1. We are as good Christians as we wish to be.
2. We should take shame to ourselves for not being better Christians.
3. Our not being better Christians is because we have not met the conditions.

Propositional Discussion

Text :—But grow in the grace . . . of our Lord and Saviour Jesus Christ (*2 Peter 3 : 18*).

Object :—To persuade Christians to growth in grace by conviction of the imperative duty of it.

Introduction :—Growth seems the order of nature. It is married to life in the vegetable, animal, and mental world. The realm of grace is no exception. No growth is reversal of order. Injunction of the text is imperative.

Theme :—Growth in grace is a Christian duty.
 I. Because commanded of God.
 II. Because growth is a law of all healthful life.
III. Because increase of grace is increase of power ; speech is mighty as it has character behind it.
IV. Because the more we grow Christlike, the more we honour Christ.

Conclusion :—Christians, you who wear Christ's name, this is not an optional thing, a mere privilege to be enjoyed or not, at pleasure ; well enough, and even desirable, but not vital. It is clearly as much a duty as faith is, or prayer. God's word makes it a test of discipleship, and binds it on our hearts as an imperative law.

EXPLANATORY DISCUSSION

Text :—For the Son of man is come to seek and save that which was lost (*Luke 19 : 10*).

Object :—To show the sinner that he need not be lost ; and yet to show him from the character of the Seeker and the cost of the seeking, what a terrible thing it is to be lost.

Introduction :—The scene—its vivid contrasts. Hosannas of the crowd followed by sneers. The despised publican seeking Jesus, and Jesus seeking the publican. Jesus the guest of a sinner, and the sinner an heir of salvation.

Theme :—The reach of the divine compassion.

Seen   I.   In the person of the Seeker.

             The Son of man, because the Son of God. God in the flesh.

Seen   II.   In the way of seeking.

             (*a*) Its humiliation.

             (*b*) Its isolation.

             (*c*) Its desolation.

Seen III.   In the person sought—"that which was *lost.*"

             (*a*) Not simply lost in error, but in sin.

             (*b*) Not simply lost to the good, but to God.

             (*c*) Not simply lost for this life, but forever.

Conclusion :—1. The lowliest and wickedest may take
hope and heart.

2. If the seeker be God, and the way
of seeking at such a cost, what a
world of meaning is put into the
word *" Lost " !*

3. If the seeker be God, and the way
of the seeking at such a cost, *what
must it be to be saved.*

PROPOSITIONAL DISCUSSION

Text :—For it is better, if the will of God should so
will, that ye suffer for well-doing than for evil-doing (*1 Peter 3 : 17*).

Introduction :—Can this be possible ? We are not
wont to think of it so. If we do wrong and suffer,
we count it our desert. If we do well and suffer,
it seems a cruel stab. But here is the word of God
telling us it is better to suffer doing good than doing evil.

Theme :—Suffering in well-doing is preferable to suffering in evil-doing.

Object :—To help Christians to a Christlike patience
when they are misinterpreted and misunderstood.

I. Suffering in well-doing is in the path of duty.
Suffering in evil-doing is in the path of diso-
bedience.

II. Suffering in well-doing is with an approving
conscience.
Suffering in evil-doing is with an accusing conscience.

III.   Suffering in well-doing is the discipline of love
—the judgment of mercy.

Suffering in evil-doing is punishment of sin—
the judgment of wrath.

IV.   Suffering in well-doing is an honour—for so
Christ suffered (Ch. 4 : 14).

Suffering in evil-doing is a shame.

Should we therefore seek suffering ?   No.

Are we doing well when not suffering ?   Yes, if
in the path of duty.

Conclusion :—Christians, let us accept suffering even
for our well-doing, if God will that we suffer, and
rejoice in it as in duty's path, and as the chastening
of a Father, and as having the Spirit of glory and
of God resting on us.   If we suffer with Christ, we
shall also reign with Christ.

EXPLANATORY DISCUSSION

Text :—" But I have this against thee, that thou didst
leave thy first love " (*Rev. 2 : 4*).

Object :—To bring lost love back by pressing home the
guilt of it, and urging the remedy for it.

Introduction :—The first word of the ascended Lord
sent back to His blood-bought church,—" He that
hath an ear, etc.," therefore adapted to any church
similarly conditioned.   Christ first *commends*, and
this is His blessed way, if He can find aught com-
mendable.   Nevertheless, He has this against the
church of Ephesus, that she has left her first love.

Theme :—First love left.

   I.   *The signs of it.*

Negatively, not a want of service, for this church was rendering service :

    (*a*) By laborious toil (v. 2). An *active* church.

    (*b*) By holding fast to the truth (v. 2). An *orthodox* church.

    (*c*) By patient endurance (v. 3). A *suffering* church.

Positively :

    (*a*) A want of ardent personal affection in service.

    (*b*) A want of joy in service.

    (*c*) A want of self-forgetfulness in service.

II. *The sin of it.*

    (*a*) When love is gone, all is gone. Take the heart out of religion and nothing is left but dry bones. " My son, give Me thy heart " is the cry of God's heart. He can take nothing less and keep His throne.

III. *The cure of it.*

    (*a*) " Remember."

    (*b*) " Repent."

    (*c*) " Do."

Conclusion :—Christians, can our blessed Lord see this sin in this church ? Let every one examine himself, applying these tests : Is it with warm personal affection and heartfelt joy we are doing work for Christ ? If the sin of having left our first love lies at our door, let us heed the warning of our Lord, and *remember*, and *repent*, and *do* our work for Christ in the glow of personal affection.

EXPLANATORY DISCUSSION

Text :—Him that cometh to me, I will in no wise cast out (*John 6 : 37*).

Object :—To persuade a sinner to cry out, " Just as I am, O Lamb of God, I come."

Introduction :—What a precious word " come " is in human language and relation. How much more precious, how unspeakably precious, in the gospel sense, when spoken to lost wanderers from God ; and when accompanied with the gracious assurance, " I will in no wise cast out."

Theme :—Coming to Christ ; its method and result.
I.   The way of coming.
  Negatively :
    1.   It is not by commencing a process of refor-
       mation.   Every sinner who comes to
       Christ will reform ; but he does not come
       to Christ by reforming.
    2.   It is not by attending religious meetings
       and joining the church.   He may do this
       and be as far from Christ as ever.
    3.   It is not by simply reading the Bible
       and offering prayer ; doing these things
       is not coming to Christ.   Men have done
       them and yet have perished.
  Affirmatively :
       It is having Christ in the thought and heart
         as the hope of salvation, to the exclusion
         of all else.

Illustrations :—A burning building, man inside, his thought on the only door by which escape is possible, saying, I must reach that door or perish. An Israelite, pursued by the man slayer, fleeing to the city of refuge. Bunyan's Pilgrim, with his eye and mind on the light, fleeing from the City of Destruction.

This involves:

> (*a*)   Looking *out*, not looking *in*.
>
> (*b*)   Looking to Jesus, not looking to self, or sin, or Church or Bible.

This is a confession :

> (*a*)   That the seeker is a sinner needing to be saved.
>
> (*b*)   That he cannot save himself.
>
> (*c*)   That no one else can save him.
>
> (*d*)   That Jesus can.

II.   The result of the coming :   Absolute certainty of Christ's welcome.

> (*a*)   No matter what the degree of previous guilt ; He will in no wise cast out.
>
> (*b*)   No matter what the decree of God ; He will in no wise cast out.
>
> (*c*)   No matter how weak the effort ; He will in no wise cast out.
>
> (*d*)   No matter how slight the conviction of sin ; He will in no wise cast out.

Conclusion :—Careless sinner, blinded sinner, outcast sinner, infamous sinner, *come* and come *now*. And He who never broke His word, will keep it with you, and welcome, pardon, cleanse and save.

EXPLANATORY DISCUSSION

Text :—One man esteemeth one day above another : another esteemeth every day alike.   Let each man be fully assured in his own mind. He that regardeth the day, regardeth it unto the Lord ; and he that eateth, eateth unto the Lord, for he giveth God thanks ; and he that eateth not, unto the Lord he eateth not, and giveth God thanks (*Rom. 14 : 5–6*).

Object :—To lead Christians rightly to understand, and joyfully to obey, the gospel law of liberty in non-essentials.

Introduction :—Absolute subjection to the will of God demanded of every Christian. But what if there be no " thus saith the Lord " to guide us ? To meet this case the Apostle gives us.

Theme :—The doctrine of Christian liberty in non-essentials.
I. The doctrine set forth.
    (*a*) There are things neither enjoined nor prohibited by God which may be done or not without affecting the moral character of the doer. Days, meats, amusements, wine.
    (*b*) Concerning these every man is to be fully persuaded in his own mind (vs. 5, 6). We are not to be forced into the groove of another's conscience.
II. The doctrine guarded and limited.
    (*a*) The Sabbath day is not yielded to this liberty.
        1. It was instituted before the ceremonial law.
        2. The reasons for its observance are permanent and universal.

3. The law of the Sabbath is imbedded in the moral law.

(b) What a man *thinks* to be *wrong*, though it be in itself innocent, is not yielded to this liberty (v. 14).

(c) What a man thinks to be *right*, if the doing cause a brother to stumble, is not yielded (vs. 13, 15, 20, 21).

(d) What a man cannot do, or refrain from doing, "*to the Lord*," is not yielded (v. 6).

III. The doctrine applied. In the exercise of Christian liberty,

(a) We are to beware of tampering with conscience (vs. 14, 15, 21, 23).

(b) We are not to judge the brother whose conscience is not as ours (vs. 3, 4, 5, 10).

(c) We are to have tender and self-sacrificing regard to the weak.

(d) We are to have supreme regard to the glory of God.

PROPOSITIONAL DISCUSSION

Text :—" Thou art the man " (*2 Sam. 12 : 7*).

Object :—To drive guilt home.

Introduction :—The circumstances.

Theme :—Sin will always return to plague the sinner.

I. Sin has a fearfully blinding power.

(a) Through passion.

(b) Through habit.

(c) Through searing the conscience.

II. God can pierce the blindness, and bring guilt
     home.
    (*a*) By His knowledge of the heart's secrets
     (Ps. 90 : 8).—Achan.
    (*b*) By His control of circumstances.
    (*c*) By His power of evoking conscience.—
     Judas, Felix.
III. He is pledged to bring guilt home to every sin-
      ning soul, (2 Cor. 5 : 10 ; Eccl. 12 : 14).
IV. Sense of personal guilt is therefore inevitable.
    (*a*) Either in the life that now is,
    (*b*) Or at the judgment.

Conclusion :—Men should welcome the preaching that
shows them their sin ; for the exposure and conviction are inevitable somewhere. Better far be convinced of sin *now* while pardon is possible, than
when probation is ended. Reckless, hardened
hearer, " Thou art the man." Self-righteous hearer,
thou art the man. Professedly Christian hearer,
grinding the face of the poor, driving a sharp bar-
gain, making the worse appear the better reason, *indulging in any secret sin*, like David, having merely
the form of godliness, " *Thou art the man !* "

PROPOSITIONAL DISCUSSION

Text :—" Because the mind of the flesh is enmity
against God " (*Rom. 8 : 7*).

Introduction :—It is a cruel mercy that lulls to
security by concealing danger. Better know the
worst if thereby we can provide against it. God's
Word lets us see what we are, that we may know

what to do. The text is one of the mirrors Scripture holds up to nature.

Theme :—The heart of man by nature is enmity against God.

Object :—By proving this truth, to show how radical must be the change of heart, if any one would be saved.
  I. The expression of authority is law.
  II. The best test of loyalty is obedience.
III. The heart of obedience is love. When born of fear or self-interest, obedience is servile and selfish.
IV. Man by nature does not obey, for he does not love.
    (*a*) He may be virtuous and not vicious.
    (*b*) He may be amiable and not morose.
    (*c*) He may be forgiving and not revengeful.
    (*d*) He may be outwardly observant of religious duties, even.
But love is deeper than all of these, involving
    (*a*) Disposedness towards God Himself.
    (*b*) Delight in His company.
    (*c*) Relish for His law.
    (*d*) Desire for His glory.
Hence, when God comes with these deeper searching spiritual requirements, the mind of the flesh rebels, and its enmity is revealed.

Conclusion :—See here the true test of what we are by nature. We must look deeper than the surface. The mischief is radical, and not a question of mere morality. It is at the roots of character. Ferocity is in the tiger *even when fondling its young.* Sin is in the mother, even when she is caressing her babe. The plague spot of sin spreads its virus, even where the fairest flowers of morality fling out their bloom. If this be so, how hopeless is reformation. How vital is regeneration. Except a man be born again he cannot see the kingdom of God.

PART THREE

THE SERMON

XVIII

ITS IDEAL DEFINITION

SYLLABUS

Introductory.—Review—embracing brief glance at the great ideas that uplift and glorify preaching,—and also the related ideals which have been found to be mighty helps to pulpit efficiency.

We are come now to the making of the sermon, and the indispensable first step is definition. What is a sermon? Different definitions by different writers. An ideal definition must have everything in it that ought to be in it, and no word in it that ought to be out of it. This will make the ideal sermon an address, a speech, a discourse, a religious discourse, a formal religious discourse, founded on God's Word, and designed for salvation, either from sin's penalty or pollution or power, *i. e.*, designed to bring men to Christ or to make them like Christ. There is no other business for a sermon.

What would follow such preaching? In some pulpits, a revolution.

XVIII

ITS IDEAL DEFINITION

INTRODUCTORY : We have already considered those great distinctive ideas, indissolubly connected with the gospel ministry, and which uplift and glorify it as the art of arts, and we found them to be preaching as its permanent function, making men Christlike its supreme aim, love its ruling spirit, the Word of God its subject-matter, preaching Christ its preeminent business, Christ crucified its central theme, everlasting life and death its eternal sanctions, and the Holy Spirit its cooperating agent.

We have also had before us those related ideals which are mighty helps to pulpit efficiency : the ideal call to the ministry, the ideal student, the ideal study, the ideal law of adaptation, the ideal way of preaching old doctrines in new times, the ideal methods of preaching, and the ideal kinds of discussion.

Let it be remembered also, that ever since the first heavenly ratification of public Christian discourse at Pentecost, the true sermon, however wanting in the enticing words of man's wisdom, has been, more often than any other instrumentality, "in demonstration of the Spirit and of power." However its form has changed, and wherever pomp and ceremonial and ritual or the crudities and vagaries and vain reasonings of philosophy, falsely so-called, have not crowded out the Word of God, the sermon has continued to occupy

275

the place of recognized and commanding importance. God has honoured it above all other products in propagating the truth and saving men. The sermon "always has been, and ever must remain, the essential complement of the idea of preaching." And preaching, as we have already seen, is the preeminent business of every ambassador of Jesus Christ. It follows, therefore, that the sermon is of paramount value and has supreme place among the means employed to extend the kingdom of Christ and edify the church.

To prepare and deliver sermons and to see that as far as in him lies these sermons get translated into the lives of those who hear them, is, therefore, the great life-work of the preacher. And he should test special fondness for this or that study by the help it directly or indirectly renders him in sermonizing. He must put the curb and the bit on any linguistic bias, or delight in philosophic speculation, or passion for antiquarian research, that makes him blind to the one purpose for which he is in the ministry ; viz., to make God's truth plain and mighty as he holds it forth Sabbath by Sabbath. No preacher can effectually shy Hebrew roots at his congregation. Nor can he lift his hearers Godward by metaphysical abstractions. Nor can he healthfully dump the musty lore of some old dead century into their lap. But he can, and should, make Hebrew roots grow many a fruitful bough in the garden of the Lord, and he can, and should, compel philosophy to be a mighty adjunct in helping him preach the philosophy of the Gospel ; and he can, and should, make all histories live again, as he writes new history with them in the hearts and lives of to-day.

Only let him keep his eye on the goal, have distinctly in mind the ideal definition of a sermon, and determine, by the grace of God, to do what in him lies to realize and make actual the ideal in his weekly ministry.

We are come now to *the making of the sermon.* We are to consider the ideals that prepare the way for, and that enter into, sermonic structure. For, sermons are not born. They are made. They are products of study and discipline. They are also products of faith and prayer, beyond a doubt—illuminations, inspirations. But "faith without works" is as "dead" here as it is anywhere. And eyes will not be opened to see wondrous things out of God's law, if they are not on the search for the hid treasures, and preparing the way for the divine illumination.

What, then, is a sermon? We need exact definition here as we do everywhere else, where construction of any kind is to be undertaken. If there is vagueness in our definition, there will be vagueness in the sermons. We cannot chisel precision out of a fog bank. Exact definition will tell us what belongs to a sermon, and will help us see that a good many things that come knocking for admittance at the door of a sermon, and that, alas! too often get in, have no business there. The absolutely indispensable quality of definition is *precision.* Definition is both inclusive and exclusive. It must include all that essentially belongs to the thing defined, and it must exclude all that does not belong to the thing defined.

From this view-point the definitions of a sermon that are found in our popular dictionaries are lamentably deficient, and practically worthless.

Here is the Webster Dictionary definition: "A discourse delivered in public (usually, by a clergyman) for the purpose of religious instruction, and grounded on some text or passage of Scripture." A parenthesis is never at home in a definition, and certainly has no place in a sermonic definition. And whether the sermon is delivered in public or in private, or not at all, it is still a sermon. And whether "delivered by a clergyman," or a clergyman's wife, or a phonograph, it would still be a sermon.

Here is the Standard Dictionary definition: "A discourse by a clergyman upon some religious topic, based on a passage or text of the Bible, and delivered as part of a church service."[1] In this definition some of the Webster errors are reproduced, and, in addition, we have this clause—"delivered as part of a church service,"—which has just as much to do with the definition of a sermon as where a dog barked has to do with the definition of his bark.

But some notable preachers, and some writers on preaching, have been little better than the dictionaries in their attempted definition of a sermon.

Dr. Shedd's characterization of a sermon as "the elongation of a text," is, of course, no attempt at exact definition, and was not meant to be. But it is the nearest to a definition of anything in his "Homiletics." It would apply to a piece of commentary or of exegesis as well as to a sermon, and it omits almost everything vital to a sermon.

Here is a definition by a distinguished scholar and

---

[1] The Standard Dictionary is exceptionally excellent in its definitions, but the ministerial heads must have been nodding when they let this sermon definition go in.

preacher, that appears at first sight to be marked by the finest analytical precision: "A sermon is a rhetorical organism evolved by a genetic process from a text, and standing in vital and obvious relation to it." But if we put this definition to the test of analysis, it will be seen to be little better than Dr. Shedd's broad characterization, and to the last degree redundant. The seventeen words following the word "organism" can better be put in four words; viz., *born of a text*. "Evolved by a genetic process," means "born," and the rest of the definition is surplusage. For it certainly adds nothing to the thought to tell us that a child born of a mother, "stands in vital and obvious relation" to that mother! Moreover, the phrase, "rhetorical organism," is indefinite. It would apply to an essay or a bit of exegesis or a piece of commentary. Pope's "Essay on Man," "is a rhetorical organism, evolved by a genetic process from a text ('What is Man') and standing in vital and obvious relation to it;" but Pope's "Essay on Man" is not a sermon, except in the loosest sense. It is a religious poem, a moral essay in rhyme; not a speech.

Austin Phelps, so long the scholarly rhetor and homilete of Andover, in his "Theory of Preaching," defines a sermon as "An oral address to the popular mind, on religious truth contained in the Scriptures, and elaborately treated with a view to persuasion." But while this definition is marked by some superior qualities, it is fatally lacking in precision. It is neither inclusive nor exclusive—the two absolutely vital qualities in definition. The word "oral" is superfluous. What it implies is implied in the word "address"— something to be spoken. If it means a spoken address

—a discourse actually uttered—then a sermon is not a sermon until it is delivered.   This is of course absurd. But still further, a sermon is not necessarily "to the popular mind."   For it might be to a body of scientists, and by their request (*e. g.*, the American Association for the Advancement of Science), and therefore properly packed to the full with technical terms and illustrations, which, while perfectly adapted to the scientific minds addressed, would be only Hebrew or Hottentot "to the popular mind."   "Elaborately treated," is another defining phrase in this definition by Phelps that is clearly without warrant.   For some most mightily effective sermons have been marked by a quietness and simplicity at the farthest remove from elaboration.

What, then, is a sermon?   Here is our answer to this vital question : *A sermon is a formal religious discourse, founded on the Word of God, and designed to save men.*   This definition is the product of a good deal of cutting and chipping and hewing.   It has had frequent class-room discussion.   Let us take it to pieces, and test it by analysis, and see if every word is in it that ought to be in it, and if no word is in it that ought to be out of it.

Beginning with the substantive, fundamental word —the thought-word : A sermon is a *discourse: i. e.*, a speech, an address ; which distinguishes it from an essay or an exegesis or a piece of commentary.   It may *contain* exegesis or commentary as positively necessary to the hearer's understanding, and contributive to the preacher's purpose.   But exegesis must not monopolize the sermon ; must never prevent the sermon from taking an *oratorical form.*   The sermon is a speech, a thing to be spoken. It is to reach and move the will.

Again: A sermon is "a *religious* discourse"; which distinguishes it from speech that is secular in its tone and spirit and subject-matter.

And again: It is "*founded on the Word of God*"; which distinguishes it from all other speech that has only human authority and sanction.

Finally, it is "designed to save men"; which distinguishes it from all other speech aiming only at instruction or reformation. This purpose of salvation— in the broad, deep, Scriptural sense of salvation; namely, salvation from sin—is the preeminent mark of the sermon, and absolutely indispensable to sermonic integrity. If the sermon is to the impenitent, then the purpose is salvation from the *penalty* of sin, by bringing the sinner to Christ—for "there is no condemnation to them which are in Christ Jesus." If the sermon is to Christians—to those who are already united to Christ by faith—then, the purpose is salvation from the *power* and the *pollution* of sin, by making the Christian more Christlike.

Of course, each may do the other's work. Such is the blessed sufficiency of divine grace. A touching appeal to the impenitent may melt a whole body of believers to tears, because of their supineness and worldly-mindedness, and may put them at once to service in seeking and saving the lost. And a searching sermon to believers may be the sword of the Spirit to smite clean through the refuge of lies where a man of the world in fancied security has been hiding himself. But in either case, and in any case, it is *salvation from sin*—either from its penalty or from its pollution or from its power.

Hence, it may be said, with all possible emphasis, that a sermon has no other business than to do this thing. If it is not designed and adapted either to bring men to Christ or to make them Christlike, then, away with it. Whatever wealth of original research it may exhibit, and with whatever charm of fascinating rhetoric it may be accompanied, for sermonic use it is as " wood, hay and stubble," and fit only to be burned.

Suppose, now, that every minister, as he begins his weekly sermonic work, should distinctly say to himself : This is an address, a discourse, a speech I am to prepare for my people. It is to be distinctly religious, having for its warrant and base the Word of God. It means changed hearts down there in the pews, and changed lives out amongst men, going to the roots of moral character—a regeneration and a sanctification, seeking either to free men at once and forever through Jesus Christ, from sin's penalty, or seeking to give them the purity and the liberty of the sons of God by freeing them more and more from sin's pollution and sin's power.

What would surely follow ? Do we not all know that in some pulpits a revolution would follow ?

Suppose again that every man of God who preaches should hold distinctly in mind the great Christian quadrangle, representing in its four sides the Incarnation, the Resurrection, the Ascension, and the Intercession of Jesus Christ, and having at its centre an uplifted and blood-stained cross—that cross giving to the Incarnation, the Resurrection, the Ascension, and

the Intercession of Christ their only meaning and their
fullest justification—then surely it would be the constant purpose and the ever-deepening joy of every
man of God who preaches to make each sermon a formal religious discourse founded on the Word of God
and designed to save men.

XIX

ITS IDEAL "CONSTANTS"

SYLLABUS

Introductory.—The "constants" pertain to a man's entire ministry. They look towards preparation for *all the Sundays*, and are distinct from the steps in preparation for the next Sunday. They are:

I. *The constant cultivation of a vivid sense of the divine realities of the gospel message.*

    (*a*) What this involves.

    (*b*) Reasons for its possession : (1) The preacher is to handle these things in his sermons. To make them realities to others, they must be intensely real to him. (2) Nothing will so arm the preacher with power.

    (*c*) How secured : By companionship—meditation.

II. *The constant cultivation of the homiletic bias.*

    (*a*) Possible to every mind. Homiletic bias is born of homiletic practice. Frequent repetition gives two things : tendency, facility.

    (*b*) Direct advantages : (1) Gives method. (2) Greater facility in grasping salient points. (3) Increasing command of materials. (4) Glow in actual composition.

    (*c*) Importance of homiletic bias. Homiletics is his business. Get insensity ; narrow the channel ; make pulpit a throne; transmute everything you touch into sermon.

    (*d*) Means of cultivation : (1) Give much thought to plan-making. (2) Take up sermons and analyze them. (3) Have a text-book, and *use* it. (4) Beware of books of skeletons : They warp originality ; their use is often immoral.

III. *The constant cultivation of familiarity with sources of material.*
The Bible, other books, living men.

    (*a*) The Bible preeminently : (1) Why the Bible? (2) With what spirit ? (3) By what method ?

(*a*) Study the text itself. (*b*) Read whole books at one sitting.

(*b*) *Other books:* (1) On the Bible. (2) Philosophy. (3) Psychology. (4) History. (5) Science.

(*c*) Living men.

IV. The constant presence of a *lofty standard of sermonizing.* Standard cannot be too high.

Consider first, the peculiar character of the times.

Consider secondly, the work a sermon is to do.

Consider thirdly, Apostolic example.

Two cautions : (1) Standard should not be simple excellency of speech. (2) The vital thing is not the *number* of sermons but the *kind* they are, and the work they are fitted to do.

These four "constants" make some things impossible :

(1) That a minister should *grow old before his time.*

(2) That a minister should ever exhaust his stock.

(3) That a minister should ever be out-of-date.

(4) That a minister should ever be afraid.

XIX

ITS IDEAL "CONSTANTS"

WE have discussed the great ideas indissolubly connected with preaching, and which uplift and glorify it as the art of arts.

We have also defined the sermon, and have sought to show that the definition is ideal: *i. e.*, inclusive of everything vital to a sermon, and exclusive of everything dispensable.

We are now to consider that which should be constant in the pursuit of this supreme art of preaching— the ideal qualities that should enter into all sermonic construction, and that should have study and care throughout one's entire ministry.

This involves those matters, by faithful attention to which the preacher is to get ready for all the Sundays; and they are to be distinguished from the immediate steps by which he is to get ready for the next Sunday. The one may be termed general preparation: the other, special preparation. The one may be characterized as the ideal " constants " in sermonic construction ; the other, the ideal "immediates" in sermonic construction.

The " constants " are as follows : the constant cultivation of a more and more vivid and abiding sense of the divine realities of the gospel message ; the constant cultivation of the homiletic bias ; the constant

289

cultivation of familiarity with the sources of materials;
and the constant presence of a lofty standard of sermonizing.

Let us consider these in their order:

I. The constant cultivation of a more and more
vivid and abiding sense of the divine realities of the
gospel message :

(*a*) This clearly involves something beyond a mere
conviction of the truth of the great doctrines of Scripture; and even something beyond a practical belief
in them, leading to the outward and ordinary consistencies of Christian life. An unregenerate man may
be convinced of the truth of the doctrines. An
ordinary Christian may have the ordinary Christian
consistencies. But surely a prophet of God should
have something more. For a minister to *fail* of an
exhibition of ordinary piety, is to cut the throat of the
best sermon he can preach, and to make preaching
utterly abortive. It is inconsistent with any true notion of the ministerial office. The preacher is to be an
example to the believer, in word, in conversation, in
charity, in spirit and faith and purity, " having a good
report of them which are without," and " not falling
into reproach or the snare of the devil." He must
have a character above suspicion.

But a truly vivid sense of the divine realities of the
gospel message involves far more than this. It means
a sacred continued commerce with the other life, leading to an ever-deepening consciousness of its realities
—a more and more vivid sense of the unseen—a walk
with God as if in the very presence of the powers of
the world to come. Underneath all preparation, pervading and filling the intellectual atmosphere as sun-

light fills and floods the material atmosphere, must be this sense of the invisible and infinite.

(*b*) *Reasons for possessing this vivid sense of the divine realities of the gospel message:*

(1) The preacher *is to handle these things in his sermons.* To make them anything like realities to others, they must be intensely real to him. He must see them with faith's eye. A man who has this clear sight and sense of eternal realities, " walks with God," like Enoch. He endures "as seeing Him who is invisible," like Moses. He *knows* whom he has believed, and to him "to live is Christ," like Paul. He is face to face with the eternal forces and facts, and he becomes the medium through which the fire and power of these eternal forces and facts are brought to men. He opens to the material world and lets down upon it the inspirations of the Holy Spirit, as he stands with a sense of God, and of eternity, and of the instant and imminent peril of lost souls, charged with these and all other realities of that unseen life, and seeking to uplift and spiritualize the souls before him by the contact and admixture.

(2) Nothing, moreover, will so arm the preacher with power. He comes to see how arms and armies and sciences and philosophies and any and all combinations of evil men are no match whatever for a God-trusting spirit. He thus learns the entire supremacy of spiritual over carnal things. To his unveiled face there come to be revealed the invisible troops of God covering the mountain ; and he *knows* that they that be for Him are more than they that be against Him.

(*c*) How is this vivid sense to be secured ? By

companionship with the invisible. By taking time to
get acquainted. Positively, there is no other way.
Brief and infrequent fellowship will not answer. The
powers of the world to come cannot be known by
snatching a mere glance at them in our set seasons of
devotion. There must be much meditation on God's
Word, brooding and brooding over it; much personal
communion with God in the "still hour," much opening of the sluices of the heart for the Spirit to pour in
His revelations. If these mighty realities of God's
spiritual kingdom are to be something more than
vague notions, or mere intellectual beliefs, we must
get into their presence and stay there, with a cry to
God for *vision*. And vision will come, and with it
will come vivid sense of eternal truths and facts: and
this means *power*. Down from these heights Peter and
Paul came, and preached, and men heard as for their
lives. And so they have ever since, when preachers
have come from these same heights. It was this that
made Luther's words " thunderbolts." Jonathan Edwards shook his parish, not because of his intellect,
but because he saw God. From out this presence also
spake Baxter and Pascal and McCheyne and Knox
and Whitefield. It was this that made Phinney the
great searcher of hearts among revivalists, and that
made Moody to rive men's souls.

No minister of Jesus Christ can preach these eternal
realities and powers, if he does not have a vivid sense
of them. He may repeat them, parrot-like, but he cannot hurl them with a John-the-Baptist earnestness, or a
Pauline energy, or a Christlike tenderness of power,
if they are not the overmastering forces in his own
soul. To make them so, he must be a good deal in

God's company. He must learn, day by day, to walk
with God. He must look long and lovingly into the
glass of the Word until he beholds the glory of his
Lord there. First and last, in all his preaching he
must seek to stand, when he preaches,—he must dare
to forego other things, that he may stand when he
preaches,—in the constant presence of things unseen.
He will not rest with an unmoved heart, while seeking to move other hearts. He will make it manifest
to his hearers that in painting the great things of God's
everlasting kingdom, he has learned to " dip his pencil
in the azure of heaven."

For helps to this vivid sense of the spiritual and
eternal, read sermons like Cheever's "Powers of the
World to Come," or Shedd's " Sermons to the Natural
Man." Go often and often to portions of God's Word,
like the eighth chapter of Romans, or the twenty-fifth
of Matthew, or the Epistle to the Ephesians, or those
portions of Isaiah which treat of the spiritual triumphs
(Ch. 25) ; of the power of God (Ch. 40); of the atonement (Ch. 53); of the blessed invitation (Ch. 55).
Spend days and days of spiritual delight and abysmal
joy in the Psalm country—and look often from Patmos
through John's eyes, and join in the new song, "Worthy
art Thou, O Lamb of God, to receive the blessing and
the honour and the dominion and the glory forever
and ever,—for Thou wast slain and didst purchase unto
God with Thy blood men of every tribe and tongue
and people and nation." But above all ponder the profound warnings and tender beseechings and heart-cries
of Jesus Himself.

And let it be remembered that this spiritual vision
of heavenly things and this commerce with them, this

constant cultivation of a vivid sense of the divine realities of the gospel message, is not a matter of great brains; nor is it dependent on scholarly research; nor is it the product of higher or lower criticism. These are unquestionable aids to great thoughts of God. But Moody, no less than Moses, "endured as seeing Him who is invisible." And Phinney, the revivalist, alike with Jonathan Edwards, "walked with God." And Whitefield, who had little of logical process, and Paul who had much, had intimate fellowship with eternal realities. And Gipsy Smith comes from out the presence as truly as Moses came, when descending from Sinai. It is not so much massive intellect as purity of heart, that sees God.

II. Another constant that should always have place in the work of preaching is the *constant cultivation of a homiletic bias.*

This bias is a tendency to the classification and orderly arrangement of materials for sermonic use; in other words, the *organizing, methodizing power* in sermonizing.

(*a*) And of this it should be said at the outset that *it is possible to every mind*, though more easily acquired by some than by others. Certainly the formation of our mental habits is largely under our own control. It is the commonest of truisms that the frequent repetition of an act will give both increased tendency to the action, and increased facility in its doing. The ease and readiness with which the mind comes to do some things through discipline and practice, are marvellous. Let the mind get accustomed to the severer processes of logic, and it will soon tend to make everything run to syllogism. Let the fancy be constantly stimulated, and at last the mind, as by instinct, will compel all ideas to take to themselves poetic forms. So an *organizing* tendency may be cultivated—a habit of mind that shall lead to classification and orderly arrangement in the use of all its materials. And this, in connection with the work of preaching, is what is here termed the *homiletic bias*— the tendency to organize in the direction of sermonizing—the constructive tendency.

(*b*) The *direct advantages* of the homiletic bias are obvious. (1) It gives method in homiletic toil. And the men of method are the men of achievement. Men that scatter shot, aim at nothing and hit it. He whose work of sermonizing is at loose ends is shorn of half his effectiveness.

(2) This bias also gives great facility in grasping the salient points of a text. The thoughts in the text and about it, will place themselves naturally in proper succession. Everything will tend to glide into plan. And out of the realm of haziness and indefiniteness, with less and less delay as the methodizing power is developed, will come the dry bones of a skeleton, instinct already with the promise and potency of life, and waiting to be clothed with flesh and blood. The mind will be by a growing bias ready for construction, and will feel no necessity of leaning on the crutches of some other plan builder.

(3) The homiletic bias also gives the preacher increasing command of all the materials furnished by his reading and study. Every book into which he dips, every department of art or science or literature he explores, every field of truth he enters for investigation will, with ever-increasing facility, be made to

yield its stores by way of proof or suggestion or illustration, and so augment the wealth and effective
power of his pulpit discourse. This strong, sermonizing tendency, this homiletic bias of mind, will compel all these materials to shape themselves so as best
to further the purpose of each discourse.

(4) Still further, this bias gives glow to the sermonizer in the process of actual composition. The
task becomes congenial. The materials are at hand.
The plan has grown into orderly shape. It has taken
clear and definite outline. The preacher has his subject well in hand; knows his aim; is not lashed into
the service by the necessities of the weak, but leaps
to it as to a delight, eager to rescue or to mould. The
plan is his own, and the freshness of it, the inspiration of it, puts oil to all the wheels of his mental
machinery, and his sermon is written in a glow.

Hence, (c) The importance of the homiletic bias. It
is just as important to the preacher as the imagina-
tive bias is to the poet. He should make everything
pour into the channel of sermonizing, just as the poet
makes everything contribute to what he deems his
divine art. Preaching is his business, and should be
his whole business. He has sacredly committed himself to it. Alexander says, "To be a great preacher,
a man must be nothing else."[1] He must forego the
reputation which comes from erudition and literature.
The channel must be narrowed, that the stream may
flow in a rapid current, and its impact produce a
mighty impression.

If sermons are constructed to secure reconstructed
manhood,—if they are built to build men in Christ

[1] "Thoughts on Preaching," p. 15.

Jesus, what other work is there like it! It should have a kind of sacred monopoly of discipline and acquisition. No other intellectual calling can be safely or wisely pursued along with it. To be efficient homiletes, successful and great in this high calling of God as preachers of the eternal Word, the whole life must be made to run towards the pulpit. It will take what there is in any man—all of it and at its best, to do the work justice. The man has never yet been seen, built large enough to go much beyond this.

The ideal ministry will therefore learn to transmute everything it touches into sermon. The ideal minister will grow organific as he grows in grace—and so develop this methodizing power as to render it year by year swifter and surer in results.

(*d*) Means of cultivation will readily suggest themselves, and should be put to constant use. (1) Give much thought to the construction of plans. Habituate the mind to skeletonizing. Organize thoughts on a text into a skeleton, and then hang the skeleton up in a text-book.

(2) Take up sermons now and then; analyze them. Study the best models,—their themes, methods of treatment, ends aimed at. See whether the plan can anywhere have improvement, compare sermons one with another by different authors, yet on the same subject.

(3) Have a classified text-book, and jot down in it all texts that make their impress and arrest attention as God's Word is read; and all texts that are flashed to the mind in meditation: *suggestive* texts, that seem laden with new riches as they go flying by. If the text-book is not within reach, use a piece of paper, an

old envelope,—anything, to make it sure that the
thought and its treatment will not be lost.   These
texts that are brought down, as it were, "*on the wing*"
—that flash unbidden to the view, and grow luminous
on the instant, are almost like inspirations; and sermonizing on them will be like the sweep of the eagle,
cleaving the air with his strong pinions.

(4) Negatively: Beware of *books of skeletons*,
called "Pulpit Helps."   They are pulpit hindrances;
snares of the devil.   They may tide the preacher over
a present difficulty—they may back him across a
stream which he is too lazy to swim, or too heavy
with the things of this world to fly over, but the fires
of homiletic enthusiasm cannot be fed with them.   As
well think of rousing the passions with the propositions of Euclid, or of heating an oven with snowballs.

Sermon plans may be studied, and should be studied,
as a matter of course; just as sermons should be
studied: as suggestive, illustrative, helpful, revealing
many a secret of pulpit effectiveness.   But to transfer
them bodily to one's pulpit without credit, is, in principle, as immoral as to appropriate entire sermons that
way.   Each is alike a deception and a fraud.

Beware, therefore, of these so-called "Pulpit Helps."
Avoid them, pass not by them, turn from them and
pass away.   For "they sleep not except they have
done mischief"; and they can hardly rest on the
library shelves of ministers of the Gospel, without
causing "some to fall."

The preacher should make his own sermon plans—
and make them often, over and above the weekly use
of them.   And the fruit of this repeated process will
be a homiletic bias of incalculable value.

III. Another of the "constants," that must have heed in any growing ministry, is the *constant cultivation* of familiarity with the sources of materials to be used in preaching. And these sources are the Bible, other books, and living men.

(*a*) First, and preeminently, *the Bible*. Familiarity with this, if with nothing else. Familiarity with this even, if need be, at the expense of all else. Any companion or pursuit that charms away from this—any study that lures our feet to other paths of knowledge from which we come back reluctantly to the study of God's Word, were better unknown. At whatever cost, the man of God should let the science or the literature or the learning go, that would keep him ignorant of the Word of God.

(1) Why should the Bible have such preeminence as a study? For the all-sufficient reason that this Word is to be the foundation and essential substance of all preaching. And both the matter of it and the spirit of it should therefore enter into the very texture of the sermon. This is not interlarding the sermon with textual citations. The sermon may be studded and starred with texts of Scripture, and yet be unbiblical. The shower of texts may simply come from a concordance. But judicious quotations are certainly to be commended. They serve to clinch an argument, and make profound impression. A clear ringing, unchallengeable " *Thus saith the Lord* " is often the end of controversy.

(2) With what spirit should the Bible be studied? Alike *with the true spirit of scholarship and the true spirit of devotion ;* as a book of sacred literature and as a book of divine authority. He makes a griev-

ous mistake who thinks it for the heart only, and not for the head. As an intellectual preparation for the intellectual work of the ministry, its habitual and careful study is indispensable. But he who uses it for the head only, and not for the heart, makes a far more grievous mistake. To neglect it as a daily manual of devotion is positively fatal.

The students of its mysteries will be sorely tempted with a lust of brain and a pride of intellect,—tempted with a subtlety and pressure of seductive power it will be hard to resist—to leave these fields of inspiration and wander elsewhere in quest of facts, illustrations, arguments and principles with which to dignify and grace their pulpit speech. But they must see to it with relentless watch and care that nothing takes them so far or so effectually away from God's Word, that they do not joyfully return to it *day by day*, to read it not only, but to give it some of their best and most painstaking study.

It should appear in their preaching that they are not only familiar with the Scriptural system of doctrine, but that they are coming to an ever-increasing knowledge of its authorities, illustrations, histories, phraseology and spirit ; so that their discourse, in all its length and breadth, shall be more and more exhibitive of the Word of God, and so that divine authority shall everywhere be stamped upon it as an unmistakable seal.

Alexander thus tersely gives his matured advice : " Cut off superfluous studies. Come back to the Bible. This rings in my ears as years go on. Consider all past studies as so much discipline to fit you for this great study. Make Scripture the interpreter of Scripture."[1] This eminent divine and accomplished scholar had a great ambition early in life to be great in classical acquisition. And his attainments were unusual. But his riper judgment made all this but stubble and dross in comparison with the Bible.

(3) By what method should the Bible be studied?

(*a*) Study the text itself, verse by verse. Not commentaries so much, though they are to be consulted and compared as accredited helps in exegesis. But study the text itself, in translation and in the original, thoroughly, critically. Dip into the deep things of God. Dip deeper and deeper. There are depths everywhere that never discover their full riches to the superficial seeker. Pore over the Word. Mine for the hid treasure. Take *single verses,* and grasp them, grapple with them, till they yield their secrets. Pay most careful heed to the *nexus* of the passage, so as to be sure of the local colouring.[2]

(*b*) Read entire books of the Bible at one sitting: especially the Epistles. Go over the ground again and again. Long trains of thought, logical connections, sweeps and drifts and pervading unities will thus disclose themselves.

Here are the materials for preaching—and the best materials. The preacher must know them, and grow to ever-increasing familiarity with them, or he cannot preach the message given him of God.

(*c*) *Other books.* But the Bible is not the only source of materials. There are other books whose enriching stores must be at the preacher's command.

---

[1] "Thoughts on Preaching," p. 56, J. W. Alexander; Phelps' "Theory of Preaching," pp. 216–219.

[2] Prof. J. M. Gray's "Synthetic Bible Study;" an excellent help.

(1) First, books on the Bible and drawn from it. Commentaries and treatises and fruits of exegetical study. These are stocked to the full with Bible lore —every page often bearing the ripest fruits of the best scholarship of the world's master minds. These must be studied. The Bible is the original fountain, and these are only issues from it. But they have been drawn from the wells of inspiration by men who knew how to reach down far and go deep. To say that "original research" must dispense with these processes and these results, is to make a fetish of a phrase, and to require the students of God's Word to do what the students in any other field would count an egregious folly, viz., to pursue their investigations as if there had never before been an investigator. What progress could there be in knowledge, human or divine, along that road !

(2) Secondly, books of philosophy, history, science, art, literature, in all its branches, are a wide and open field.

Philosophy : not to preach it, but for discipline and method, to help one the better to preach the philosophy of God in the Gospel; and to help make accurate the constructive tendency of which we have spoken.

(3) *Psychology :* that we may know what we are; and knowing what we are, may know what other men are, and how we may best reach them with God's truth.

(4) *History :* for illustration and proof. God is writing history, and every page of it must confirm the pages of His Holy Word. " History is philosophy teaching by example," it has been said. Nay, more.

It is God, in the march of providence, illustrating His truth.

(5) *Science :* true science is full of God : is " packed with confirmation strong as proof from Holy Writ," that He is in His world, its builder and maker.

In fact, materials are furnished from every department of human knowledge. And the most diversified knowledge can be, and will be, made tributary to the pulpit, just as the preacher understands the art of transmuting these common metals into gold.[1] But he should dare always to be ignorant of many books, that he may thoroughly know some books : and, first of all, and more than all, his Bible. Other books only as they shall make him a better exegete of *the* Book.

(*d*) *Living men.* Here also are to be found rich and varied materials, contributive to pulpit efficiency. Next to a knowledge of God's Word, what can help a preacher so much as a knowledge of the human nature that is before him every Sabbath, thinking, feeling, wondering, hungering, yearning, doubting, hating ? " Know thyself." But know others also. Psychology is important here. But *mix with men.* Be observant. Get at their dispositions. Discover their prejudices and needs. Learn what they are thinking about. Do not leave humanity outside the study, or at the foot of the pulpit steps. Let its wants set back into the sermon, and determine the sermon's bent. Touch, with the touch of personal presence and companionship, its great throbbing heart. A man shut up forever in his study is a monk in a cloister—

[1] For a fine illustration of this combination, see " The Ascent Through Christ," by E. Griffith Jones.

barring his clothes. Gather materials from out among men everywhere—from their lives, their characters, their business, their pleasures ; from their thoughts and hopes and fears, as these find expression. Henry Ward Beecher once said, " A minister who walks down a whole street and sees nobody—who only looks inside of himself—is but half a minister." This may be an overstatement, but it has truth at the bottom of it. Surely, if we would do any wise soul-winning, we must know the way of talking to men, and coming into sympathy with them. And in order to this *we must know men.*

IV. Another " constant " in sermonic construction is the constant presence of *a lofty standard of sermonizing.*

The preacher must set and keep his model sermon far before him and above him always. Then let him point his arrow towards *that sun ;* and though the arrow fall short of it, it will fly that way.

The standard of sermonizing cannot possibly be too high. As reasons for this high standard :

Consider first, *the peculiar character of the times.* Once the pulpit was a kind of popular educator, preacher, teacher, printing-press, in one. The most that great bodies in the community learned they got from the pulpit. It is not so now. The pulpit cannot rely on the information it gives, for its place of power. Other enginery thunders at its work of diffusing knowledge, with a celerity, and sweep and reach of power no ministry can possibly vie. Other professions are now abreast of the clerical in all knowledges. Society is intensely active. Men think quickly, sharply, complexly. There are varied and complex forces behind them and surrounding them that make them so think. Into the midst of this whirl and hum must now be thrown—one day in the week—the sermon.

Consider, secondly, *the work a sermon is to do*. It is to arrest these thronging activities, stay the stress and press of these underlying and out-pushing forces, make men pause and think, get hold of them, spiritualize their carnalities that have been moved upon all the week, bring divine and eternal realities to bear down upon them, and get such a leverage that their souls shall be lifted away from everything mean and sordid, and shall be transformed by other and better presences than have thronged about them and often possessed them in the weekly whirl of business and social life.

"Thirty minutes to raise the dead in"! as Ruskin puts it.

Once understand this, and a man's whole soul will go out into his sermon every week, and into the effort to make it all it ought to be as a word of eternal life and death.

The danger lies in the temptation to be satisfied with inferior homiletic preparation for the pulpit. There is need of being kept toned up to constant effort at improvement. There is need of the constant presence of a high ideal. Let the standard be always set furlongs forward of all actual achievement. It will serve as an incitement and inspiration. "Now I am growing old," said Thorwaldsen, "for I am satisfied with this work which I have completed." Men do not grow old while the stir and call of a noble and yet unrealized ideal is in their hearts.

But consider, thirdly, *apostolic example*. It is there

on record, for each man who preaches, to strive after
and imitate.

Paul's standard of preaching was high. He attempted nothing in an off-hand, careless way, as if the
work were easy, and his conception of it something
that his abilities could easily meet. How he struggles
with the impotency of language to express himself.
" Who is sufficient for these things," he cries. His
work was ever above him. " It exhausted and mocked
the mean sufficiencies of human resource. It scorched
and consumed him like an altar fire."

Two cautionary words must close this discussion.

(1) The sermonic standard should not be one of
simple excellency of speech—not that which is to be
reached by the mere sentence maker. God forbid that
a preacher of the Gospel should aim at anything like
that! Let Vinet's weighty words be a perpetual guide
and warning here. " I affirm," he says, " that the
desire of speaking well, the literary point of view, just
in proportion as it has ascendancy over a minister,
degrades his ministry. I affirm that the preacher is
not, in the highest view, a man of literature. I affirm
that there is a seductive intoxication in the use of
speech, which should be feared. . . . To avoid
this evil, a sure way is to hold Art in contempt. But
God has not made our way so easy. . . . It is
between the idolatry of Art and the contempt of Art,
that God has required us to walk. Neither an
anathema on Art, nor Art for Art's sake; but Art for
God's sake, is what we insist upon."

And this must be the insistence of every man of God
who preaches. He will strike this golden mien, and
be kept from idolizing his tools (which are his ser-

mons), if abidingly and vividly conscious of the work
they are to do; and that they are nothing but sounding brass and tinkling cymbal save as they are designed and fitted to do that work—which is reaching
and saving men.

(2) The second cautionary word is this: The vital
thing, whether in preparation for the ministry, or in
the actual work of the ministry, is not the number of
sermons one makes, but the kind they are, and the work
they are fitted to do. Just as it is not so much how
many times we pray, as what our praying does for us.

Therefore, let not the preacher be ambitious to pile
up manuscripts, either on his way to the ministry or
while in the ministry. It is far better to have few
sermons of the right quality, and the ability, from
study and discipline, to make them, than to have many
sermons written in the vanity of a foolish rapidity, as
if they were productions that could be rattled off at
any hour on short notice by a mere intellectual
machine. Remember the old fable: "*One—but a
lion*"! Set the standard high. Then work up to it.

Here then are the four ideal "constants" in the
study and practice of the homiletic discipline; or the
divine art of preaching the Gospel. Let us once more
group them, and in grouping them, see how they make
some things impossible. These indispensable and
peerless "constants" are:

The constant cultivation of a more and more vivid
and abiding sense of the divine realities of the gospel
message.

The constant cultivation of the homiletic bias.

The constant cultivation of familiarity with the
sources of materials.

And the constant presence of a lofty standard of sermonizing.

See now, as we look these "constants" in the face, how they make some things impossible.

(1) They make it impossible that a minister should grow *old before his time*. Nature has indeed set limits to efficient age. But, far within those limits, ministers are sometimes charged with outliving their usefulness, preaching old sermons, living in the past, lacking in adaptation. But a minister in the constant cultivation of what we have here named would make such a charge ridiculous.

(2) They make it impossible that a minister should ever *exhaust his stock*. Under these "constants" he would be forever *replenishing* his stock.

(3) They make it impossible that a minister should ever be *out of date*. How could he be a constant student of the *Bible*, of *other books* and of *living men*, and ever become "a back number" in the ministry of the Word of God?

(4) They make it impossible that a minister should ever *be afraid*. It is the *absence* of these "constants," and not the presence and use of them, that makes a compromising and a cowardly ministry.

XX

ITS IDEAL "IMMEDIATES"

SYLLABUS

The ideal "immediates" are the steps to get ready for next Sunday. For the best preparation, every preacher must take these steps.

I. He must get a distinct conception of the theme to be treated, *i. e.*, he must know *what he is going to talk about.*

   (*a*) The theme should *include* what he is going to say, and *exclude* everything else.

   (*b*) The text is not ordinarily the theme.

   (*c*) The theme should have an exact expression in words.

II. A distinct conception of the *object* to be accomplished, or an answer to the question, *Why* am I going to talk about this theme? Four possible *generic* objects : (1) To instruct the understanding. (2) To convince the judgment. (3) To exclude the sensibility. (4) To persuade the will.

   There are many *specific* objects, and *one* of *these* must often be determined on, for the best results. Sorrow, shame, fear, etc., *dissuading* passions—anger, hope, love, gratitude, etc., *persuading* passions. Sermons will often be completely changed by the particular feeling the preacher would arouse.

   Here is the *core* of effective sermonizing.

   Consider the *advantages.*

   (1) Without aim it is impossible to do one's best.

   (2) A distinct specific object would go far to shape the plan of treatment.

   (3) It is essential to the truest unity.

III. A distinct conception of *the plan*, or an answer to the question, How am I going to talk about this theme so as to accomplish this object? Objection to plans; that the thought lacks spontaneity. Plan binds. But learn from the general—the architect—the engineer. They *never* work without a plan. A lot of thought is not a sermon, any more than a heap of stones is an arch, or a house, or a barn, or a steeple.

   Plan leads to three things :

(1) A clear knowledge of what belongs to the subject.

(2) An adjustment of parts according to their relative importance.

(3) Natural and orderly succession, *i. e.*, sermonic unity.

Two observations, (*a*) The plan may be modified if found defective. (*b*) Plan should vary with the theme and object.

IV. The collecting and arranging of materials.

(1) What materials shall be used? The best material is what the preacher has made his own by past reading and study. The next best is from immediate study.

(2) How to be gathered?

(*a*) Make the earliest possible selection of theme.

(*b*) Refer to parallel passages of Scripture.

(*c*) Make brief notes of the fruit of your own meditation.

(*d*) If not material enough, *read* judiciously—chew—assimilate. Do not *cram*.

(*e*) *Borrow* outright if necessary, but let it be *known* you are borrowing.

(*f*) In quoting poetry, drop the stale and useless prelude, "As the poet says."

V. Quickened personal interest and sympathy. Think and think. Pray and pray.

VI. The actual writing.

(*a*) With audience before you, is the fundamental specialty.

(*b*) If written rapidly, *review*.

(*c*) Don't make your work *patch*-work.

XX

ITS IDEAL "IMMEDIATES"

WE have considered the ideal "constants," involving sermonic preparation for all the Sundays. We are now to consider the ideal "immediates," or the steps to be taken in preparation for the next Sunday.

Conceding the utmost variety of mental characteristics and making all allowance for differences of constitutional temperament, are there not certain requisites indispensable to the best weekly preparation for the pulpit? Is there not a theory of preparation of universal application, which every man, whatever his tastes or habits or idiosyncrasies, may adopt and carry out, with increasing profit to himself and to his hearers? We hold there is such a theory. We hold there are steps to be taken in the construction of a sermon that form the best method of preparation, and that are essential to the best results.

I. One indispensable step in preparation is a clear, distinct conception of the theme to be treated; or an answer to the question, What am I going to talk about?

Until the preacher gets this question definitely answered, he should go no farther. He must have a theme and should know precisely what it is. And that he may know that he knows, he should put it in words. If he can't put it in words, discussion is hopeless. If his theme is in a haze, everything else will be : his introduction, his arrangement, his proof, his object, his hearers, himself ! It must be vividly outlined in his thought, and given a precise verbal form.

(*a*) The theme should not simply *cover* or *include* what he is to say. It should *exclude everything else.*

Repentance, *e. g.*, is not the theme of a discourse which is designed to show *the necessity* of repentance, if one would not perish. It does not fix a boundary to the subsequent discussion. And a theme must do that if it is to tell the truth.

(*b*) The text, as a rule, is not the theme. It simply contains it. The theme lies in the text, and should usually be its very core. But the text and the theme are by no means synonymous. When the preacher has his text, he is commonly only on the road to his theme. Take the text (Heb. 2 : 3) : " How shall we escape if we neglect so great a salvation " ; and three or four themes may be got from it according to the emphasis given the leading words. " Mere neglect of salvation is certain ruin " would be a theme where the emphasis would fall on the word " neglect." Melville has a great sermon on this text, taking for his theme, " The greatness of salvation an argument for the peril of its neglect," which is the precise thought of the inspired writer.

(*c*) The theme *should have exact expression in words*. The preacher should not be satisfied with a general idea. Let him take time to be definite. It will often require time, and that too when the preacher may think he ought to be dashing on to the construction of the sermon, which must be ready, *nolens volens*, for the swiftly approaching Sabbath. Let the theme

be stripped of everything redundant. It is the
epitome of the discourse—the germ, out of which the
whole structure is to grow. It should be concise—explicit; phrased with painstaking care. One may be
perfectly sure the thought is vague, so long as he cannot give it exact expression. *Put it in words. Put
it in words.* Time taken, no matter under what pressure or call from other quarters—in getting a clear,
distinct conception of the subject, is time saved. In
each preparation for the pulpit, the first words written
should invariably be *the exact wording of the theme :* or
an answer to the question, What am I to talk about ?

II. A second indispensable step in immediate preparation is a clear, distinct conception of *the object
to be accomplished*, or, an answer to the question,
Why am I going to talk about this theme ? What is
my purpose in the use of it ? If I have a distinct end
in view, what is it ?

There are only four possible, immediate, generic objects the preacher can have in view, viz., to instruct the
understanding, to convince the judgment, to excite the
sensibilities, to persuade the will. He may have any
one of these before him, or more than one, or all.
One may be chief and the rest subordinate. *Instruction* may sometimes demand supreme place. The
nature of the theme, its setting in God's Word, the
condition of the hearers, may make it imperative that
instruction shall be the leading object of discourse.
But instruction may be required only in a very
modified degree, or not at all. Conviction may be
chief—or excitation. Invariably, and often domi-
nantly, *persuasion* should be distinctly aimed at.

Under these four generic objects, instruction, conviction, excitation, persuasion, there may be many specific objects. And some one of these more specific objects it may be the purpose of the preacher to secure.

For example ; suppose conviction to be the object. But conviction of what ? Of a truth of God ? of duty ? or of sin ? And then again, What particular truth of God ? What specific duty ? What kind of sin ? The discussion of the theme will be changed completely by the determination of any one of these several objects. The preacher will not produce conviction of a truth of God by the same road that he will produce conviction of duty, or of sin. He will convince of truth by logical process, by arraying the Scriptural and other evidence, appealing chiefly if not wholly to the understanding. He will convince of duty or of sin, by storming the conscience, by appeal to the feelings, by an exhibition of God's claims.

So with *excitation* as an object. There should be a further limitation of object to the particular feeling or passion to be excited. Sorrow, fear, shame, humility, are the *dissuading* passions. Anger, hope, love, gratitude, emulation, ambition, are the more *persuading* passions. While joy, esteem, compassion, are what may be termed the intermediate.

Now what is it, that the theme has been chosen to arouse ? What does the preacher in handling it most wish to arouse ? The sermon may be totally changed in its tone and material and structure, as one or another of these specific objects is decided on.

And *in every case* the object is to be considered in relation to that final object of every sermon, the determination of the *will* of the hearer *Godward*.

For example : Suppose the text to be, " The soul

that sinneth it shall die" (Ezek. 18 : 4). And suppose the theme drawn from the text is, "The doom of the finally impenitent."

Now, if the preacher's object were to excite *fear*, he might have the sermon show the irreversibleness and awfulness of the doom.

If his object were to excite *sorrow*, he might have the sermon show how the sinner tramples on God's *heart;* and cite in illustration Christ's tears and heart-broken cries over Jerusalem.

If his object were to rouse the *conscience*, he might have the sermon show the terribleness of sin as against the Sovereign God.

Or, if his object were to excite *hope*, he might take the awfulness of the doom, the flagrancy of the sin, the holiness of God, and show how they are all magnified in the wondrous way of pardon, by which the chief of sinners may die in Christ and live forever.

But in *every* preparation for the pulpit, a distinct conception should be had of some definite object to be accomplished. Of all the sinners from lack of purpose, a *purposeless pulpit* is the chief.

The advantages of having a definite object :

(1) *Without aim it is impossible to do one's best at any toil.* It is as true of brain-work as it is of hand-work. It is not in human nature to get absorbed in vague, indefinite effort. Unity in aim is the very life of invention. Having no object in view, the mind has no spring—no stirring incentive. There is nothing to marshal its energies. This-one-thing-I-do inspiration is wanting. There is no focus-constraining convergence.

(2) Again; this distinct conception of the object

will go far *to shape the plan of treatment.* The
preacher is now after a plan that will do a certain
thing. He knows what he wants. Hence the greater
likelihood of his getting it, and the greater facility in
the process. Having determined on his object, much
is at once decided that otherwise would be left in un-
certainty. The kind of plan, the form it shall take,
the amount of explication or proof or appeal it shall
contain, will be largely determined by the object
aimed at, and this will help immensely in the construction of the plan. So much is gained in knowing
just what one wishes to accomplish.

Suppose men made new tools as some men make
new sermons, with no idea of the definite thing to be
done with them,—how would they go to work? A
man making a tool must know what the tool is for.
When he knows that, the plan of it is often half-
formed. *Sermons are tools.* But imagine a man in a
workshop busy with some device quite beyond ordinary conjecture. A friend drops in and asks,
" What are you about, man?" And the workman
replies, " Oh, I'm trying to make a tool." " But what
kind of a tool?" the friend asks. " Well, I don't
quite know," answers the workman; " haven't decided. But I thought I'd try my hand at a new tool."
At this the friend fairly bursts with laughter. And
the workman, quite nettled at his friend's jocoseness,
says, " See here, I don't mind telling you. I want a
tool that will *make a hole.*" " But what kind of a
hole?" " Oh, I haven't bothered my head about that.
I simply meant to enlarge my *kit of tools!* " And
whether round hole or square hole or triangular hole,
or big hole, or little hole, was to him of no consequence.

He had a gimlet and an auger and an awl and a chisel, but he was after another tool that would make a hole! Query: Is not this the way sermons are sometimes made? The minister wants another sermon, and he simply goes to work and makes it, simply to add to his kit of tools, with no distinct, definite, commanding purpose whatever. God may bless such a sermon, but only as He blesses "the weak things to confound the mighty, and things that are not to bring to nought things that are, that no flesh may glory in His presence."

(3) Another advantage in having a definite object is this: It is *essential to the truest unity.*

Unity is the very life of discourse. Nothing can atone for the want of it. Everything must be subordinated and made subservient to this, as we shall see in subsequent discussion.

But singleness of subject will not give unity. Certainly not in its highest and best form. There must be an object also—a terminus *ad quem* as well as a terminus *a quo*, to which the mind shall be rigidly held, and which shall be steadily pursued throughout the discourse. It is here, perhaps more than anywhere else, that young sermon makers are apt to fail. But, alas, we all know there are homiletic sinners who have grown old at this bad business.

They take a subject. They are to make a sermon to cover twenty or thirty pages of manuscript. They give themselves to writing, with no clear, distinct, commanding object in view, that they are bent on accomplishing. The discourse will have truth in it, important truth—it may sparkle with brilliant flashes of genius—nevertheless, what is it after all but an ac-

cumulation of dead words, " cemented together by the
lifeless rules of grammar," if there is no single governing purpose running down through it, and dominating
the entire discussion. The focal point to which all the
lines of the sermon converge, is absolutely vital to the
highest sermonic efficiency.

III. A third requisite in immediate preparation for
the pulpit, is the *plan*. With a subject and an object
distinctly determined, the question that now faces the
preacher is: How am I to treat this subject so as to
accomplish this object? This means *plan*—plan of
some kind—that shall work everything up into one
compact organism, that shall set the parts together in
climacteric order, that shall present a natural and
orderly succession, exclude irrelevant material, and
make the different lines of the discourse grow hot as
they converge to one burning focus—this is without
doubt essential to the most effective sermonizing.
Just in proportion as the plan of treatment is clear,
comprehensive, and cumulative, will the sermon be
impressive, and adapted to its end.

Labour at this point is commonly imperative. Now
and then a plan will be flashed to the mind as by inspiration. But the mind does not ordinarily work
with this electric swiftness. Often it will be only
after the severest study that an outline will be reached
at all satisfactory. There will be struggles with obscurity and confusion. The subject may be enveloped
in haze, and the thought chaotic—leading to half truths,
side truths, irrelevant truths. There will be *seeming*,
and sometimes *real*, want of harmony, want of unity,
want of logical connection. But *labour*—persistent,
thoughtful, hard labour, will bring order out of the

chaos—and it will *always pay*. Labour here is well spent, however severe—and time here is well employed, however long—until the skeleton is given its proper shape.

Doubtless the preacher will sometimes be tempted to forego the plan, because of the difficulty of organizing it. Both the subject and the materials will so seem to baffle effort to make them take order and shape in a well constructed plan, that the preacher may be inclined to go on without a plan. Shall this be done? *Never!* Think; study; organize. Leave the work awhile, and return to it. These little "rests," or changes of occupation, are wonderful helps to clarity of vision. The preacher returns to his task, and often finds that what he left a fog-bank, is now shot through and through with sunlight.

The objection urged against a preconceived plan is this: A fixed plan is a restraint—it cramps and limits the mind's movements, and trammels thought. Alexander says, "To write by a plan is, in some degree, to bind the thought to a given track. He is most likely to arrive at what is original and new, who, like the river, ' wanders at his own sweet will.' "[1] And he lays it down as a canon of composition: " *In writing or speaking, throw off all restraint.*" [2]

He betrays the secret of this preference, however, and, at the same time, the folly of it, in an item labelled sermonizing, thus: "I have just finished a sermon. I am not pleased. I was hampered throughout by a preconcerted *skeleton*. Thus it worked. Things would arise in my mind, and flow into my pen just at the right place (!) but I could not use them, *because they*

[1] "Thoughts on Preaching," p. 45.   [2] *Ibid.*, p. 32.

belonged to another head (!) The result was, the articulation was broken, the flow was interrupted, the work became a Mosaic." [1] Illustrating thus his further word, that "the current is often stopped at the very moment when it begins to gush." [2]

The best answer to Alexander is Alexander. How could things rise in his mind and flow into his pen " at *the right place*" if they "*belonged to another head.*" If they belonged to another head they were in the *wrong* place. If they were in the right place, they *could not belong to another head.*

Is a crowd an army? Is a heap of stones an arch? Is a lot of ideas a sermon? Other things being equal, a discourse is powerful in proportion to the *order* reigning in it. The *place where* you put a thought or thing, makes a mighty difference in the effectiveness of use. Suppose a man had an arm where one of his legs ought to be, and the leg was socketed at his shoulder-blade—what kind of a man would he be for doing things? Ideas in speech must be so arranged that they shall be best fitted to do things. This means *plan.* An architect will never start to build without a plan of the building. A civil engineer surveys his route before he authorizes construction. A general studies the situation, and lays out a plan of campaign, before his army goes afield. Should a minister ever prepare and preach a sermon without a sermon plan?

A discourse without plan may produce effects. So may a lawless mob. But face that mob with disciplined policemen or troops, one-tenth its number, and there is no more the mob can do. A sermon with a

[1] "Thoughts on Preaching," p. 29. [2] *Ibid.*, p. 32.

mob of ideas may have some power. But that same sermon, with those same ideas transformed from a mob into a disciplined, unified battalion of thoughts, arranged in the interests of *climax*, will be *fitted* at least to do great things for God. To have all the power of which discourse is capable, it must have adjustment, proportion, a governing purpose, an end— all its parts mutually aiding and sustaining one another.

Prearrangement leads to natural and orderly succession: *i. e.*, to organize sermonic unity; leads to clearer knowledge of what really belongs to the subject; leads to an adjustment of parts according to their relative importance.

The lack of prearrangement, the disuse of skeletonizing leads to a rambling and diffusive style; the law of association is the only law: and we all know what will-o'-the-wisps that law will start an undisciplined mind in chase of.

Observation (*a*) The plan need not be binding in the entire composition of the sermon. It may be seen in the progress of the work, from increased familiarity with the subject, and in the glow and inspiration that may come from contact and insight, that the end in view—the determined object—may be better accomplished by some modification or readjustment. Let the modification be freely made.

Observation (*b*) Plans should vary with the subject. There should be no procrustean bed for plans. But their construction should invariably precede the construction of the sermon.

IV. A fourth requisite in immediate preparation for the pulpit is the collection and arrangement of sermon materials. This involves answers to two questions : What materials shall be used ? and by what method shall they be gathered and arranged ?

(1) What materials shall be used ?

Clearly such as will give the sermon plan or skeleton an appropriate body. In other words, that which will best unfold the theme and accomplish the object.

The absolutely best material for the sermon is unquestionably that which the preacher has already made his own by past reading and study, it having been so taken into his mind as to become the very chyle and blood and fibre of the intellectual and moral man. This inwrought and digested material is beyond a doubt the fittest for use, for it is the man's own. He has made it so, not by memorizing, but by those mental processes of absorption and assimilation which make the thoughts we feed on as veritably our own as the food we eat.

Happy the man who has stored away by reading and study, and observation, treasures of literature and art, principles of philosophy and ethics, facts of history and biography—and, above all, incidents, precepts, parables, personal histories, principles, truths and facts from God's Word, with which to clarify and fortify and illustrate his theme—and who has the faculty of marshalling them to his service, when occasion calls for their use.

But few men can thus trust wholly to their past for materials with which to give body to discourse. Henry Ward Beecher often prepared his Sunday evening sermon Sunday afternoon. But this would have been impossible if he had not formed the habit of regular study and continual observation. He went

through the world with his eyes open. He himself
says, " I do not believe that I ever met a man on the
street that I did not get from him some element for a
sermon. I never see anything in Nature which does
not work towards that for which I give the strength
of my life. The material for my sermons is all the
time following me. I am tracing out analogies, which
I afterwards take pains to verify, to see whether my
views of certain things were correct. I follow them
out in my study, and see how such things are taught
by others."

This capacity of resource may be cultivated by every
one. Spurgeon had it to a degree somewhat remarkable. He, too, went through the world with his eyes
open, always gathering material for his pulpit. Here
is the advantage of careful reading and of ever-widen-
ing research. Especially here is the immense profit
of the constant critical and devout study of the Scriptures.

But the stock on hand is by no means always equal
to the demand. The thoroughly digested and assimilated material may fall short of meeting the weekly
need.

Hence the *balance* of material must be got by
reading and study and observation *on the week in
which the sermon is to be written.*

(2) A few suggestions that may be helpful in gathering and arranging material for sermonic use :

(*a*) Make the earliest possible selection of the theme,
the very first of the week, so that every suggestion,
fact, illustration that may be met with, as bearing on
the subject, may be put to use.

(*b*) Refer to parallel passages of Scripture, and critically examine and compare these. Scripture is often the best interpreter of Scripture. What God has said upon the subject must be helpful in understanding and enforcing it.

(*c*) Put upon a loose slip of paper brief notes or catch-words of your own thoughts on the subject, together with such illustrations and practical conclusions as may occur to you from past reading or observation.

(*d*) If this supply is not rich enough, read with judicious care other authors on the same subject, or on a subject closely akin to it.

All this, however, with one rigid and conscientious purpose scrupulously adhered to: to wit—to profit from this help *only and solely by letting the matter digest in the mind,* and then to write freely with no further use whatever of the authors consulted, and in entire forgetfulness of their phraseology and method. Unless the matter is made one's own by reflection and thorough digestion, the user must either give explicit credit for its source, or be guilty of using " stolen goods." Provided one digests while he reads, turning the thought over and over in his own mind, he may read with profit even in immediate preparation for the Sabbath. But to *cram* before writing—to make the mind " a mere warehouse for other men's thoughts," is most pernicious.

(*e*) Borrow, outright, if there is occasion for it. If you know of something belonging to another, that is forceful and impressive—borrow boldly: but let it be known to your hearers that the thing borrowed is not manufactured at your own mill.

(*f*) In quoting, quote nothing that will not give

weight to the discourse, either in itself, or in view of its
authorship. And in quoting poetry, give the rhyme
without that stale and useless prelude, "As the poet
says." Take it for granted the people know poetry
when they hear it and know that you are not a poet.

(*g*) Just one more suggestion. Arrange the materials according to the plan, under appropriate heads.
Some will go under one head. Some under another
head. Some under no head. In this latter case, resolutely set the material aside. Use may be found for
it on some other occasion. There is absolutely no use
for it here.

V. A fifth requisite in immediate preparation for
the pulpit is a *quickened personal interest—a lively,
living sympathy.*

Somehow this must be secured, or the highest success in preaching is impossible. The truth preached
must not only get into the preacher's head, but into
his heart—and be a living experience, a glowing
enthusiasm, an intense reality, or preaching will be
largely a dead letter. The preparation of the preacher
must go on side by side with the preparation of the
sermon. "Interest is the law, the spring, the life of
eloquence." Adolph Monod makes the eloquence of
the pulpit depend on "inward conception and feeling." Alexander says, "The great reason why we
have so little good preaching is that we have so little
piety."[1] "Build a big fire in the pulpit," as we have
already said, was Moody's way of heating a cold
church. But hear the flaming apostle of feeling who
so long swayed the hearts of his Brooklyn church.
"Hundreds and hundreds of times as I rose to pray

[1] "Thoughts on Preaching," p. 9.

and glanced at the congregation, I could not keep
back the tears.   There came to my mind such a sense
of their wants—there were so many hidden sorrows—
so many doubts, so many perils—there were such histories—not world histories, but eternal world histories
. . . and it seems as if God permitted me to lay
my hand on the very Tree of Life, and to shake down
from it both leaves and fruit for the healing of my
people."[1] Such living, personal sympathy in the pulpit,
makes a mighty pulpit.   Power is along no other road
so often and so surely.

VI.   There is a sixth requisite in preparation for
the pulpit, provided the preaching is to be from a
manuscript—and this is the *actual writing*.   Three
suggestions here may not be without value.

(*a*)   The writing should be done *with the audience
mentally before the preacher*.   This is the fundamental
specialty of all public discourse.   It is for the ear—
not for the eye.   It is therefore to be caught " on the
wing."   It is a bird of passage.   It must be understood as it falls from the preacher's lips, or it will not
be understood at all.   It is not a text-book, to be
studied and studied, until its meaning is perfectly apparent.   The preacher therefore must dare to be
plain.   His meaning must look the audience in the
face.

(*b*)   Whether the sermon should be written rapidly,
or with painstaking care, will depend upon the temperament of the writer.   But if one " writes with
fury," he should "correct with phlegm."   Robert
Hall prepared with great care.   John Foster's sentences sometimes cost him hours of labour.   Albert

[1] Beecher's " Lectures on Preaching," p. 47.

Barnes wrote rapidly, and when he once began the sermon, the scratch of his pen could be heard with scarce an interruption until the sermonic work of the day was ended.

(c) The writing *should not be patchwork.* Continuity is so vital a matter, that certain hours should be kept sacred to the preparation of the sermon. Frequent interruptions are the open door to sermonic crazy-quilts.

Here, then, are the ideal "immediates" in sermon-making—the subject, the object, the plan, the gathering and arranging of materials, a quickened personal interest and sympathy, and the actual writing. These are the "what," the "why," the "how," the kind of material, the *personal* equation, and the verbal form to be considered in preaching the Gospel of the blessed God. Are they not vital to an ideal ministry? Must not each one of these steps be taken in any ideal preparation for next Sunday?

XXI

ITS IDEAL "CARDINALS"

SYLLABUS

These are qualities of inner structure, not of verbal form; they are *unity, order,* and *movement.* They enter into the very life and soul of sacred discourse.

Unity

1. Its *nature.* It is born of diversity—one out of many. It is not the mere contact of connected truths. It is consistent with great variety.

2. Its *necessity.* Founded in the very nature of rational discourse. Discourse is one—not many. Essential in painting and architecture. A deeper necessity in the sermon.

3. Its *demands :* (*a*) singleness of theme ; (*b*) of object; (*c*) and the use of that which will tend both to develop the theme and accomplish the object.

4. Its *advantages :* (*a*) stimulates inventive faculty ; (*b*) secures definite impression ; (*c*) tends to cumulative force and effect.

5. *Violations :* (*a*) needless explanation ; (*b*) digression, that does not give increased momentum ; (*c*) all ideas, though growing out of the subject, if they do not contribute to the *end* in view.

Order

1. Its *necessity.* 2. Its *demands,* (1) comprehensively, (2) specifically : (*a*) in narration ; (*b*) in description ; (*c*) in division ; (*d*) in argument ; (*e*) in meeting objections; (*f*) in pressing motives.

3. Its *advantages*—To the preacher : (*a*) his mind grows orderly ; (*b*) grows fruitful.

To the sermon : (*a*) makes it intelligible; (*b*) gives it power.

To the hearer : (*a*) increased pleasure ; (*b*) increased facility of remembrance; (*c*) increased profit.

Movement

1. Its nature. 2. Its demands. 3. Its importance. 4. Its hindrances. (*a*) *Isolation of ideas* as they first come to the mind. (*b*) *Prolixity ;* excess of treatment. (*c*) *Digressions.*

Unity, order, movement, each is great ; no one is the greatest.

Power is the crowning attribute—and power, under God, lies only this way.

XXI

ITS IDEAL "CARDINALS"

THESE are qualities of inner *structure* rather than of outward verbal form. They pertain to the sermon as a whole. They are capital or "cardinal," because they enter into the very life and soul of sacred discourse and, humanly speaking, are decisive of results in the public proclamation of the Word of God.

These inner vital qualities are *unity, order* and *movement.* And we venture to affirm that apart from divine agency there is nothing in the entire field of homiletic discussion that would so contribute to pulpit efficiency, as the constant and masterful command of these three structural qualities of sacred discourse.

UNITY

1. *Its nature.* Unity is born of diversity. It is one out of many. It results from union. It is not singleness or sameness of idea, but combination of ideas for convergence and single effect. It is not the mere contact of connected truths. All the great truths of Scripture are connected. Repentance implies faith, and faith implies regeneration, and regeneration implies original sin. But the connection of these truths would not justify their treatment in any one sermon. Connection at the source alone is not the highest unity—not sermonic unity. But connection at the

terminus as well. Both divergence and convergence. The star scatters rays. The lens gathers them to a burning focus. The two represent a discourse marked by true unity.

Unity, therefore, does not consist in a collection of good remarks, though all drawn from one subject. They may lead away from the subject, and so lead the hearer away. To conserve and promote unity, they must be convergent, and so cumulative of momentum and power.

On the other hand, true unity is consistent with great variety, and even contrast. A single effect may often be greatly enhanced, by combining things most diverse. For example: in dwelling upon the importance of saving a soul, what increasing and immeasurable sense of its importance would be gained by dwelling upon such diverse considerations as the anguish of a soul unsaved, the joy of all heaven over one soul saved, and the passion of the cross it behooved Christ to suffer that one soul might be saved. Unity is not marred but heightened by these wide contrasts.

2. The *necessity* of unity. It is founded in the very nature of rational discourse. Discourse is one— not many. It is a flow. In unity therefore lies its very life. Its ideas, however varied, are vitally related. They are fused, and run like molten ore. They constitute, or are born of, one theme. A true discourse never has themes. Unity is demanded by the very nature of mind. It belongs to the poem and the drama. It is essential in painting, in architecture, even in landscape gardening. It is a deeper necessity in the sermon.

3. The *demands* of unity. They are three, and they are imperative.

(*a*) Singleness of theme. This lies at the foundation of all true unity. It is the first and broadest condition, one theme—and every thought, every illustration, *every* thing in the sermon, subservient to it.

(*b*) Singleness of object. All rational discourse has an object. It is an address. It has respect to others. It is mind to mind for some purpose. A single leading object must be fixed upon, and steadily pursued throughout, in order to unity. The true sermon will always have an end—a purpose outside of itself—to be accomplished. Just as this is single, specific and controlling, will the discourse have unity. Lines will all converge. Ideas will all bear one way.

(*c*) Another demand of unity, and growing out of singleness of theme and object, is the use *only of that which will tend both to develop the theme and accomplish the object.*

Nothing is to be admitted into the sermon that is not made rigidly subordinate and subservient to this twofold work. The thoughts and illustrations are to be narrowed to the single theme and still further narrowed to the uses to which the theme is put in securing some single leading object.

This demand of unity will be best secured by writing out both the subject and the object before proceeding to write the sermon ; and then by challenging each thought that knocks for admittance to the sermon, and asking whether it consists with the chosen theme and end, and can in any way throw light on the one, or promote the other. If "Nay"—then *no admittance on any terms whatever.*

4. *Advantages* of unity.

(*a*) It stimulates the *inventive* faculty of the preacher. Compelling not only a subject but an object, it gives the mind a spring and impulse in toil. For it is not in the nature of mind to put forth its best activities without aim. To think without a purpose is to think feebly. To wander at one's own sweet will, untrammelled by the demands of unity, may seem delightful and suggestive to the young writer, but it is the sure road to superficiality. No rich ores will betray their hiding-places to such thinking. Unity of aim reacts upon invention and arouses it, and so gives it command of materials that would otherwise never heed its call, or reveal themselves to its search.

(*b*) Unity secures definiteness of impression. *Disconnected* thoughts are like a whirl of sparks. They may be brilliant and beautiful; but they come and go leaving no distinct impression. *Connected* thoughts —thoughts that are fused and made a living whole by one common animating purpose, are like a pointed tongue of flame.

Disconnected thoughts are like dead words strung down the dictionary. *Connected* thoughts, born of one theme and convergent to one object, are like those same words put in a living sentence. The impression from the string of words is confused and vague. The impression from the living sentence is clear and definite. Vinet says, " Attacked by a crowd of mutually self-neutralizing impressions, we are made captive by none, and fixed to nothing."

(*c*) Unity tends to cumulative force and effect. It leads to concentration, blow on blow, in one spot. Thus a wall is breached, an enemy's line broken, a cause carried. Thus is discourse made effective. It gathers momentum as it proceeds. Each succeeding thought promotes the impression of its predecessor— for they tend the same way, look to the same result, converge to one point. The blows all have one aim, and the truth goes home with ever-cumulating power.

5. *Violations* of unity.

(*a*) All explanation or exposition of the text not necessary to bring out the theme and lead to its clear apprehension, is a violation of unity.

(*b*) All digression that does not turn again into the main stream of thought and give it increased *momentum*, is a violation of unity.

(*c*) All ideas and figures, however brilliant, and though they grow out of the subject, if they are divergent from the one dominant purpose and end, are violations of unity.

ORDER

1. The *necessity* of order in discourse.

It "is heaven's first law." God is a God of order, and not of confusion. His works and ways are by method. Order is the handmaid of effectiveness. The human mind as by instinct demands order, and dreads chaos. The apostle says, "Let all things be done decently and in order." A mass of unsightly material, by an adjustment of order, is made a beautiful edifice. A rabble, under order's law, is changed into an army. The different parts of the body must have their true place, if the body is to have effectiveness and symmetry. Not less is order a necessity in the sermon. Vinet goes so far as to say, "There is no discourse without it." Certainly the preacher who has

no order in his sermon, is flinging to the wind the law
of adaptation.

2. The *demands* of order.

Comprehensively, order in discourse demands of the
preacher what Horace says it demands of the poet,
"that he just now say what ought just now to be
said." "Ut jam nunc dicat, jam nunc debentia dici."
In other words, that every part of the discourse take
its right place, as the result of judicious arrangement.

Specifically : (*a*) Order in *narration* demands regard to *time*. Events should be so narrated as not to
mix and confuse the dates of their occurrence.

(*b*) Order in *description* demands regard to *affinity*.
Man, for example, should not be described by
mingling confusedly the different parts of his nature,
as intelligent, lymphatic, social, æsthetic, bilious,
logical.

(*c*) Order in *division* demands regard to *relation*
—as of whole and part, cause and effect, antecedent
and consequent. In enumerating, *e. g.*, as divisions,
the evidences of true godliness in Malachi 3 : 16. The
order in the text is not the true succession.

(*d*) Order in *argument* demands regard to three
things. (1) Regard to the different classes of arguments. An argument from experience should not
be thrust in between two speculative arguments.
Proofs of various kinds should be classified and
grouped, as internal, external, historic, experimental :
and not be hurled at random in promiscuous and confused mass.

(2) Regard to the dependence of arguments on
one another. Sometimes an argument presupposes
another. Then it should always follow.

Sometimes one argument explains another, prepares the way for it, throws light upon it, is vital to its best effect. Then it should always precede. Whether an argument goes before, or follows after may make just the difference between weakness and great weight, *e. g.*, prove the antecedent probability of a thing, from the nature of the case, or on general principles, and the direct proofs will then come in with greatly increased and more conclusive force. Show cause why God should interpose with a revelation, and then the internal evidence of the divine authenticity of the Scriptures will have tenfold weight.

(3) Regard to the state of mind of the hearers. If they are filled with skepticism, a relatively weak argument at the outset would be a waste of breath. Let the best, the strongest blow, be struck first. To make the final impression strong in such a case, recapitulate, *reversing* the order, and thus get the power of climax.

(*e*) Order in meeting objections demands regard to their application. If the objection applies to a certain division of the discourse, it should be met on reaching that division. If the objection applies to the main statement, and is already known to the hearer, it should be met at the outset. Otherwise, the hearer, having the objection in mind, and not its refutation, would not be likely to listen to the argument without prejudice. This unanswered objection would constantly recur to him, and prevent the argument from having its full weight. If it be deemed best to defer the answer to objections, until the direct positive proof has been offered, reference should be made to the objections, and suspension of judgment asked, until they are fully considered.

(*f*) Order in pressing motives demands regard to antecedent knowledge and conviction on the part of the hearers. *These ground all motives and appeals.* Men must see clearly *what it is* that is pressed as a duty, and they must be convinced that it *is a duty*, before they are urged to its discharge. The most affecting exhortations are a waste of breath, where there is no sense of oughtness.

3. The *advantages* of order.

They accrue to the preacher, to the sermon, to the hearer.

Here are some of the advantages to the *preacher*.

(*a*) His mind grows orderly. Methodizing makes him methodical. Systematizing makes him systematic. He is cured of rambling. And digressions at last become an impossibility.

(*b*) His mind grows *fruitful*. Order enriches. It helps memory by the law of association. The suggestive faculty becomes fruitful in furnishing materials. Contemplating ideas in their proper connections is the sure way of commanding the reserved stores of memory. He will discover little, who knows not whither he is going or what he is in search of.

Here are some of the advantages to the *sermon*.

(*a*) It makes the sermon *intelligible*. Perspicuity in style is not enough to give clearness to discourse. It must have proper arrangement. The successive remarks may be clear enough. Each idea may be readily grasped as presented. But if the succession is confusing, without natural order, with no regard to logical and oratorical method, the total impression will be that of an indistinct mass. We wonder sometimes that the pews take in so little of the sermons—hear so little understandingly. But when we think of the confusing, blinding sins of the pulpit against order, the wonder suffers an immense contraction.

(*b*) Order gives the sermon *power*. An arch of stones is stronger than a heap of stones. A built ship, buttressed and ribbed, beam to beam, is stronger than the loose timbers. So ideas, arranged according to the laws of association and logic, are much mightier than when thrown out in a disconnected, illogical way. Such ideas mutually aid and sustain one another. Part is adjusted to part for the best effect. But when lacking in orderly arrangement, they not only give each other no support, but often actually neutralize each other's power. They are not tied together by the living ligaments of a pervasive purpose. They are put forward without method. Ideas are deferred when they ought to be treated. They are anticipated and partially expanded before the way is prepared for them to have their full effect. They are dropped and then resumed. They are thrust into the midst of others, severing a close and needed connection. They are not grouped, marshalled, compacted. There is advance and recession—no coherence. Nothing weakens a discourse like these breaks, uncertainties, returns, digressions, partial presentations—these "*many almosts.*"

A sermon thus constructed may have power. So may a mob. But how a mob melts away before a little band instinct with order, moving by method!

But the advantages of order to *the hearers* are as marked as those accruing to the preacher and to the sermon.

(*a*) Increased *pleasure* is one of these advantages.

Order makes truth more *beautiful*.   Just as a collection of precious stones is made more beautiful, when,
by the magic of good arrangement, it is changed into
a rich mosaic.   And the mind takes pleasure in beauty ;
rejoices in it.   Confusion is distasteful.   Chaos is re-
pulsive.   Order is pleasing.

(*b*)   Another and a great advantage to the hearer,
is *facility of remembrance*.   Try to remember fifty
words with no connection—no natural succession.
How difficult !   Now wheel those same words into
line by constructing out of them connected and living
sentences ; and how easily memory masters them.

Mere contiguity is of little service in recollection.
But one idea following another by some well-defined
law of association is greatly helpful.   Let order reign
in the sermon—let its various points have a natural
and true succession, and *the sermon will stick*.

Hence comes (*c*) *increased profit*.   Hearers are edi-
fied, other things being equal, just as the sermon sticks.
No food so feeds the flock as that which is distinctly
remembered ; which the mind can carry away from
the sanctuary for the heart to feed on, afterwards.
This sometimes makes just the difference, and all the
difference, between failure and success in a pastorate.
A sermon may not be profound or brilliant.   But it
may be, and should be, characterized invariably by
order.   And with order so important, it is an inexcusable sin and shame for any preacher to make sermons without it.

MOVEMENT

1.   Its *nature*.   It is that quality by which the sermon bears the thought onward and the hearer with it.

It compels movement, and is therefore itself movement.

2. Its *demands*. As connected with discourse it involves both continuity and progress. *Continuity :* the movement should be continuous ; for a break means suspension and a pause. *Progress :* for all true discourse has an end in view ; and there may be movement on a pivot—reasoning in a circle—splutter in a puddle. Movement is the living energy of the living soul poured along the channels of speech for the attainment of some definite object. It is the quality that makes the difference between a river and a stagnant canal. And like the river's movement, it is neither always at the same rate, nor in a straight line. Sometimes there are obstructions to be removed, necessary digressions to be made, and even apparent *recessions.* But like the river, whose goal is the sea, the sermon will move with a steady constancy towards its end, turning aside to obviate an objection, to explain a difficulty, to summon a support, only to reach the goal the surer and the sooner.

3. The *importance* of movement. Its value can hardly be overestimated. It is the attending and animating genius of climax. No great effects by discourse are possible without it. It is the thing that most stirs souls, lifting them out of the ruts of daily procedure, changing their spiritual plane, exalting and bettering them. It has characterized all immortal speech. Horace says of Homer, " *Semper ad eventum festinat* "—he always hastens on to the event. Lord Brougham says of Demosthenes, " He is never found making any step, in any direction, which does not advance his main object, and lead towards the conclusion

to which he is striving to bring his hearers." Beyond a doubt, he only is the true orator who gives his hearers the exhilaration of a forward motion. It is the steady, unceasing sweep of thought, gathering force as it proceeds, until it is a mighty torrent, that constitutes effective speech, that takes great audiences off their feet, melting their wills into one, and stirring them with a common feeling and purpose.

4. The hindrances to movement.

(a) The isolation and independence of ideas as they first come to the mind in thinking on any particular theme. The ideas are from different sources, of different kinds, for different purposes. While they remain thus, they make oratorical movement—a constantly progressive flow—impossible. They must be given a connection, a continuity—they must be welded or fused. Theremin says, " As they first present themselves they are hard, brittle, separate particles; the mind must seize them—and by grinding them incessantly upon each other, crush them, until the friction kindles the mass, and they run like molten ore."

(b) *Prolixity* is a hindrance to movement. This is excess of treatment—undue expansion, turning over and over the same idea. Revolving is not progressing. Care should be taken lest, in being brief, one become obscure. But as soon as the thought is fully and fairly before the hearers, it is time for the preacher to leave it, and pass on. Every word after that is a sin against movement. It is continuing to explain what is already clear. It is pursuing details in description that add nothing to the effect. It is making men forget the object of an illustration in a too great expansion and elaboration of the illustration itself. The steady flow of discourse is retarded and checked by every needless repetition, by wire-drawn and tedious explanation, by hammering away at an idea after it is once fairly driven home.

To avoid this, let description seize and present only the salient points, let narrative pass from incident to incident in a quick succession, let instruction add thought to thought, let argument confirm argument, each tending to deeper conviction, and *let the preacher stop when he is done!* Why go on banking the river after it has reached the sea!

(*c*) Digressions are a hindrance to movement. They compel a pause, a suspense of progress in the true path of discussion, and a turning aside for the consideration of something more or less foreign to the end in view. However tempting and however full of instruction, such asides should be left for a subsequent occasion. So important is it that the mind of the hearer should be borne along from point to point, so requisite is this to the best oratorical effect, that the preacher should regard "every thought, every word, that does not bring him nearer the goal, as a weakness, a fault—and cast it from him."

Unity, order, movement, these three; but the greatest of these is—well, it is impossible to say. They stand side by side—the three cardinal qualities of the sermon. They mutually help one another. Discourse without them is shorn of half its power. No one of them can be neglected without seriously impairing efficiency. Impression may be made without them, but by no means the highest and best. Good may be done, but not the most good. It will pay to toil for these qualities. And toil will be necessary. Unity and order and movement are not born. They are made♦ To have a single purpose dominate through the whole length of the sermon, from the first words of the introduction to the final appeal—to have order reign throughout, every thought and illustration, every incident and argument marshalled to its place—and to have a constant flow—a steady onward progress in the sermon, bearing resistlessly to the goal—*hic labor, hoc opus est.*

But *power* is the attribute crowning all a minister's accomplishments ; and power, under God, lies only this way. Is it not worth while, therefore, to make every sermon with scrupulous regard to the demands of unity, order, and movement ?

Seeing is believing. Let us look at a sermon plan by Mr. Spurgeon, in the light of these ideal cardinals.

Text :—He that hath no money ; come ye, buy and eat.—*Isa.* 55 : 1.

Introduction :—God is here represented as a merchant offering his wares, viz., "the Lord Jesus Christ," "everlasting love," "heavenly edification," and "everlasting safety."

Theme :—Buying without money.

I. The description of the buyer, "he that hath no money."
    1. His fancied stock of innocence is all gone.
    2. His imaginary righteousness turns out to be counterfeit.
    3. His procuring power is gone.
    4. His stock with which to trade is gone.
    5. He cannot pay his old debts.
    6. He cannot meet his present expenses.

II. The selection of this particular buyer.
    1. He needs mercy most.
    2. He is such an one as will exhibit in his own person the power of divine grace.
    3. The Lord thus makes evident the freeness of His grace.
    4. He is the kind of man that will listen.
    5. When he gets mercy he will prize it and praise it.

III.   The invitation "come and buy."   In buying there are three or
four stages.
1.   Desiring to have.
2.   Agreeing to terms.
3.   Appropriating the goods.
IV.   A few things by way of assurance.
1.   It is not God's way to mock men.
2.   God is under no necessity to sell His benefits.
3.   There is no adequate price we could bring to God for
His mercy.
4.   All supposed conditions are supplied in Jesus Christ.

This outline is by the great London preacher, who in his day was a
prince of God in preaching.

The *Introduction* to this plan is appropriate ; and the theme is per-
fectly legitimate.   But the *Plan* is a hodge-podge.
I.   The first head and its discussion are happily suggestive.
II.   The second head is absolutely indefensible.   The sub points 1,
2, 4 and 5 are simply a further " *description of the buyer*," and
should have gone under the first head.
Moreover, sub points 1 and 4 fail to commend themselves.
As to the first, "he needs mercy most" ; no one sinner needs mercy
more than another sinner.
As to the fourth, "He is the kind of a man that will listen";
millions of sinners that have "no money " do *not* listen.
III.   The third head is " The Invitation."   But under this head
Spurgeon does not discuss the *invitation at all*.   He simply
discusses the *conditions of sale*.
IV.   The fourth head, "A few things by way of assurance," seems a
kind of afterthought, tacked on, and not born of the discussion.   It should be a conclusion, drawn from the whole discussion, and mighty with appeal.   Thus Unity, Order and
Movement are all, and repeatedly, and flagrantly violated in
this sermon plan.
If now we should take the very same materials that are in Spurgeon's plan, and arrange them in the interests of these cardinal qualities, without the addition of a single new thought, an ideal plan something like the following would emerge :
Text :—He that hath no money ; come ye, buy and eat.—*Isa.* 55 : 1.
Introduction :—Here is the strangest transaction under the sun.   A
merchant is offering his wares.   The wares are of exceeding value, be-

yond all price, and the buyer has nothing to buy with.   God is the merchant.   All the riches of grace and glory are the merchandise. The sinner is the buyer.

Theme:—Heavenly merchandising.

I.   The buyer—the sinner—he is "without money."

    1.   His fancied innocence is spurious.

    2.   His fancied righteousness is worthless.

    3.   He is loaded with old debts.

    4.   He can't borrow; for he has no credit.

    5.   Although an utter bankrupt, he is the only kind of buyer who is asked to this sale.

II.   The merchant—the faithful and gracious God.

    1.   Faithful—It is not His way to mock men.   He will deliver the goods.

    2.   Gracious—He sells of grace—not of necessity.   It is not a forced sale, and grace is all that makes this sale possible.

III.   The goods—pardon, peace, adoption, security, victory in this world, and in the world to come life everlasting.

IV.   The conditions of sale.

    1.   Desire for the goods.

    2.   Acceptance of terms.

    3.   Actual appropriation.

Conclusion:—Sinner, this is heavenly merchandising.   Heaven, pardon, peace and everlasting life are offered you here for nothing. Do you want these wares?   Then just believe this heavenly merchant. He deals in infinite values.   Millions of buyers have testified that He never played false with a customer.   He has just what you need.   He is eager to sell.   Agree to His terms, and take the goods, without money and without price.

Here are Spurgeon's rich materials all reproduced, but they are arranged according to the laws of effective discourse, and dominated throughout by Unity, Order and Movement.   And the gain in definiteness, sequence, and climax is unmistakable.

XXII

ITS IDEAL TOPICS

SYLLABUS

Three things that help to settle this question of topics—the preacher's *office*, *commission*, and *aim*.

I. The *range* of topics. (*a*) Limited by the Word of God. (*b*) Not every text of Scripture holds a proper topic for public discourse. (*c*) The Scriptural limit excludes all *secular* topics. (*d*) Leaves scant room for controversial topics. (*e*) Does not leave *large* room for apologetics. (*f*) No room for *philosophical topics;* but room for *philosophy.* (*g*) Nature of preaching would keep out philosophical topics, but not philosophy.

II. *Variety* of topics. (*a*) Regard should be had to variety. (*b*) Two general classes of topics; for rescue work, and construction work. (*c*) More minute division—doctrinal, ethical, biographical, historical, topics of Christian socialism, political topics, topics of Christian benevolence. Duty of the pastor to present these topics. Particular *method* to be left to the individual judgment.

III. The *proportions* in which these various topics should be presented. Proportions must vary according to local conditions.

IV. *Methods* for securing varied and Biblical proportion. (*a*) Keep a classified list. (*b*) Go through a prescribed course between communions. (*c*) Have regard to three things: system of truth; needs of flock; personal preference.

Comprehensive summary.

1. Proclaim truth rather than combat error.
2. Be assertive, aggressive, rather than defensive.
3. Preach on important topics, rather than on those of minor moment.
4. Choose topics from the *Word of God always.*

XXII

ITS IDEAL TOPICS

THREE things, fairly considered, will go far to settle this question of topics for the pulpit : the preacher's *office*, *commission*, and *aim*. The preacher's *office*. He is called in the Word of God a *herald*, a proclaimer—a public messenger. The herald does not create his message : he carries the message of another, and commonly of one in authority —his superior, whose absolute right to have the message transmitted with sacred fidelity, is not open to challenge. With the message from God, how utterly beyond the herald's province to take from or add to the message with which he has been entrusted. The preacher is God's herald. And as such, he has a message to deliver—neither more nor less. He changes it, makes light of it, mutilates it—at his peril.

The preacher's *commission*. It is found in the last words of instruction given by Jesus to His disciples : " Go ye, and make disciples of all the nations . . . teaching them to observe all things whatsoever I commanded you." [1] And again : " Go ye into all the world and preach the Gospel to the whole creation." [2] That this is what all preachers for all time are to teach and preach is clear from the added words of Jesus, " Lo, I am with you always even unto the end of the world."

So Paul, when called of God to the ministry, felt

[1] Matt. 28 : 19–20. [2] Mark 16 : 15.

349

that this was the one exclusive message he had to
deliver, as an ambassador for Christ, saying, " *Christ
sent me to preach the Gospel.*" [1]   And in setting Timothy into the ministry, Paul charged him before God
and the Lord Jesus Christ to " preach the Word " ; [2]
i. e., the Word of God—the message which God would
have all His appointed and anointed heralds proclaim.
So those early preachers went everywhere preaching
the Word of God.   It was this that whole cities came
out to hear, and that mightily " grew " and " prevailed," and that was not " bound," but was " living "
and " powerful," and by which those early preachers
went " everywhere triumphing in Christ Jesus."

The exact limit of this Word is " all Scripture."
This is the preacher's message—his only message.
He is to go everywhere, holding forth the word of
life—of salvation—of *God*.   The word of science is
not that.   The word of history is not that.   The word
of philosophy is not that.   These may illustrate, explain, vivify the truth of Scripture ; but to make these
the substance of the message, is clearly transcending
the right of a " herald."

The preacher's aim.   It is salvation in the largest
sense : reconstruction of manhood.   The preacher is
to reach and find his man, and then build him up in
Christ Jesus.   This is his constant, absorbing, inspiring purpose, and it has only one possible way of accomplishment—by *the truth of God as accompanied
by the Spirit of God*.   The Holy Spirit convicts and
sanctifies men only by the truth—and by the truth,
not as it is in Socrates or Plato or the stars or the
philosophies—but as it is in Jesus—the Christ.

[1] 1 Cor. 1 : 17.   [2] 2 Tim. 4 : 2.

If this, then, is the office and the commission and the aim of the preacher—if he is simply a *herald* of God sent to deliver a certain specified *message* in order to *salvation*, there can be no doubt that much concerning "Topics for the pulpit" is already settled; much that will throw light on our path as we consider the *range* of pulpit topics, their *variety*, and the *proportion in which the varied topics should be used.*

I. The *range of topics.*

(*a*) The range is limited to the Word of God. The Scriptures furnish the only legitimate themes of pulpit discourse. With these "the man of God may be complete, furnished completely unto every good work." [1] He must look to his instructions, and follow them. If God has provided a word for him, and has said "*Preach this Word,*" he has just this to preach, neither more nor less.   He ceases to be a *herald* when he travels beyond his instructions.   He does not preach the *Word.*

It may be truth he preaches—important truth : but so long as it is truth beyond the range of Scripture, he is without divine authority or sanction in preaching it, and thus divests himself of his high and sacred function as an ambassador of Jesus Christ.   Inspired truth, given of God for salvation, should invariably mark pulpit utterance.   Topics not lodged in any single text or passage of Scripture may be for the elevation of society and the promotion of morals, and the advancement of civilization, and they should have thorough treatment, and doubtless they should have it often, and by Christian ministers, but *not in sermons with the Word of God for their text.*   For the text

[1] 2 Tim. 3 : 17.

thus becomes a mere figure-head, and a false one. It has nothing to do with such a discourse, and the divine Word is dishonoured by being placed there.

(*b*) While the range of topics is thus limited to the Scriptures, it is *not to be inferred that every text of Scripture furnishes a proper theme for pulpit discourse.* There are texts obviously local and secular—statements of fact having no spiritual import, narrative portions, obituary notices, statistical records, and the like, which good judgment and taste would never bring into the pulpit. As 2 Timothy 4 : 13, "The cloak that I left at Troas with Carpus, bring with thee."

(*c*) This Scriptural limit of the range of pulpit topics *rigidly excludes all purely secular topics :* as, for example, the *merely* scientific or philosophical or social or political. Secular benefits come to society and the state from preaching ; but they do not come from preaching on secular themes. Christianity is weakened as a social and civilizing power, just as *secularity* characterizes its pulpit ministrations. It gets its ground leverage from man's need as a sinner, and from its power as a salvation, and the leverage is gone, just as these *are lost sight of, in secular themes.*

It was when rationalism ran mad in Germany that "sermons were preached everywhere upon such subjects as the necessity of industry, the ill-effects of lawsuits—that Christmas was taken advantage of to connect the sad story of the child born in a manger, with the most approved methods of feeding cattle ; and the appearance of Jesus walking in the garden at the break of day on Easter morning with the habit of rising early and taking a walk before breakfast."[1] Homiletical instruction on silk worms has been given from the pulpit; on substitutes for sugar and coffee in a time when these articles were scarce; on the Christian mode of cultivating red beets, and the pious method of raising tobacco.

All such topics are of course barred out of the pulpit. But much of the sensational preaching of to-day comes in the same category. Texts are torn from their exegetical nexus, and made to do service in the behalf of themes, with which it would be a gross affront to the Spirit of inspiration to say He ever connected them. Think of the pathetic scene where Christ is weeping over Jerusalem, and imagine the mental and spiritual make-up of a man who could use that scene, so full of pathos and tears, for a sermon on "the relative advantages of city and country life"![2]

(*d*) This limit of the range of topics to the Word of God, leaves scant room for *controversial* topics. There is little, if any, space in the divine Word devoted to polemics. The truth is directly pressed with cogent argument, and every variety of fact and illustration. The more of this direct inculcation there is in sermons, the more they will be like the Scriptures in bold and unembarrassed statements. To carry controversial themes into the pulpit, and to bang away at opposing theories, is often to suggest doubts where none before existed. *Error is commonly best combatted by the direct inculcation of truth.* Fill the hearers' minds with *truth*, preached directly, balancedly, boldly,

[1] Hagenbach.

[2] Advertised and preached in one of our city churches this past year.

with clear Scriptural warrant, and errors will find it hard to get lodgment.

To rush into the pulpit with a reply to the book or scientific review the preacher has just been reading, may be the very means of publishing error of which the congregation have never heard; and the error may be remembered when the antidote is forgotten. Doubtless notice should be taken of current criticism upon Christian faith and doctrine; but doubtless this notice should be taken *outside the pulpit*. Printed attacks should be answered by printed defenses. Send the antidote where somebody has flung the poison. If a vicious attack on evangelical truth has appeared in some paper or periodical, send a reply through the same channel. It will do far more and better service than a dozen sermons, for it will reach the audience the vicious attack reached. Sometimes a doctrinal error may have so pervaded a community as to justify its complete exposure and refutation in the pulpit; but the occasions are exceedingly rare when the sanctuary should be turned into an arena of *ex parte* debate. Men do not come to the house of God to be fed on the reputation of skeptics; skeptics even of whose existence probably nine-tenths in every audience have no knowledge. Surely not at the flock within the fold is the minister to cast " the bristling missiles that ought to be hurled at the wolves without."

(*e*) This limit of the range of topics does not leave large room for *apologetics* in the pulpit; *i. e.*, *evidences of Christianity* and *defense against assailants*. Now and then an explorer with his spade does wonders for God's truth. He turns up unimpeachable witnesses that may well be heard from the pulpit.

But beyond a doubt much may be left to the self-
evidencing power of the truth. Christianity is its own
evidence. Some things may well be taken for granted.
This is the way of God's Word, and it should be the
preacher's way. After nineteen hundred years it can
hardly be necessary or desirable to convey the impression that the Christian religion is a thing yet needing
to be proved. Doubt of ability to hold the fort will
surely be born of constantly building fortifications for
defense. Pulpit themes should be largely such as can
be carried directly to the conscience and the heart.
In Christianity, to show, to exhibit, is often to demon-
strate.

(*f*) But how does this Scriptural limit of the range
of topics for the pulpit affect *philosophical* topics?
Are they barred from pulpit discussion?

As the pulpit is the place where Christianity gets its
most constant and conspicuous official public expression, the question occurs whether the philosophy that
underlies all our thinking, and that does so much to
shape it, is to make itself heard in the discussion of
philosophical *topics* in the pulpit; or whether that
philosophy is simply to be a background upon which
all our preaching is set? The latter, beyond a doubt.
Philosophy of some sort every thinking man will have.
Popular modern thought has given it immense sweep,
from the philosophy of the unconditioned soaring
among the infinities to the philosophy of the brigade
of bread and butter. But confining ourselves to the
stricter definition, the treatment of knowledge as
knowledge, let us consider by way of example, "the
innate idea of God" in the human soul. Left to itself,
fetich worship may be the product. Developed by

pure reasoning, and in such a man as Spinoza, panthe-
ism may be the outcome.   Developed exclusively by experience and inductive reasoning, and we may reach a
God of human passions.   Theologians have founded
religion in the feelings, and promoted a kind of irra-
tional mysticism.   Others have so exalted the divine
will as to make God's *fiat* the basis of all distinction
between right and wrong, thus giving ground for the
atheistic charge that "Theism makes a *capricious will
supreme.*"   A necessarian lands logically in materialism—and man becomes "a puppet, that moves according as its strings are pulled."   Schleiermacher's philosophy shaped his theology.   He was intensely subjec-
tive.   Feeling with him was a stronger reality than
speculation.   His philosophy flamed up everywhere in
his preaching.   And men like Bushnell, F. W. Robertson, Maurice, and Müller were often drinking at this
fountain.   True or false, philosophy will strike up into
the pulpit.

But philosophy in the pulpit is one thing.   Philosophical *topics* in the pulpit is quite another thing.
The minister must *look out* what kind of philosophy
gets into his pulpit, and *keep* out of his pulpit philosophical *topics*.

If it be contended that philosophical topics stand
vitally related to Christian truth, that they are implied and suggested and taken for granted in Scripture,
that they are God's great thoughts written in the
structure of the soul, and that therefore they should
have place in the pulpit, the sufficient answer is that
God's great thoughts are in the rocks, the stars, the
flowers, the soils—everywhere; but this is hardly a
reason for presenting geological, astronomical, botan-

ical, and agricultural topics in the *pulpit*. Some of these have vital relation to Christian truth, but we are not commanded to preach them.

> " Earth's crammed with heaven
> And every common bush afire with God ;
> But only he who sees, takes off his shoes ;
> The rest sit round it and pluck blackberries." [1]

This is beautiful poetic thought and beautiful Christian sentiment, but it furnishes no reason why we should go into the pulpit and preach on vegetation ! There are " tongues in trees," and " books in the running brooks " ; but there are no " sermons in stones," Shakespeare to the contrary notwithstanding. Sermons have the Word of God for their base and source. The Bible, and the Bible alone, is at once the source and the test of all the matter of preaching. The matter of preaching is the whole faith. Scripture is exhibitive of the whole faith, and " Christ is the watermark on every page."

Another point in support of the contention that philosophical *topics* should not go into the pulpit is the *nature of preaching*. That which is essential, which all the discourses of the Bible have in common, and which all our sermons should have in common with them, is that they proclaim the will of God. Doing this out of and according to the Scriptures is preaching. The pulpit is not an academical chair, and the church is not a philosopher's lecture room. A character of urgency should dominate in it. By this is not meant that it is to be simply a cry of alarm. By no means. But it is not a study, a contemplation, by *eminence*.

[1] Mrs. Browning.

Its fundamental specialty is *persuasion*.   This cannot
be too often emphasized.   The sermon is nothing if it
does not bear on the will, to move it Godward.

Nor is it meant that preaching is to be narrow in
its range of resource—that there is to be no familiarity
with scientific and philosophic thought.

But this is meant—that preaching is the direct, bold,
urgent, oratorical presentation of the truth of God ;
and this is meant—that every whipster in theology
and smatterer in science or philosophy is not to rush
into the pulpit fresh from some book or review article to demolish Huxley or Spencer or Mill or Haeckel ;
and this is meant—that the sanctuary is not to be
turned into an arena of *ex parte* debate—that the
" apologetic " and the " conflict-reconciliation " business, as a *pulpit* business, has been greatly overdone.
Preaching has such a character of urgency, and is so
much a proclamation of will to will, that it seems the
very climax of absurdity for a minister to enter the
pulpit and undertake there to lay philosophical foundations for his hearers' " primary beliefs " !   For example, Harris says : " Man cannot inquire respecting
the personality of God till by studying the constitution of man, he has found out that man is a person." [1]
This is true, philosophically, and Harris is right.   But
imagine a preacher on the plea of furnishing a basis
for intelligent belief in God and His personality, coming before the congregation and saying, " My dear
hearers, I am come this morning to prove to you that
each one of you is a person."

Yet the preacher should do just this thing if
philosophical topics are to be at home in the pulpit.

[1] " Philosophical Basis of Theism," p. 3.

For the idea that man is a person, is the very bottom idea in philosophy. And if you are going to lay the philosophic foundations of a stable faith, you must begin there. Which needs to be proved in the pulpit just as much as the existence and personality of God —*just as much!*

II. *Variety of topics.*

(*a*) Studious regard should be had to *variety* in the choice of topics, as greatly contributive to pulpit interest and efficiency. The best thing palls on the taste if long continued; *e. g.*, eight or ten sermons on the peril of delay in conversion would be apt to breed satiety, to say nothing of the peril of a sinner's waiting eight or ten weeks to hear what the peril of delay is! Sermons are not to be made, as it has been said they used to make ships in Maine—by *the mile:* and when they had an order for a ship they cut off so much timber, rounded up a stern and a bow, and sent it!

(*b*) The two *general* classes of topics that should have large place in the pulpit are, topics designed for *structural* work in life and character—adapted to growth and edification—to build men up in Christ Jesus; and topics designed for *rescue* work—chosen for the express purpose of conviction and conversion: looking to the *immediate salvation of souls.*

If the first of these are exclusively handled in the pulpit, the Gospel becomes only food for the saints— a word of instruction.

If the second class are exclusively handled, the Gospel becomes simply an appeal to the impenitent—a cry of alarm. He who is a pastor must frequently, and throughout his entire ministry, treat both of these general classes of topics. His whole responsibility can in no other way be met. The *evangelist* may give himself largely, and even exclusively, to awakening sermons, summoning men to repentance and a new life. But the pastor—the shepherd, put in charge of the fold, must feed his flock as well as seek the lost. And he will best feed his flock, who so fills them with the spirit of Christ, that they will all be seekers of the lost—going out and compelling men to come in. Therefore, no imagined or real success in winning souls, however marked the success, should keep a pastor always hammering away at the ungodly. The flock will suffer and grow lean and weak and sickly, if they do not die, under such treatment.

On the other hand, it should be said with equal positiveness, that no imagined or real success in comforting, guiding, feeding the flock, should keep a pastor always furnishing supplies to the saints. Like his Lord, he should be filled with compassion for the lost, and he should seek to save them. He should long for souls and get them, and rest not without frequently having this seal of God upon his ministry.

How does his commission read ? Go and *make* disciples and *teach* them. Who gave him the right to bisect his commission ? How can he stand in the place of his Lord, and in the presence of unsaved souls, some of whom are before him every Sabbath, and have no compassion on them ? And if he have any compassion in his heart, how *can he keep* it there, and never let it get into his sermons ?

Rescue work and construction work—every pastor should be at both in every year of his ministry. He should seek for lost souls, and care for them after they are found; and so save to completeness—gather and build, *gather and build, gather and build,* so long as God lets him preach His Word.

(*c*)   But there is a further and more minute division of topics, into doctrinal, ethical, narrative, biographical, social, political, and topics of Christian benevolence.

Doctrinal topics.   How should these be preached ? As doctrines lie at the base of the Christian system, they should have frequent treatment in the pulpit. They inform the understanding, give intelligence to conviction, furnish firm anchorage to faith, and lay broad and deep foundations for Christian culture and Christian life.   A true stability in Christian character is impossible without them.

As an *objection* to doctrinal preaching, it is urged that doctrines are dry and cold; and the people want something that will touch and move the heart.

This objection arises partly from a misconception of the *relation* of truth to emotion; and partly from a common *fault of treatment* of doctrinal topics.

The *misconception* is in divorcing truth from emotion, as its ground and cause.   No emotion, unless it be merely animal or evil—no *rational* emotion, can move a rational being except as it is *grounded in apprehended truth.*   If light without heat is cold: heat without light is blind.   It is truth clearly apprehended that excites feeling and volition.   And nothing stirs so profoundly the human heart, and therefore so nourishes and renews emotion, as the great and mighty ideas that lie imbedded in *Christian doctrine.*

But the objection also arises from a common *fault of treatment* of doctrinal topics.

Doctrinal sermons are too frequently divested of the flush and throb and energy of real life, and rattled in the pulpit as mere skeletons, or theological barebones.

Three things borne constantly in mind will correct this fault of treatment. 1. In the use of doctrinal topics, the *oratorical* demands upon the preacher are to prevail, rather than the demands of scientific and exact method. The science should be science popularized: the logic, logic on fire.[1] The technical phraseology of the school, naked abstractions, theological formulas, themselves needing explanation, should be avoided; and everything should be made to assume rhetorical and concrete form.

2. The whole power of doctrinal themes should *be made to bear in practical directions.* It is a maxim needing constant reiteration and emphasis; that "doctrines should be preached practically and duties doctrinally."

3. Doctrines should be preached *in the connections* in which they are set forth in the Word of God. See how the doctrine of election is everywhere made to include the *means* as well as the *ends* (John 15 : 16 ; Eph. 1 : 4 ; 2 Tim. 2 : 13 ; 1 Peter 1 : 2). See also how precepts are linked with promises, how faith is linked with life, pardon with penitence, redemption with renewal.

But this counsel is not given as if there were to be tolerated any abatement, even by so much as by one jot or tittle of the claims of God's truth. Disguise nothing, withhold nothing, cover up nothing that God

---

[1] Tyndall could present a strictly scientific topic to a popular audience with thrilling interest.

has bidden His heralds to preach, however unwelcome to the natural heart. Dare to preach all the truth —to declare the whole counsel of God—to displace all half tints by vivid colouring—to divide hearers, and to divide all mankind into two classes, and only two, as far as vital relation to the Gospel is concerned : the friends and the enemies of the truth—the children of God and the children of the devil. But avoid needless offense and the useless arousing of opposition, by the employment of technical theological terms, liable to be misunderstood, and against which ignorant prejudice may already exist.

How then should doctrinal topics be preached ?

Frequently, boldly, distinctly, oratorically, practically, in their Scriptural connections, and with warmth of conviction. So preached, they will do more than all else towards building up an intelligent and stable body of believers in Christ Jesus.

Ethical topics.—They embrace all those duties growing out of man's relation to man and to God ; their nature, limits, obligations, and motives. They stand related to doctrinal themes as works to faith. As faith is dead without works, so are doctrines dead without duties.

Three points should be borne in mind in preaching upon ethical themes.

First that the specific, sweeping and imperative claims of *the divine law* are to be preached. But, mark you, preached, not that men may obey and live ; but that they may see the impossibility of obedience by nature, and *be led to Christ* to find in Him the righteousness that may meet the law's demands. God's commandment is " exceeding broad " and its vigorous lines must be drawn faithfully across the conscience and heart. Mere vague or general discussions of depravity will fail of producing that sense of sinfulness and helplessness and hopelessness, which will lead a sinner to the Lamb of God.

The second point to be borne in mind in preaching on ethical themes is, that the specific sweeping and imperative claims of *Christian obedience* are to be preached. For Christ is a Master as well as a Saviour; and Christianity is a life as well as a belief—a rule of practice as well as a rule of faith. But it is distinctly to be borne in mind by the preacher, and made ever clear to the hearer, that Christian obedience is preached, not as a ground of justification, but as a *proof of having been justified.* The true child of God has been created in Christ Jesus *unto good works,* and he is to be fully taught as to what these good works are.

And the third point concerning ethical themes is that they are to be presented as *not so much the moralities of natural religion ;* but rather as having evangelical basis and evangelical obligation *by reason of Christ's cross.* It is a *gospel* system of ethics the preacher is to enforce. The natural claims and advantages of virtue may indeed be shown ; but always as subordinate. The chief stress and glory and power of ethical themes should be got from Calvary.

Narrative, biographical and historical topics.— These are derived from Biblical incidents, parables, biographies and personal records, that put truth in concrete form. The fact that they are in the Scriptures in such abundance, makes their frequent use legitimate in the pulpit. They often furnish setting for a great doctrine or a great duty : and by means of which such doctrine or duty may be the more impressively exhibited and enforced, because vitalized by personality and so freed from all abstraction. They make truth lifelike and vivid; Christ and the woman of Samaria at the well; Christ and the woman that had sinned; envy and Haman; pride and Naaman; penitence and Peter; Christian compassion and Christ's tears; the matchless parables; how vividly these all embody and illustrate truth.

But all such use of incident and story, should be vivid, graphic, brief—not in too great detail, bringing out only the salient essential points, and leaving room for pressure of argument and appeal.

Topics of Christian socialism.—There is such a thing. And it is clearly distinguishable from what is known as modern socialism. The latter has a certain spirit of brotherhood, and it aims to lessen the frightful inequalities that prevail in social and industrial life. But it is at war with *individualism,* with *competitivism* and with *capitalism*; and its chief aim seems to be improvement in material conditions rather than in intellectual or spiritual, thus giving it a materialistic aspect.

On the other hand, *Christian* socialism has no war with individualism; or with competitivism; or with capitalism. Christianity *exalts the individual,* offers *eternal reward for competitive effort,* and insists simply on accumulated capital's *consecration.* In Christianity there is nothing held more sacred than the individual—his rights, his privileges, his talents, his acquisitions. God wants no machine work. He lets each individual will *keep its throne.* And He distinctly offers reward for competitive effort. "Thy pound hath gained ten pounds; have thou authority over ten cities." "Thy pound hath gained five pounds; have thou authority over five cities." And again: "Thou hast been faithful over a few things; I will make thee *ruler* over many things." And as to *capital*—it is not with the possession of capital nor with its use, but with its abuse that Christianity is at war. The record in Acts 4 : 32–35 is sometimes cited as an instance of absolute community of goods. But it simply proves that the early Christians held their possessions in *trust* for the Lord. "Not one of them said that ought of the things which he *possessed*, was his own;" *i. e.*, of course *while still possessing it*. If anybody lacked, the others who had abundance sold enough to meet the immediate need. Ananias and Sapphira were punished, not for withholding their goods, but for lying about them. Christian socialism makes no war on capital. It only demands that it be *used for the glory of God* in the good of men. The converted Karen who visited this country years ago, was in spirit a Christian socialist. He had been given a small purse of gold, and when boarding the ship for his return home he was asked why he had not used some of his money to buy little memorials of his visit to take back with him. He held up the purse, and said, "*This no me money—this Jesus Christ's money*."

When a millionaire sits loose to his millions after this fashion, looking upon his millions as Jesus Christ's millions, and when he proves his faith by his works, never asking, "Who is my neighbour?" but, finding a man anywhere with the blood of the human race in his veins and in need of help, is a *neighbour to him—*

he is the true representative of Christian socialism. And when his time to die comes, he will go to bigger riches than he ever had here ; for of such is the kingdom of heaven.

Political topics.—Shall *political* questions be carried into the pulpit ? If they clearly involve a great question of morals for which a clear and unmistakable, " Thus saith the Lord " can be found against them in Holy Scripture, of course they ought to be taken into the pulpit. That they are in politics is a shame to our citizenship. For the pulpit to be silent about them would be a deeper and darker shame to our Christianity. That they have drifted, or have been dragged into politics, does not change their *nature.* It is only the more incumbent on the part of God's heralds to let God's voice be heard in the matter. Fear of giving political offence by pulpit utterance should shrivel before the fear of giving God offence by pulpit silence.

Let the question be clear—the case unchallengeable —like the Sabbath question, the saloon question, the question of financial honour, the question of an unholy war, Mormonism, communism,—anything that through the greed of power or lust of license or fear of adverse vote, has been allowed to fasten itself on the body politic, and to gnaw away at the moralities and the decencies and the safeguards of society and the home —and pulpit silence on that question is simply recreancy to a sacred trust. It would seem as if the Church of God had had lessons enough on this subject, and had eaten enough of the fruits of such folly, to keep her forever free from any and every entangling alliance with policies or powers, that would make her dumb in the presence of a great iniquity because it had somehow got into politics!

Topics of Christian benevolence as related to the Boards of the Church.—They represent the College Board, the Board of Ministerial Education, of Home Missions, of Foreign Missions, of Freedmen, of Church Erection, of Publication, and the permanent committees on Temperance.

The College Board aids in planting, endowing, and equipping educational institutions under Presbyterian control—so that all the instruction shall be in harmony with the Christian faith.[1]

The Board of Education helps young men through these and other institutions into the work of the ministry.

The Boards of Home and Foreign Missions and of the Freedmen, give the men their fields, and, when needed, help support them.

The Board of Church Erection helps in the building of houses of worship for these mission fields.

The Board of Publication and Sabbath School Work equips these mission churches with books and tracts, aiming especially through its Sabbath School Missionary Department to reach *the children.*

The Board of Ministerial Relief relieves the wants of God's ambassadors who have come to infirmity and old age; and after their decease looks with reverent care after their destitute widows and children.

At first blush it would seem as if these benevolences

---

[1] It will be understood that the boards of benevolence here referred to are the officially authorized agencies of "The Presbyterian Church in the United States." Other denominations may have different agencies.

were too many. But we tried consolidation a few years ago, and the scheme failed. It gave us neither more money, nor greater efficiency, nor wider interests.

1. These benevolent schemes of the Church are her *missionary* schemes—the agencies by which she seeks to obey her Lord in preaching the Gospel to every creature. They are more or less interdependent, they have been born of experience and manifest need, arching the ministry from the cradle to the grave of ministerial life.

2. These benevolent schemes can be efficiently prosecuted only by constant and liberal giving. They cost money for their prosecution : and money must be had. And what so vitally concerns the Church, concerns *all the churches*, and *each individual member* of all the churches. Hence the duty of all to share, according to ability and as God has prospered them, in securing this steady and generous supply of funds to meet the ever-recurring, and often increasing, needs of our various benevolent boards.

3. No liberal Christian giving can be sustained in any church without intelligent and definite knowledge of the need to be met. As human nature is constituted, men *must see the need*—be brought face to face with the actual necessity, before they will adequately and continuously meet it. It is the law of the human mind to be moved by what is seen and known. And this is not only according to human nature, but according to Scripture. Paul placed the need of the poor saints at Jerusalem before the churches of Galatia and Corinth, and then appealed to them to give. Jesus represents the righteous as *seeing* Him hungered and athirst and naked and sick and in prison, in the

persons of His disciples, and so giving food and drink and clothing and ministry. In neither case, and in no case in all the Bible, is giving made to depend solely on abstract Christian principle. Some Christian men do indeed set apart to the Lord a tenth, or a fifth, or a third of their income, as a matter of principle; but these are comparatively few, and even these must judge to what objects their money shall go. And this judgment, to be intelligent, must be based upon knowledge.

The Church, therefore, to give constantly and liberally, *must be informed—must know the facts, the work done and to be done, the agencies to be employed, the expenses to be incurred, the successes already achieved, and what promise there is of results.*

4. A thorough knowledge on the part of the Church of this missionary and benevolent work will depend on *the fidelity of the preacher in presenting month by month and year by year from the pulpit, the various causes.*

A large service has been rendered by the able and faithful secretaries of these boards, who in addition to their laborious office-work, have ransacked the continent in the interests of the different boards, visiting churches and presbyteries and synods, their minds crammed to the full and their hearts aflame with the mighty things God is doing through these respective mission and benevolent agencies of our beloved Church. But what are a few secretaries among eleven thousand churches!

Something also has been done and can still be done by periodicals, printed circulars, and religious newspapers; and these have been, and should continue to be, freely employed to increase the knowledge of the people as to this great work of extending the Gospel.

But many cannot be induced to take these publications. Many who take them neglect to read them. And even when they are read, the facts they set forth lack the life and vividness and impressiveness of these same facts marshalled and grouped in connection with some truth of God on the Sabbath day by the living preacher.

5. Hence, and with a kind of irresistible pressure of moral obligation, comes the conclusion that it is the duty of each pastor to keep himself thoroughly informed concerning the great causes in our scheme of Christian benevolence, and, from time to time, to exhibit their vast needs, their open doors, their many signal successes, as constant and heaven-approved claims upon the sympathies, the prayers, and the contributions of his people.

6. The particular *method* may be left to the individual judgment. But the plan of publicly designating a particular Sabbath in the year for each one of the eight or ten benevolent boards or committees of our Church, and of presenting more or less fully *on that Sabbath* the claims of the cause, is recommended as on the whole leading to the best results.

III. The *proportions* in which these various topics should be presented from the pulpit.

(*a*) Generally speaking, in *biblical* proportions: "according to the proportion of faith."

Doctrinal topics should be first of all. In one form or another these should be made the *basis* of

pulpit ministration. For example : Any attempt to
mend the morals of men, that does not insist on a recreation—a new birth ; that does not make distinct
recognition of the divine scheme of human recovery
from guilt and sin, will be a failure.

The great themes of Christianity are what should
engage the minister's chief thought and study. How
otherwise is he to succeed in engrafting a divine life
on human nature. Let him swing away from the discussion and practical enforcement of the distinguishing doctrines of sin and grace; God's topics—all of them
—the fall, the promise, the cross, faith, sovereignty, the
judgment, heaven, hell—and he will inevitably lose
the lever by which alone, "he may raise up the very
roots of human life," and throw away the only
power by which the ruined soul may be restored to
God.

Alexander says, "A man should begin early to
grapple with great subjects. An athlete gains might
only by great exertions. So that a man does not
overstrain his powers, the more he wrestles the better ; but he *must wrestle*, and not merely take a great
subject and play with it."

Ethical themes should be intermingled with doctrinal ; and both doctrinal and ethical should be set
forth in narrative or historical robing, in Biblical proportions, and Scriptural harmony.

(*b*) The *proportions* in which topics should be
used must somewhat vary with the condition of the
hearers. Special needs will of course require special
provision for them. And now and then an urgent demand of some sort will justify a minister's *bulging*
with a certain class of topics for a period, a great

exigency requiring exigent, persistent, relentless effort to meet it.

IV. Methods for securing varied and Biblical proportions.

(a) Keep a classified list of topics preached on, and consult it from time to time, to see whether the proper proportions are being regarded.

(b) Go through a kind of prescribed course between communions, e. g., if young converts have for the first time taken their covenant vows, two or three sermons designed to help and strengthen these new-born disciples would very appropriately follow the communion service.

Then sermons to feed the flock, to establish Christians in the faith, to comfort them under trial and affliction—sermons for Christian *growth*.

Then sermons to stimulate to Christian *service*—and especially to be busy in personal effort to seek and find and bring to Christ—sermons for Christian work.

And now sermons to the impenitent—inviting, loving, faithful, searching sermons, that mean *now*.

(c) Have regard to three things in any extended preaching in order to keep the balances, and avoid bulging.

(1) Have regard to the *system of truth*.

(2) Have regard to the varied and specific *needs of the flock*.

(3) Have regard to *personal predilection*—last and least, but by no means to be wholly overlooked.

A comprehensive summary of this whole talk on topics :

1. Proclaim truth rather than combat error.

2. Be assertive and aggressive, rather than defensive

3. Preach on important topics, rather than on those of minor moment.

4. Choose topics from the *Word of God* ALWAYS.

A SIMPLE METHOD OF CLASSIFYING SERMONS.

I. Sermons to Christians.
    (*a*) Instruction. 卌,卌,||
    (*b*) Consolation. ||
    (*c*) Stimulation,—
      By promise, ||| By privilege, ||| By love, 卌
      By command, 卌   By duty, |||| By fear, 卌,|
II. Sermons to the impenitent.
    Probing, 卌,||| Warning, 卌,卌   Inviting, 卌,||

Here is a record of forty sermons to Christians. Imagine this to be the record of an actual pastor in the field. A single glance reveals some very positive leanings. He leans to *instruction*: he would make his people *know*. He is little given to *consolation* or *comfort*. He bulges large with *stimulation*; but he would impel by the hard, the severe, the fearful, rather than by the winsome and tender and loving.

And the record shows twenty-five sermons to the impenitent. But gospel *invitation* has not even a *third* of the sermonic stock. He is evidently too much bent on *driving* men into the kingdom, and not enough given to *winning* them.

Some such simple device as the above—a brief analysis, or sermonic classification, and a simple stroke of the pen for every sermon preached—would wonderfully help the preacher to balance and true proportion in sermonizing, keeping him from bulging, or from what may be characterized as the homiletic "goiter."

XXIII

ITS IDEAL QUALITIES OF STYLE

SYLLABUS

I. What is style? Style and elocution. Style and diction. Style and thought.

    Hence (a) In order to write well, one must think well.

         (b) One may think well and write badly.

II. The value of a good style.

    (a) Complete force means complete expression.

    (b) Especially important for the pulpit.

III. Objections urged to study of style.

    (a) It makes a man artificial—a mere student of words.

    (b) Men have been mighty in speech without it.

    (c) Few hearers know what good style is.

IV. The different properties of style.

    (1) The fundamental property: that the style be true—to thought—to thinker.

    (2) The *absolute* properties.—These pertain to language itself; are fixed and inflexible. Euphony, harmony, rhythm, and grammatical purity.

    (3) The *relative* properties are various; limited here to *perspicuity, precision, energy*, and *beauty*.

Perspicuity

1. Its nature: It means the quality of *being seen through; transparency, clearness.* Of what worth is force or beauty so long as the preacher is not *understood*.

2. Special reasons for *perspicuity in the pulpit:*

    (a) The dominant thing in preaching is *instruction* in order to conviction and persuasion. But instruction is impossible where the instructor is not understood.

    (b) Obscurity may mislead—and to mislead here is *perilous*.

    (c) The variety of mental capacity in the audience.

3. Means for the attainment of perspicuity:

    (a) The thought must be clear to the preacher.

(b)   The preacher must look at style from the *hearer's point of view*.

(c)   Must cultivate *exactness* in the use of words.

(d)   Must pay heed to proper arrangement of words and sentences. The use of *relative* words must be carefully discriminating. In reading, one can study out the meaning. In listening to a speaker, this is impossible.

(e)   Must read perspicuous writers.

Precision

The property that gives thought *sharp outline*. It has respect to number of words. Perspicuity to kind of words. Illustrated by scene-painting. Involves right use of *brevity* and *expansion*. *Brief repetition, apt illustration*, its chief aids. Omitting nothing necessary : discarding everything superfluous.

Energy

This is the quality of style that makes thought *impinge*. It comes : (1) From *energy in the man*. The men of intense speech are the men of intense conviction. (2) From *directness*. Hence the sententiousness of proverbs. (3) From use of figures of speech—especially tropes. Personification and apostrophe are figures of intense energy.

Beauty

This is the quality that commends discourse—makes it pleasing, winsome. (1) It is internal, and generic; goes deeper than embellishment ; enters into entire sermonic structure, in the form of unity, propriety, tone, simplicity. (2) Beauty is also *external* and *specific*— that which embellishes; the flush and splendour of style, born of a delicate fancy or a brilliant imagination. But it must be *useful* beauty, ornamenting construction. Blossoms are *developed*—never *tied* to the apple tree.

Two other qualities should mark the style of pulpit discourse : *Scripturalness* and *dignified simplicity*—the one born of a soul saturated with Biblical truth ; the other born of a sense of the divine proprieties in handling the things of God.

XXIII

ITS IDEAL QUALITIES OF STYLE

IN considering the matter of style, it is vital that we first attend to some distinctions and definitions.

I. What is style?

Style is the art of expressing thought in language. Just as colour gives to thought a body in painting, and marble gives to thought a body in sculpture, and sound gives to thought a body in music, so language gives to thought a body in literature. Style has to do with this body. It is the form of the form.

Style and elocution.

Style was formerly used as synonymous with " elocution." And ancient rhetoricians applied the word "elocution" to the second of the two general divisions of rhetoric, of which "invention" is the first. The etymology of the word sanctions this use. But elocution has come to be applied to oral delivery. And style is now commonly understood as denoting the art of expressing thought in language.

Style and diction.

Style and diction are sometimes used interchangeably. But diction is of narrower signification, and has reference chiefly to the grammatical qualities of discourse—to purity and accuracy. Style is a more elevated and comprehensive word, embracing those qualities which mark the taste and genius of the writer.

Style and thought.

There is a real and vital relation, in some essential qualities, between a man's thought and his style. In this sense, Buffon's statement is true that "style is the man." It represents his mind. His thought penetrates and animates his style and goes far to determine its outward form and character, as the organic body of which his thought is the possessing and vivifying spirit. Language is more than the mere dress of thought. It is the living body, vitalized, animated and given a special form and character by it.

Hence, (*a*) *In order to write well, one must think well.* For ideas alone form the groundwork of style. If the spirit be dull, the body will surely lack expression. Just as no eye flashes and no face glows, so no words burn, where there is no fire within.

But, on the other hand, (*b*) One may think well and write badly, and, in this sense, Buffon's oft-quoted maxim, "style is the man," is not true. Where the art of thinking has received special attention, and the art of expression none at all, a man may think great thoughts, yet be able to give them no eloquent embodiment in language. Language is a study. Its use is to be learned. We are not born masters in the art of verbal expression, any more than in the art of painting or sculpture.

II. The value of a good style.

(*a*) A thought can only be given to others with complete force when it has complete expression. And this is style. Its value, therefore, can hardly be over-

estimated.   For it is simply rendering the thought as
perfectly as possible.   In its best form, it is exhibitive of whatever force, grandeur, dignity, beauty there
is in thought to instruct, convince and move men to
feeling and action.   What brooks it, therefore, how
we think, or what we think, if we do not know how
to express our thought?

(b)   A good style is especially important for the
pulpit, for there the speaker is delivering the Word of
God; and it is preeminently due to God's thoughts,
that they be given fit embodiment.   If care ought to
be taken by the lawyer in legal documents, and by
the physician in medical treatises, that their ideas
may be set forth with verbal exactness, much more
should the gospel herald make his style the perfect
medium of what he is bidden of God to communicate
to men.   This is a moral matter as well as a matter of
taste.   The preacher has no right to obscure the message by a bad style; to speak of divine things in a
way that impairs their efficacy and belittles and be-
clouds them.

A bad style is *not true*—not true to the writer, not
true to the subject.   And what right has a preacher
to use the false, in dealing with the things of God?
If it be said, "The *thoughts* should speak," the answer
is, It is the bad style that hinders them from speaking.   Beyond a doubt, truth often fails of its best
impression, because of the imperfect form.   And many
a hearer is made indifferent and inattentive, or sharply
critical and censorious by a bad style.   "It is much
better to write so as to make a critic turn Christian,
than so as to make a Christian turn critic."

III.   But objections are urged to this study of style.

(*a*) It is objected that such study will make a man *artificial*—a mere student of *words*, of *outward forms*. The form will draw attention from the subject. Therefore let words come as they will. Ideas are the chief thing.

Well, it is not to be denied that a man may be borne away by this study of style, so as to become at last merely a cunning worker in words, a manufacturer of pretty sentences and high-sounding phrases. There is a subtle influence exerted by the pomp, harmony and decorum of fine language, which is likely to make itself felt, and which unquestionably ought to be feared and resisted.

But surely the remedy is not to be found in ignoring style and turning our backs upon it. To hold style in contempt will certainly keep any preacher from the seductive intoxication of the art of verbal expression. But it will also keep his thought from reaching his hearers in all its completeness. Thought can be given its full worth and weight only when best expressed. And its best expression is nothing more or less than the style that it is proposed to hold in such contempt.

The remedy is in *keeping the end of good style constantly before the mind*. That end is to convey the thought in *the fullest, clearest, most direct, most forcible way to others*. Substance can never be sacrificed to form, if the form is always sought for the sake of the substance. The verbal body is our care only because of the ideas with which we would animate it. The best style is that which will best embody those ideas. Instead of being made artificial or false, therefore, by the cultivation of style, a man will be intensely real and true, just as he keeps the end of style in view—the making his thought intelligible and powerful.

(*b*) Again, it is objected that men have been mighty in speech without this devotion to style. Aristotle speaks indifferently of it. Paul paid no attention to it. Pascal is on record as saying: "True eloquence is the contempt of eloquence." The pulpit gives repeated instances of grand effectiveness without aid from style.

But as to Aristotle it may be answered, a clearer, truer style would have made his work doubly valuable. He is his own best refutation. As to Paul, while he allowed himself some digressions and some obscurities, so that unquestionable defects may be seen in his style, yet be it remembered he himself distinctly said, "I had rather speak five words with my understanding, that I might teach others also, than ten thousand words in a tongue." And again: "Except ye utter by the tongue speech easy to be understood, how shall it be known what is spoken? for ye will be speaking into the air." Now just so far as thought is conveyed in words not fully understood, it is conveyed in an unknown tongue. As to Pascal, his word is simply rhetorical extravagance.

But, after all, the great thing is to be powerful. Power is the attribute crowning all a minister's accomplishments. Write as Paul did, if thereby you can be as mighty as he. If the mere blind, unstudied promptings of your nature lead you to effective speech, let the study of style go. So that the *end* is reached, it matters little by what way. Drive truth home as **Paul did,** go triumphing everywhere in Christ as he

did, and nothing more need be said. But the question
is, Will you do it? Will a man carry as heavy a load
when it is flapping about loosely as when it is packed
and adjusted?

(c) Once more: It is objected that few hearers
know what good style is, and hence time here spent is
time wasted.

But the object is not to impress hearers with the
style, but with the *truth*. If their attention is drawn
to the style, then the style is defective. The purest
atmosphere is that which brings out the stars, not that
which preaches itself. If the preacher's object be to
win admiration for his chaste and perfect form of
speech, then the objection might hold good, and the
fact that few in any congregation can appreciate a
faultless style, would be a reason for not spending much
time in its cultivation. But if the art of verbal expression be studied for *truth's* sake, so as to render
thought as perfectly as possible, and this end be really
secured, so that men take in the thought without effort just as they see the stars on the clearest night,
what does it matter whether fifty hearers, or five,
know anything of good style. Keep it constantly in
mind that expression is to be studied, not for the sake
of expression, but for the sake of the idea, embosomed
in expression.

IV. The different properties of style.

(1) The fundamental property is this: that the
style *be true*—true to the thought, true to the thinker.
This is comprehensive of many other properties ordinarily enumerated in works on rhetoric. And all other
properties are important as they have this for a base.
Without this essential merit, speech is a deception.

(2) The absolute properties pertain to language itself. They are fixed and inflexible, independent of speaker or subject. They are determined to style by the unchangeable laws of language. They are chiefly oral and grammatical, and are founded on accent, pitch, the sounds of words, their forms, their connection and their meaning. They are usually denominated euphony, harmony, rhythm, and grammatical purity.

The place for their discussion is in a work on rhetoric. But perhaps it should be said with reference to grammatical purity, that proximate standard is good use, which is opposed to *obsolete* use, *provincial* use, *individual* use, and *foreign* use, or use derived from another language. The sanction making good use should be *wide, reputable, present*. Where use is clearly divided, the preponderance should be given to the greater weight of authority.

(3) The relative properties of style are various. Our discussion must be limited to the leading properties in this class, and that have peculiar relation to the pulpit. They are *perspicuity, precision, energy*, and *beauty*.

PERSPICUITY

1. Its nature. We preach to benefit men. Men can be benefited only by the truth. To benefit by the truth, truth must be made intelligible. The quality in style that makes truth intelligible is therefore the prime quality. It is of first importance in all discourse. This quality is *perspicuity*. It is the Latin word *perspicuitas* transferred almost bodily to our language, and means, of course, as its etymology indicates, *transparency*. It is the quality of *being seen through*, and as applied to style means a style in which

there is no obscurity; which lets the hearer see the
thought just as the thinker thinks it.

Clearly this is at the foundation of all effective
style. Style should be stripped of everything—cut
and pruned rigorously and remorselessly until it exhibits the exact reality of the thought it embodies, and
so carry that thought straight to the understanding.
Why speak at all if we do not speak to be understood?
Of what use a body that lets no soul through it? The
contemptible affectation that would avoid plain, simple speech and clothe thoughts in large and high-sounding words, and interlard discourse with unfamiliar,
foreign and classic phrase, for the sake of producing
the impression of learning and profundity, ought to be
despised by every preacher of God's truth. It is the
resort of shallow minds. They stir up the mud so that
no one may see the bottom of their shallowness. Uneducated minds are imposed upon by the obscurity,
mistaking it for something profound. But the best
hearers discover the superficiality and are disgusted
with the affectation. But even if the device were
wholly successful, what a miserable and shameful resort for men commissioned of God to *teach*, where
teaching may be decisive of eternal destiny![1]

When a man is obscure, *because of his subject*—beyond the intellectual grasp of his audience—it is an
impeachment of his judgment. Such an obscurity
saves his honesty, because the obscurity is not assumed
for the sake of false impression; but it is a reflection
on his common sense. Gospel themes should be
adapted to the comprehension of the hearers. An il-
literate, uncultivated congregation, unused to evangel-

[1] 1 Cor. 14 : 9.

ical preaching, needs to be instructed in the first principles of the Gospel—to be fed on the milk of the Word. The deeper, harder, more difficult subjects should not be discussed before babes.

But it is perspicuity of *style*, rather than of subject, with which we have now to do. And there is no property of style so desirable, so absolutely essential. Energy and brilliancy, vividness and elegance are important, and they demand and should have diligent cultivation, but never, until a speaker has laid the foundation for them in *clearness*. Of what worth are force and beauty, so long as a man is not intelligible! Nay, how is force possible where one is not understood! How much power over an audience has a man speaking in an unknown tongue?[1]

Aim, then, at perspicuity. Before all else seek simplicity. Be determined that your hearers shall understand you, that not a soul shall be left in doubt of your meaning. Sacrifice the choicest sentence, give up the finest word, let the glittering beauties go that look so fair to you, hew away at your style at whatever cost, until you make it so transparent that your whole thought will go right through it and *strike*, impressing other minds just as it impresses yours. Fichte

---

[1] We have all read of the old Scotchman who did not like plain speech, but was happiest when he encountered a man who could "joomble the reason, and confoond the judgment." Per contra, here is an incident concerning Dr. N. S. S. Beman, which I had from his own lips while associated with him as Junior Colleague at Troy. The Troy Presbytery met somewhere in the far North woods. And the region was all agog to hear the famous Trojan preacher. When he had finished his sermon, and the congregation was dismissed, an old woman walked out of church, saying, "La me! Is that your great Dr. Beman? Why, I could understand every word he said."

once wrote a philosophical tract entitled : " An effort
to compel the reader to understand." A preacher
must not only have ideas ; *he must make his hearers
have them.* He must compel the contact of his ideas
with their minds by a style so clear, so perspicuous,
that men cannot listen to his words and fail of his
thought.

2. There are special reasons for perspicuity in the
pulpit :

(*a*) The dominant thing in preaching is *instruction
in order to conviction and persuasion.* But how is instruction possible, where the instructor is not understood ? What power can the preacher have to persuade men and influence their wills, if he is not clear ?
There may be obscurity in the poet, the painter, the
sculptor, for their end is not persuasion but pleasure.
But the discourse of the preacher should be as clear as
sunlight, for he seeks to move men by the truth. And
the souls of men will never yield to the truth, while
they are engaged in the labour of understanding what
is spoken. The effort on the part of the hearer to
understand keeps the truth from grappling with the
conscience and prevents its full effect on the heart.

(*b*) A second special reason for perspicuity in the
pulpit is, that *obscurity may mislead.* And to mislead
here is perilous. It may prove of infinite consequence.
As we value men's souls we must speak plainly on
these things. The heart is prone to pervert the truth
of God. The preacher must see to it that he furnishes
no excuse for this guilty perversion. If a physician's
prescription should be written with care and clearness,
lest a poison be administered for medicine, how ought
clearness to be studied by the man of God, lest he be

misunderstood, and mislead a soul to its hurt and ruin.

(*c*) A third special reason for perspicuity in the pulpit is the variety of mental capacity for comprehending truth that is found in almost every congregation. It is rarely a select audience of picked minds. The scientist writes for those more or less familiar with his work. He addresses persons of some degree of mental maturity. But the preacher addresses all classes of minds, and all degrees of culture. The children, the uneducated, the ignorant, the dull, and lethargic in thought, as well as the educated and intelligent—persons of every grade of intellect, and of every age of life,—wait on his ministry. Above all others, therefore, the preacher is solemnly bound to use great plainness of speech, so that he may feed the whole flock. He should strive after clearness as the supreme attainment in style.

3. Means for the attainment of perspicuity :

(*a*) First of all *the thought must be clear to the preacher*. Clear conception is vital to clear expression. The man who does not distinctly grasp his own thought, will find no words to make it plain to others. By what possibility can he give what he does not possess !

(*b*) The looking at one's style *from the hearer's point of view* will also help to perspicuity. The preacher must put himself, as far as possible, in the hearer's place and then ask himself : "If I were in his place, with his limitations, would this sentence be perfectly plain to me ?" Perspicuity in style must have respect to the condition and posture of the hearer—to the circumstances of the common mind ; and the difficulties of that mind in grasping truth must, as far as possible, be anticipated and provided for.

(c) The cultivation of precision—exactness in the use of words. The study of words, with reference to their precise shade of meaning and the constant choice of them, based upon this difference, will go far to give perspicuity to style. There are no two words of exactly the same signification in our language. And if there were, it would be every man's duty to deny one of them a place in good society. No language can be enriched by the superfluous.

Regard for precision (1) will prevent the use of the same word in two senses in the same connection ; (2) will prevent the use of a word in such a connection that it may have two meanings ; (3) will prevent the use of a general word when something specific is meant. Precision will weed discourse of everything ambiguous or equivocal—and so serve to make style perspicuous.

(d) A further means of perspicuity is the proper arrangement of words and sentences. This gives each paragraph, each sentence, each word, its true place, which must of course contribute greatly to clearness. In fact, the utmost exactness of expression will be of little avail in conveying the thought, without *effective order of arrangement.* The use of relative words often leads to obscurity, because their place in the sentence leaves it doubtful as to what they refer. The pronouns *who, which,* and *that* are frequently so far from their antecedents, as to lead to ambiguity or obscurity. In reading, one can study out the connection, until it is made clear. But in listening to a speaker this is impossible. The connection must be apparent, or it is lost altogether ; for the sentence or paragraph perishes with its utterance. The proper handling of relative words is therefore of great importance, in order to clearness.

The particular should precede that which is more general.

Modifying words should be kept in close proximity with the words to which they belong.

Ordinarily, the verb should lie between its subject and object.[1]

The sense should not be too long suspended. Break up a sentence, rather than introduce long parenthetical clauses. Change clauses into complete and separate sentences, rather than drive on a whole flock of clauses to the close of a single sentence.

(e) A fifth means of perspicuity is *reading perspicuous authors.* Paley is an example of directness and clearness. Baxter and Bunyan and Franklin are remarkable for their simplicity. Robert Hall is always clear, while characterized by energy and eloquence. Theodore Parker is crisp and sharp. You cannot fail to understand him. Studiously avoid Hooker and Barrow and Jeremy Taylor and Chalmers and Melville and Storrs and such like, as writers whose style is unworthy of any imitation, until you have laid for yourself broad and deep this *foundation* of style—*perspicuity.*

If you are already stilted, florid, obscure, ambitious, high-sounding, a solicitous student of fine expressions,

---

[1] " And thus the son the sire addressed."
" The duke yet lives that Henry shall depose."
" I declare thee, O Pyrrhus, the Romans to be able to conquer."

It is impossible to determine, in these separate sentences, which is subject and which is object.

a lover of gaudy verbosity, taken with the trumpery and moonshine of superficial rhetoric, get off your high horse at once. Do not disdain to go on foot. Come down to the pedestrian style. Speak your thought in the simplest, clearest, most straightforward way. Let the imbecile elegancies of Blair, says Dr. Alexander, be an everlasting beacon to the student of homiletics. Say " life," instead of " the vital principle " ; " heat," instead of " caloric "; " teach," instead of " inculcate " ; " yield," instead of " succumb " ; " blame," instead of " inculpate "; " lost soul," instead of " ruined immortality." And if you have occasion to remind your hearers that there is not one Gospel for the rich and another for the poor, do not inform them, as a young preacher once did his hearers, " that if they would not be saved on general principles, they would not be saved at all." By all means, and before all else, be perspicuous.[1]

PRECISION

If style is the body of thought, it is something

---

[1] For clear, vivid description, the fight of Christian with Apollyon outmatches any other of its kind in literature. Here is a sample of its plainness, vividness, and strength, telling of the beginning of the fight : " Then Apollyon straddled quite over the whole of the breadth of the way, and said, ' I am void of fear in this matter ; prepare thyself to die ; for I swear by my infernal Den that thou shalt go no farther ; but here I will spill thy soul.' "

The Simplicity of Greatness.—Many years ago the licentiates of Princeton Seminary were in the habit of preaching at a station some distance from that place. Among their habitual hearers was a sincere and humble, but uneducated Christian slave, called Uncle Sam, who on his return home would try to tell his mistress what he could remember of the sermon, but complained that the students were too deep and learned for him. One day, however, he came home in great more than a medium. It needs therefore some other property besides clearness or transparency. Body must have *form, distinctness of outline,* what is here termed *Precision.* We see through the style when it is perspicuous, as we see through the clear air, or through transparent glass. But style does more than reveal, it bounds and limits, gives fullness and definiteness of form. Thoughts need not only to be seen through a clear medium, they must have distinct shape, be clear cut and sharp in outline. Precision is the property in style that gives thoughts this form. It forbids alike the use of what is superfluous, and the omission of what is necessary. It has respect to the number of words, while perspicuity has respect to the kind and order of words. It not only limits words in a sentence, but sentences in a paragraph. It is the judicious mingling of conciseness and amplification.

Style may be perspicuous, as clear as the purest air, every word used with such precision, and in such order, as to leave nothing ambiguous or confused, yet it may have superfluous detail, not clouding the meaning, but taking away the sharp, clear edge of the thought, so that it does not appear *in vivid, living form.*

This property of style may be illustrated by a reference to scene-painting. There the artist throws aside the detail of miniature. He seeks bold outline. His

good humour, saying that a poor unlarnt old man, just like himself, had preached that day, who he supposed was hardly fit to preach to the white people; but he was glad he came, for his sake, for he could remember everything he had said. On inquiry, it was found that Uncle Sam's "unlarnt" old preacher was Rev. Dr. Archibald Alexander, who, when he heard the criticism, said it was the highest compliment ever paid to his preaching.

pencil strokes bring out the salient features and give distinctness of form. An instant and vivid impression is his object; that which may be caught at a glance. For the scenes are constantly shifting, and the minute elaboration of cabinet painting would fail of the definite effect of this boldness of outline in scenic representation.

Now the orator, the preacher, is a verbal scene-painter. He speaks for immediate impression. His thought cannot be studied. It should strike the ear and the mind on the instant, just as scene-painting strikes the eye. A vivid style will thus flash his thought out to his hearers. It will be bold word-painting. It will not tolerate verbosity, however clear. It will allow no elaboration not requisite to distinctness of form. It will rigorously check deviations, diversions, flights of any kind, however exquisite in themselves, that do not vivify the main thought with bold and living outline.

This property of style requires the *right use of brevity and expansion.* We may abbreviate to obscurity. We may expand to prolixity. The happy mien gives precision. Not as brief as possible. But the briefer the better, so that the thought be given distinct form—a kind of living embodiment. Extreme conciseness brings a too swift succession. There is not a sufficient detention of the thought before the mind, to enable the mind fully to apprehend it. The scene must tarry till the mind has taken it in, but as it is a *moving, shifting* scene, on its passage, there must be nothing for the mind to take in, save what is essential to the complete apprehension of the idea. A wearisome prolixity is even worse than undue brevity. For the preacher is an orator. And every oration is essentially *a movement, a progress,* each part of it a step *towards the determined end.* It should be on wheels, not on a pivot : going forward, not in a circle, the thought kept just long enough before the mind for its thorough apprehension. Vividness lies between a too terse, compact style and mere multiplication of words—mere verboseness. Barrow was the compactest of sermonizers, and so no ordinary congregation could keep up with him. It was sometimes like hearing read aloud the solution of some difficult problem in mathematics, to hear one of his sermons, compressing, as they sometimes did, into the fewest possible words the greatest possible amount of thought.

To steer clear of this Scylla, and at the same time to avoid the whirling Charybdis of useless verbiage and tiresome expansion, let there be *brief repetition and apt illustration.* Brief repetition in the same, or somewhat different form will detain the thought and round it out and give it definiteness. A great advocate once repeated an argument so many times, in his address to the jury, that the judge called him to account. "My learned brother," said he, "you have repeated that eleven times already." "True, my lord," was the reply, "but your lordship must remember that there are twelve men on the jury." Of course, it will not do to repeat to the number of our hearers ; but it is a virtue to reiterate one's meaning where the point is important and the statement concise ; and by varying the form of the thought to make sure the hearer gets it.

Apt illustration will also flash a truth to the hearer, where extended and prolix elucidation will utterly fail. It sharply outlines a thought, as no multiplication of words possibly can outline it.

It is only in the proper handling of conciseness and expansion, omitting nothing necessary and discarding everything superfluous, that we secure *vividness ;* or that property of style which gives to thought a distinct and living form.

ENERGY

This is the property in style which gives it force. *Perspicuity* reveals the thought to the hearer. *Precision* gives to thought fullness and definiteness of form. *Energy* makes it impinge, or strike the hearer's mind with *power.* It is force in style, strength, vim, the quality that compels movement and gives momentum to thought, as it passes from speaker to hearer.

In order to energy of style, there must be (1) *energy in the man.* *He* must be energized, if his style is ever to be energized. There may be an affectation of energy in style, but it will be the ass in a lion's skin, easily detected. Energy, put on, is the most miserable of affectations. Forceful speech is born of forceful soul. And the soul of man is mighty, just as it is possessed, energized, and made mighty by some object of thought. There is nothing so stimulative, so energizing, as the truths of the Gospel. As these are taken into the mind, and firmly and clearly grasped, permeating the man's moral, as well as his mental nature, will he become energetic. And the energy of his spirit will then flow out into his style and make that forceful and mighty.

First of all, then, if one would have energy of style, he must get the substance of revelation inwoven into the very texture of his spirit. He must get imbued with the living Word, if he would make Biblical knowledge not simply an intellectual perception and a memory, but a profound experience. The men of intense speech are the men of intense conviction. When the feelings are strong, they will naturally find energetic expression. Words will be "winged and armed." Speech will be a real action of will on will —a bearing in on men to carry their judgments and their hearts. Energy thus becomes "the life of eloquence—that which gives it breath and fire and power." It subdues men by a mastery which the preacher himself acknowledges. It is not he, but the truth, that possesses him. The words he speaks unto men, "they are spirit and they are life." His mission is to lay hold of the perishing. And if in the closet he pleads with God with wrestling energy of spirit, in the pulpit he will plead with men with wrestling energy of style.

(2) Energy in style comes from directness, conciseness. When we are bent on the accomplishment of an object, we seek the shortest road. Curves and circumlocutions retard movement. Brevity helps energy. It reaches the end sooner. The thought is more swift and strikes with greater power therefore. If you wish to deliver an energetic blow, you strip the branch of its foliage and make it a naked club. Hence the sententiousness of proverbs. They are short, sharp, decisive. Much is crowded into little and every word tells.[1]

---

[1] Sydney Smith's advice is: "Run your pen through every other word you have written; you have no idea what vigour it will give your style."

Here is another protest against too many words. It is rough but pointed.

> "When you've got a thing to say,
>   Say it ! Don't take half a day.

Words of *Anglo-Saxon origin* favour directness and therefore energy, because they are often shorter, more specific, and have greater power of association. Anglo-Saxon grew sadly out of fashion in the eighteenth century, through the influence of Johnson and Blair. They were made models for the English pulpit, and its style was sadly vitiated and enervated by the *sesquipedalia verba* of the one and the " imbecile *elegancies* of the other. Dr. Johnson's sonorous sentences took the fancy of declaimers, and they forsook the pure Anglo-Saxon for his magniloquence. Macaulay brings out the contrast in a fine example from Johnson himself, whose style in familiar intercourse was often quite the opposite of that he used in his more studied papers. In one of his familiar letters he says: " When we were taken up-stairs a dirty fellow bounced out of the bed on which one of us was to lie." But in recording the same incident in his " Journey to the Hebrides," he says: " Out of one of the beds, on which we were to repose, started up at our entrance a man black as a Cyclops from the forge." He once said of a periodical, " It has not wit enough to keep it sweet," and then, as if he had committed an offense by such plain, terse speech, he added: " It has not

When your tale's got little in it,
Crowd the whole thing in a minute.
Life is short—a fleeting vapour—
Don't you fill an eight-page paper
With a tale, which, at a pinch,
Could be cornered in an inch !
Boil her down until she simmers;
Polish her until she glimmers.
When you've got a thing to say,
Say it ! Don't take half a day."

vitality enough to preserve it from putrefaction." It is worth our while, now and then, to sacrifice a little dignity on the altar of plain and pungent speech.

The Scriptures are rich with energetic Anglo-Saxon. And Dr. Shedd says they do not contain a single abstraction. Certainly they are specific rather than generic, and hence they are full of a living energy. Take this example: "*There is no work in the grave whither thou goest.*" How terse and strong it is. But paraphrase it, after the manner of some modern preachers, and read: "There is no possibility of activity in the grave whither thou art wending." Again: "If God so clothe the grass of the field." What strength and directness! But read: "If an overruling Providence so adorn the vegetable productions of the field." What weakness and verbosity!

Dr. Gregory, the writer of Dr. Hall's life, says: "In one of my early interviews with Mr. Hall, I used the word 'felicity,' three or four times in quick succession. He asked, 'Why do you say "felicity," sir? Happiness is a better word, more musical and idiomatic English, coming from the Saxon.' 'Not more musical, I think, sir.' 'Yes, more musical, and so are words derived from the Saxon generally. Listen, sir: "*My heart is smitten and withered like grass.*" There's plaintive music! Listen again, "*Under the shadow of thy wings will I rejoice.*"' 'Yes, but "rejoice" is French.' 'True, but all the rest is Saxon, and "rejoice" is almost out of tune with the other words. Listen again: "*Thou hast delivered my soul from death, my eyes from tears and my feet from falling.*"' 'All Saxon, sir, except "delivered." I could think on the word, "tears," until I wept.'"

The English Archbishop Sharpe (d. 1714) advised all young divines to combine the reading of Shakespeare with the study of the Scriptures, and he is credited with the declaration that the Bible and Shakespeare made him Archbishop of York.

(3) Energy in style comes also from the *use of figures of speech*, especially tropes. Metonymy imparts energy to style by representing the object so as to individualize it, making one word stand for another, cause for effect, container for thing contained, etc., as sceptre instead of dominion, Milton instead of his writings or poems, the crescent instead of the Mohammedan power, the grave instead of death.

Metaphors conduce to energy. They give an animation and vigour unmistakably felt in public discourse. David, describing his slanderous enemies, says: "Their teeth are spears and arrows and their tongue a sharp sword." How this energetic speech sinks to tameness and feebleness by making David say of his enemies, "The slanders of their tongues cut and mangle a good name, as spears and arrows and a sword lacerate and mangle the body."

Comparisons contribute to energy if they are brief. If elaborate, they weaken rather than strengthen style, and draw attention from the subject to the comparison itself. Jeremy Taylor was copious in comparisons with great amplification and beauty, but it would be dangerous to imitate this "poet of theology." And even the extended comparisons of his gifted genius are far less effective than the brief, terse comparisons of Scripture. Take his "Thus have I seen a cloud rolling in its airy mansion," or "So have I seen a lark soaring," etc., and contrast it with John's vision of

Jesus: "His eyes were as a flame of fire, and His voice as the sound of many waters;" or with the Psalmist's description of the ungodly: "They are like the chaff which the wind driveth away." How beauty dominates in Taylor and strength in Scripture.

Personification and apostrophe are figures of speech, contributing to vigour in style. They are figures of intense energy, full of action, making speech alive. Thus Shakespeare personifies the morn "walking o'er the dew of a high eastward hill"; and the Psalmist personifies the floods lifting up their voice, and clapping their hands; and the prophet, the mountains and hills "breaking forth into singing."

Apostrophe, especially, is full of feeling and gives great boldness and vigour to style. But to be effective, it must appear unstudied, the natural language of emotion and perfectly at the speaker's command and therefore always brief. He cuts a most ridiculous figure whose eye is on his manuscript, while he is addressing some invisible being as if he were present.

These are the principal sources of energy in style—energy in the man; directness and brevity in the use of specific, vernacular and Anglo-Saxon words; and figures of speech.

If the preacher would move men and convince their judgments and carry their wills, if he would bear in on them with persuasive and mighty power, if he would *save them*, he must toil for this property of style. A luxurious loiterer in sacred composition, an indulger in wanton dalliance with imagination, a dresser-up of beautiful things and useless charms, in the mere and the constant effort to be fine, has no business in the pulpit and no call to the ministry.

BEAUTY

Beauty in style is that property in discourse which *commends it to the taste of the hearer.* The beautiful is the perfect in form. As it respects the form of discourse, it is internal and generic as well as external and specific.

(1) It is internal and generic. It goes deeper than embellishment. In this sense, the whole construction of the sermon is an æsthetic procedure. There are elements of beauty that lie beneath its surface, that pervade it, enter into its entire structure, such as *unity, propriety, tone, simplicity.* If these are not present, all the decoration and studied dress of thought in the world will not make discourse beautiful.

There is no beauty in mere congregated atoms; in elements heterogeneous and complex. Assimilate these elements, combine them, unify the mass, give them tone by putting into them a living energy, make them dynamic instead of atomic, and inevitably there will be these three qualities—clearness, strength, beauty. And while not the greatest will be beauty, but rather the least, yet beauty will be present, not attached from without, but developed from within ; not extrinsic, but inherent, arising out of the very structure of discourse.

(2) But, secondly, beauty is *external* and *specific,* not pertaining to discourse as a whole—beauty in the common acceptation as related to style. It is that which *ornaments* and *embellishes* style, its decoration, adornment—the flush, the splendour, the aroma of style. It is perspicuity, vividness, and energy, lighted up and made a gratification to æsthetic taste by the delicate touches of a playful fancy or a brilliant imagination.

But as utility lies at the base of all sacred discourse, and is its only motive and end, the style of the pulpit admits of only useful beauties ; nothing for mere ornament, nothing for display, in the mere desire to please. The beautiful must be always and resolutely subordinated to the useful. Just as in architecture, so in discourse, the beautiful must be always developing and never running counter to structure. Language is an instrument, not an end. The *end* of sacred discourse should have our chief solicitude. And beauty in style should have our solicitude at all, only as it is promotive of the end. Or, as the architects have it, we should ornament construction, never construct ornament. The question never should be, " Is this or that a *striking expression ?* " but " Does it make the *meaning* striking ? " Any ornamentation or embellishment, any flowery diction or brilliant word-painting that allures the hearer's attention from the *great object of* discourse to the beauties of language or imagery in the discourse, is meretricious and faulty. It may gratify the taste and amuse the imagination, but it will never " call the conscience to discharge its severe and awful functions." " All flowers of language should spring out of the subject itself, just as natural flowers spring out of the earth. Images and figures should be naturally connected with the subject, as a bough and its twig, or as a blossom and a leaf, spring necessarily, as it were, from such a particular root, or such a stem." [1] Let the preacher scrupulously avoid all positive blemishes in style, all offenses against good taste. But beware of betraying a fondness for ornaments. Blossoms should not be *tied*

[1] Herder, "Theologie," p. 71.

to the apple tree. Ornaments sought for, far and wide, and tacked on to discourse, are not an exhibition of the preacher's subject, but of the preacher.

In addition to these four leading properties of style —Perspicuity, Precision, Energy, and Beauty—there are two other qualities that should be named *as especially demanded for the pulpit :*

SCRIPTURALNESS

The style of sacred discourse should be pervaded and enriched by the very letter of the Word of God. Apt quotations of Scripture should gem the sermon and give it a distinctive character, as the preaching bidden of God, not in words which man's wisdom teacheth, but which the Holy Ghost teacheth. The English Bible has been aptly styled a " well of old English undefiled," and its very language should be frequently the language of the pulpit.

But Scripturalness in style does not mean simply apt quotation, for this could easily degenerate into mere pious patchwork. It means that flavour of style which comes from having the preacher's *soul thoroughly imbued with Biblical truth.* The expressions and images and figures of the divine Word should be *fused* into the discourse. And they will be, in exact proportion to the preacher's absorption of the truth of God into his own heart and life as a living energy, and to the extent that he is steeped and saturated with its spirit.

DIGNIFIED SIMPLICITY

Simplicity is the opposite of complexity, of artifice, of vain conceit. It has respect to the matter, the

manner and the motive of sacred discourse. A dignified simplicity demands ease and naturalness, the ornaments springing spontaneously from the theme, the
language lifted above the puerile and trivial. It forbids all pompous periods, all affectation, all courting a
grin or breaking a jest for the sake of the grin or the
jest, all descent to the claptrap of the platform or the
slang of the street. It is *appropriateness in speech*, as
connected with the dignities and sanctities and grand
ends of the gospel ministry.

XXIV

ITS IDEAL DELIVERY

SYLLABUS

I. The *importance* of a good delivery in preaching.

II. The *neglect* of delivery.

III. The *acquisition* of a good delivery.

IV. The *sources of power* in effective delivery.

Posture. Should be *erect, manly,* with every part of the body ready for service. Diaphragm, lungs, throat must have free play.

Gesture. 1. An immense aid to expression. 2. Should be adapted to the individual. 3. All gesture should be the unpremeditated language of nature, *i. e.*, it should not be gone through with before the mirror, just prior to public service.

Question 1. But if fit gesture is so important, should it not be studied? Certainly. But the study should be with some other discourse than the one to be delivered, otherwise it would beget mannerism.

Question 2. But are not the very *faults* of some men the language of nature? Yes—but nature *awry.* It needs to be made natural.

4. Suggestions for improvement in gesture.

   (*a*) Study the philosophy of gesture. Note the action of children.

   (*b*) Have an intelligent friend hear and criticise in private.

   (*c*) Practice before the glass. There the minister can see his awkwardness.

   (*d*) Recall the delivery in some quiet hour after the service, and emphasize anything misplaced or overdone.

   (*e*) Pay constant heed to the five great laws of gesture. (1) The law of motion, (2) of succession. (3) of economy, (4) of consistency, (5) of significance.

Voice

The vital thing on the physical side.

1. Every voice may be improved. 2. Every voice has a character. 3. The powers of the voice. 4. Practical hints in use of voice.

(*a*) Begin quietly. (*b*) *Use conversational* tone frequently. (*c*) For sympathetic effects, use tones between base and tenor. (*d*) To rouse and fire an audience, use loud tones of upper register. (*e*) Beware of sustained loudness. (*f*) For *preserving* the voice : Good food, pure air, deep breathing, vocal exercise.

The intermediate sources of power in delivery

Emphasis ; oratorical style ; use of Anglo-Saxon words ; familiarity with the manuscript.

Emphasis. (*a*) How defined. (*b*) How determined. (*c*) How given.

Oratorical style. The sermon is for the ear—to be caught on the wing. It is an *address*.

Use of Anglo-Saxon words. These have vim, point, pungency.

Familiarity with the manuscript. Helps to this : bold hand-writing ; previous study.

Mental and spiritual sources of power in delivery

Ideas. The basis of all effective delivery. *Feeling* : shall we assume feeling ? No. May we use the *language* of feeling ? Yes. But argument with real pathos means power. How is feeling to be cultivated ? By reflection. By giving play to it. By not fearing it.

Earnestness. 1. Its basis is profound conviction of personal responsibility to God. 2. The specific conditions are : (*a*) the presence of a worthy object ; (*b*) an earnest desire to accomplish it.

But there can be no *real* earnestness in delivery except as the preacher is an *earnest man.* A prevailingly trifling spirit is fatal to all earnestness.

Authority. This comes from a sense of being God's messenger, and speaking in the name of God the things of God.

From all this two things follow : 1. That delivery is a spiritual work, needing the help of the Spirit of God. 2. That the preacher should prepare for it, by *prayer* as well as by meditation.

XXIV

ITS IDEAL DELIVERY

OUR consideration of the "constants" and the "immediates" in the preparation of the sermon, and our weighing in the scales of a just balance the sermonic qualities of inner structure and of verbal form, have brought us to the actual delivery.

Delivery in preaching can only be fully treated in a work on elocution: and it properly belongs there. But it is so vitally connected with effective pulpit discourse, that it demands and deserves important place in any discussion of an ideal ministry. And this introductory thought suggests as our first point for consideration:

I. The *importance* of a good delivery.

Most men know *something* of its importance, and are commonly ready to concede it. Very few, probably, have an adequate conception of its value. Consult any acknowledged authority, and what is the testimony? Simply this, in substance: *delivery is the chief thing in eloquence.* Quintilian, Cicero, Demosthenes, Socrates, Æschines—they are all one way. Let a word from Demosthenes and Æschines suffice. Demosthenes, when asked for the greatest excellence in oratory, answered: "*Action.*" When asked for the second and third excellence, he gave the same answer. Now, what he meant—what the Greeks meant—by *action*, was precisely what we mean by *delivery*.

Æschines read at Rhodes the great oration of Demosthenes, and his hearers expressing their unbounded admiration, he exclaimed, "And what if you had heard him deliver it himself!"—thus ascribing the greatest power of that oration, not to its rhetorical excellence, but to its delivery.

But we need not go back to these high ancient authorities in proof of the importance of a good delivery. We all know of able, godly men, who have been virtually buried from public notice, because they did not know how to give their thought effective expression, while others with half their intellectual ability, have wielded prodigious power. Whitefield shook two continents. But it was not by his *sermons*. It was the way he delivered them. John Foster was one of the most unpopular of preachers; yet how his commanding ability as a writer has compelled acknowledgment. Henry Ward Beecher attributed very much of his success in preaching to the rare thoroughness with which he had cultivated those things essential to good delivery. While on the other hand, the poor elocution of Dr. Wm. G. Shedd, made the splendid products of his intellect less effective by his living voice than by the printed page.

The best sermon ever written may be spoiled in delivery. A very inferior sermon, well delivered, will often prove more effective every way than a much abler sermon badly delivered. It will not be well, therefore, for the preacher with an affluence of empty pews facing him every Sabbath to lampoon the public for running after the man of words "around the corner," until and unless he himself not only has ideas, but knows how to make them tell mightily in public speech,

II. The *neglect* of delivery.

It is painfully manifest. Good speaking, in the pulpit, is rare. The kind often heard would not be tolerated, if it were not for the sacredness of the theme and the office. Rhetoric is taught in all our colleges. Elocution has comparatively an insignificant place. Of weak, dull, clumsy, insipid, drawling, soporific, monotonous, turgid methods of delivery in the pulpit, we have a surfeit. Of kindling, glowing, natural, animated, forceful, eloquent, effective ways of driving truth home, alas, what lack! It is the standing reproach of the ministry. It is a crying evil and shame, if not a positive sin. Men preach as if it were a canon with them to handle the grandest truths in the dullest manner; as if pulpit utterance needed a kind of paralysis to keep it staid and solemn! Preachers will give out these blessed verities of the Gospel in a dull and dreary way to empty pews, and attribute the emptiness to total depravity! Now " total depravity " has a good many things to father, but it isn't the father of empty pews. If such preachers would alter their mode of preaching, and self-denyingly go to work to learn some of the ways of effective public speech, in many cases they would gain an audience. A crowded house may not be a proof of successful preaching; but a church virtually empty—the emptiness conspicuous in great spots—is an unmistakable proof of something else! What avail is it to have an important message to deliver, if nobody can be prevailed on to hear it! And where was ever the man who knew how to say a good thing, and had it to say, who failed of getting ears to listen to his talk! Surely the neglect of this matter is without apology.

III.   The *acquisition* of a good delivery.

It is possible, beyond a doubt: except when the defect is so radical that it should keep one out of the ministry altogether.

(*a*)   If there were just one model, and it were requisite for every man to conform to that model in all particulars, then most men might despair of a good delivery.

To attempt to change the whole manner of one man into the whole manner of another, would inevitably result in that which is artificial and false.   Good delivery is simply impossible *on those terms.*

(*b*)   But effective delivery is consistent with the preservation of *the most marked and varied individuality*.   Indeed, a man to be eloquent, *must* be *himself*. This attempt at servile imitation, this gesturing and posturing and vocalizing, in calculated and mechanical compliance with certain arbitrary rules, has led to that insufferable affectation and mannerism by reason of which the Art of Delivery has been loaded with reproach.   With not one whit too much indignation, Cowper says,

> "In man or woman, but far most in man,
> And most of all in man that ministers
> At the altar, from my very soul I loathe
> All affectation."

Gladstone, in one of his London addresses, thus emphasized the value of a preacher's being true to his own individuality: " Let the preacher never forget the reality of the man; let him never become a conventional being; let him never adopt the mere slang of religion.   Let him retain his reality as a man."

And he goes so far in his advocacy of naturalness and reality in preaching that he cites in this same address some notable preachers of his time whose manner *in their cases* he would not have altered in the slightest degree—because it so unquestionably revealed and stamped their individuality.[1]

(c) But while *keeping individuality*, faults may be modified, infelicities of manner removed, the voice given flexibility and compass and purity of tone; and in this and other ways, a marked—in some cases a marvellous—improvement may be made in the delivery of the sermon.

IV. *The sources of power in effective delivery*, and the processes by which power may be secured.

[1] *From a London address by Gladstone:*

Dr. Newman, when I was an undergraduate at Oxford, was looked upon rather with prejudice as what is termed a Low Churchman, but was very much respected for his character and his known ability. He was then the vicar of St. Mary's at Oxford, and used to preach there. Without ostentation or effort, but by simple excellence, he was constantly drawing undergraduates more and more around him.

Dr. Newman's manner in the pulpit was one about which, if you considered it in its separate parts, you would arrive at very unsatisfactory conclusions. There was not very much change in the inflection of the voice; action there was none. His sermons were read, and his eyes were always on his book; and all that, you will say, is against efficiency in preaching. Yes, but you take the man as a whole, and there was a stamp and a seal about him; there was a solemn music and sweetness in the tone; there was a completeness in the figure taken altogether with the tone and with the manner which made even his delivery, such as I have described it, and though exclusively with written sermons, singularly attractive.

Well, now I will take a great jump, and go to another very notable and very admirable man—I mean Dr. Chalmers. I have heard Dr. Chalmers preach and lecture, and I think I have heard him speak. Well, now, being a man entirely of Scotch blood, I am very much attached to Scotland, and like even the Scotch accent, but not the Scotch

A full consideration of these would require an elaborate treatise. Perhaps the very elaborateness of some of our systems of elocution has defeated the end they had in view. Moreover, they have ignored some of the prime sources of power in delivery : and have been too exclusively devoted to technical rules, and to the physical instruments.

The problem is a mental as well as a physical one. On the *physical* side we have *posture, gesture*, and *voice*. Heed must be paid to these if we would have good delivery.

POSTURE

It should be erect, manly, with every part of the body free for instant response to every call of thought

accent of Dr. Chalmers. Undoubtedly, the accent of Dr. Chalmers in preaching and delivery was a considerable impediment. Notwithstanding that, it was all overborne by the power of the man in preaching—overborne by his power, which melted into harmony with all the adjuncts and incidents of the man as a whole; so much so that, although I would have said the accent of Dr. Chalmers was distasteful, yet in Dr. Chalmers himself I would not have it altered in the smallest degree.

I will take another example. I am afraid no one here recollects hearing Mr. Sheil. If anybody recollects him, there is nothing which I can appeal to; but if you will consider a tin kettle battered about from place to place, producing a succession of sounds as it is knocked first against one side and then against the other, that is really one of the nearest approximations that I can make to my remembrance of the voice of Mr. Sheil; and there, again, in anybody else I would not, if it had been in my choice, have liked to have listened to that voice, but in him I would not have changed it, for it was part of a most remarkable whole, and nobody ever felt it painful when listening to it. There was a peculiar character—a sort of half-wildness—in his aspect and delivery; and his whole figure, and his delivery and his voice, and his matter were all in such perfect keeping with one another that they formed a great parliamentary picture.

or feeling. This is the *normal* position to which the body should return after any temporary deviations demanded by action. There will thus be opportunity for the fullest play of diaphragm and lungs, the fullest expansion of the chest, and the fullest vocal expression. A lounging, lazy attitude in the pulpit is not only disrespectful to the audience, but it is wholly out of keeping with the character of one who has come to deliver a message from God. Social etiquette bars it out of the drawing-room. A sensitive conscience will bar it out of the pulpit. Especially should the diaphragm be kept free. Its muscles are what may be termed the roof of the stomach, or the floor of the lungs. These muscles are the pumping apparatus, by which breathing is made possible in swift, strong, inhaling or exhaling drafts of air. They are the secrets of vocal power. Therefore the diaphragm should be left free for the fullest play. Neither side nor front should be clamped or doubled up. Take heed to posture. Let it be erect, dignified, natural.

GESTURE

The attempt to follow rules here, in technical detail, would lead to insufferable affectation, and mannerism. But here, even more than in posture, there are some things unchallengeable, and which it is worth every minister's while to heed.

1. Gesture is an immense aid to expression and so to impression. In fact, and without dispute, impression is limited only by the power of expression. And the power of expression is almost limitless. Quintilian says, "Gesture is more impressive than the voice." No man gives vent to warm and animated

feelings with his mouth alone. Who has not seen a man talking from head to foot, through every possible medium of expression! If the preacher were representing Christ at the Judgment he surely would not need to shout the sentence of condemnation—but lifting his arm and pointing his finger, after a brief but emphatic pause, he would quietly say—" Depart." And the thunder would be in the gesture and the silence. Without doubt, fitting gesture emphasizes and intensifies vocal expression. Mark Antony wrought the passion of his hearers to the highest pitch, by *uncovering* and *counting* the wounds of Cæsar. And surely the persuasive power of Paul's speech before Agrippa was intensified, when he lifted up his chains and said, " Except these bonds ! " Whitefield's hands, stretched to heaven, his lifted eyes full of tears, his whole body quiveringly suppliant, gave his words tenfold power.

2. Gesture should be adapted to the individual. It cannot be rigidly prescribed. What would be fit in one person would be out of place in another. Chrysostom, the golden-mouthed, of Antioch and the fourth century, the prince of patristic orators, held his audience spellbound. It is said that every time he struck his left palm with his right forefinger, as he did when excited, some heart surrendered to the irresistible power of his eloquence. Massillon, the great French preacher, frequently joined his hands, sometimes crossed them on his breast, and occasionally even on his forehead, which is said to have had a surprising effect. Hooker, one of the foremost preachers of the Reformation age, stood stone still in the pulpit. Where his eye was fixed at the beginning of his

sermons, it was found fixed at the end. Bourdaloue, another French preacher of commanding eloquence, stood in a grand and noble posture, but kept his eyes closed.

Now suppose some tyro in preaching, hoping for like marvellous effects in the pulpit, should set himself to striking his left palm with his forefinger, like Chrysostom—or to crossing his hands on his forehead like Massillon, or to fixing his eye like Hooker, or to shutting his eyes like Bourdaloue. We see the absurdity—and we see the point. The mere copyist will be apt to make a sorry picture. *Gesture should be adapted to the individual.*

3. Hence all gesture should be the unpremeditated language of nature; *i. e.*, it should so be *at the time of actual delivery.* It should not be gone through with before the mirror, determined on there, and then carried by memory into the pulpit. Such gestures will inevitably be artificial. They are got up to order, made for the occasion, without the emotion or feeling to prompt them, and they will be like the body without the spirit—dead: as much unlike and beneath nature, as the forget-me-not of the shop is unlike and beneath the forget-me-not of the meadow.

Question 1. As fit gesture is so effective an aid to speech, *should not the preacher study and practice it?* Beyond all question. But the study should be on any other composition than the one he is about to deliver. Gesture, at the time it comes to birth, should be the outlet and expression of feeling—feeling that does not find its full vent in words. It cannot be this, if it is the result of attitudinizing before the glass. Looks and hands and postures should speak the unpremeditated language of nature.

Question 2. But are not the very faults of some men the language of nature? Certainly. But nature *all awry*. It needs to be made natural. Therefore, something should be done to lop off her excrescences, and to mend her awkwardness.

4. Suggestions for improvement in gesture.

(*a*) Let there be first a *careful study of the philosophy of gesture*—of that correspondence we see everywhere between emotion and action. Let the action of children be carefully noted. Watch them when they are at play. See how naturally they give expression to feeling. Hear a good speaker as often as possible, and study his manner and action; mark the effects; get at the secret of his power.

(*b*) Have an intelligent and sympathetic but absolutely faithful friend, hear you in private, and criticise and make suggestions as you proceed.

(*c*) Practice before the glass also. There one can see the awkwardness of his own movements. Nothing is more absolutely honest than a good mirror.

But *never use for either of these exercises the discourse about to be used in the pulpit*. These exercises are solely to *form the habit* of appropriate gesture. This drill and training and study are not to get one ready for next Sunday: but for all the Sundays. Leave the actual delivery of each discourse to the hour and the occasion. *Let the gestures make themselves*. They will take on fitness and naturalness, just as the speaker has been disciplined by long antecedent study and drill. The *study of delivery must not be in the process of delivery*, but antecedent to it, and in connection with other discourse. This process will ere long make it impossible for the speaker ever to use a welcoming gesture, when a forbidding or repellent action is demanded; or a gesture with the fist when it ought to be with the finger; or a broadside gesture when it ought to be a thrust as sharp as pointed steel.

(*d*) One thing more. Recall the delivery of the discourse in some quiet hour after the service. Doubtless some erroneous emphasis, some unnatural action, some strained tone of voice, will come to mind. If so, determine by the grace of God that it shall not occur again.

Avoid all mannerism—such as much adjustment of hair, much arrangement of coat, much handkerchief! Be natural. And if nature is awry, mend nature, by quiet processes of discipline.

And only do things that are *needful*. For example: do not let the arms go sprawling in the air in violent gesticulation like the arms of an old-fashioned windmill whether there be much breeze or little.

In fine, *all action in the pulpit should correspond to state of soul, and be the outgrowth and legitimate expression of thought and feeling.*

(*e*) Last of all, but possibly most of all, pay constant heed to the five great laws of gesture : the law of motion, of succession, of economy, of consistency, and of significance.

(1) The law of *motion*. *Passion* is eccentric—from the centre. Examples : "*Away* with him : *Away* with him." He *spurned* the bribe. "From my very soul I *loathe* all affectation."

Thought is accentric—*to* the centre. "As he was thinking—*thinking*—THINKING." And each word wraps the man more and more within himself. And he seems lost to everything, in the intensity of his meditation. Soliloquy is illustrative of this self-centering emphasis. The stage ranter will *shout*, "To be, or not to be—that's the question," just as if he were *making a speech*. The real actor will seem to be so absorbed in the meditation, as to be lost to all sense of an *audience*.

Love is concentric—*about* the centre. It is welcoming, enfolding, embracing, and the gesture will be in keeping with the emotion.

(2) The law of *succession*. The *eye* will speak first, flashing instantly the feeling of the heart. So look will precede gesture. And gesture will precede speech. Change that succession : and see what absurdities appear.

(3) The law of *economy*. What perspicuity, precision and vividness secure in speech, this law of economy secures in action. It corrects *waste* of power—not two hands where one would suffice ; not a gesture for every varying shade of thought. Not too frequent use of the same gesture. Don't be always sawing the air with the arms.

(4) The law of *consistency*. Eye, hand, face, voice should all *tell the same story, e. g.*, if the speaker is representing the lightning *flashing across the heavens*, the lightning will be in the *eye*, and in the swift-moving hand, as well as in the words.

(5) The law of *significance*. This is the demand for *adaptation* of gesture to thought and emotion.

Voice

The vital thing on the physical side of the problem of delivery is the voice. Success in the pulpit is simply impossible, unless the speaker makes himself heard, and well heard. If he or his hearers are under constant strain in the effort to speak or hear, the result will inevitably be a vacant pulpit, or vacant pews.

Cicero says, " For the effectiveness and glory of delivery, the voice doubtless holds the first place." The preacher is to speak every Sabbath. He must have a voice. The message, the mission, the occasion, the consequences, plead " trumpet-tongued " for a *good* voice.

This is not the place to go into minute details about the voice. The reader must again be referred to a good work on elocution, and a good drill master in voice culture. But some things cannot be out of place here.

1. Every voice may be improved. There is nothing more capable of improvement. Innumerable instances could be cited where the speaking power has been developed fourfold, by proper exercise.

What wonders have been done in its development in singing. What sweep and volume, what power and sweetness, have been given it by judicious training. The same painstaking effort would produce like marvels in giving the voice resonance and force and range for public speaking.

The Greeks had a distinct class of teachers called *vocists*, whose course of training in the use of the voice was most protracted and laborious. They had their pupils walk, run, climb, lie on their backs with weights

on their chests, declaiming meanwhile to strengthen
the voice. Cicero's eminence in vocal power, in that
most eloquent age of the world's history, would never
have been possible without painstaking drill. Patrick
Henry gave systematic daily study and practice to the
art of discourse.

2. Every voice has *a character*—an *individuality*,
just as its owner has. If a debate is going on in the
next room, and the door is ajar, and you are familiar
with the speakers, you can name each one as you
hear his voice, whether he entreats, commands, in-
structs, denounces, or threatens. The voice should be
built, just like the man—along the line of *individuality*. This shows the folly of all attempts at *imitation*
in the use of the voice.

3. The powers of the voice are length, breadth,
compass, stress, and flexibility. *Length* is ability to
continue the sound—to prolong it. *Breadth* is ability
to give it *volume*. *Compass* is ability to go over wide
range up and down the scale. It is essential to the
grandest effects; especially to the command of the
chest tones. Only this quality of voice can give that
variety of pitch and inflection which ever-varying
thought and feeling require. And, when used, it
makes dead monotony impossible. *Stress* is striking the vowels with a quick, sharp, explosive
utterance—Beecher called it "lunge" in preaching. It is a sort of trip-hammer stroke with lightning in it.

And the crowning glory of these powers of the
voice is *flexibility*, in which are the very life and soul
of expression. It is the power of passing with
ease from one key to another, through the whole

range of tone, from bottom to top, and from top to bottom.

4. Some practical hints in the use of the voice in the delivery of a sermon.

(*a*) *Begin quietly.* In all ordinary cases, use just enough voice to be heard in the farthest part of the room, *and no more.* If, at the outset, pitch and strength are taken that would fit the more animated parts of the discourse, two things are absolutely sure, —monotony in the pulpit and weariness in the pew. What possibility is there for climax, if one roars in the introduction !

(*b*) Make *frequent use of the conversational* tone. *Talk* to the audience. In all conversational passages, in quiet narration, in the persuasive and encouraging parts of the sermon—*talk.*

(*c*) For *sympathetic* effects, use the tones lying somewhere between the base and the tenor. It is the contralto voice that is oftenest full of tears. To draw men, avoid the loud tones and the declamatory style. Don't shout. Use the quiet and natural inflections of the voice. *Sympathy* wins. And sympathy is moist, tender, implies nearness.

(*d*) For denunciation, invective, triumph, anger and for inspirational effects, to rouse and fire an audience, use of course the loud tones—and more commonly the loud tones of the upper register. Ring the voice against the roof of the mouth, bring the mouth's resonant cavities into full use, if you would have the voice travel far. The sharp ringing tones will stir the blood, and send it tingling along its courses, as no bass tones will, however grand and deep. The tenor tones are more resonant and penetrating, as shown by the

way in which one calls another at long distance. The
voice then, naturally and inevitably, not only takes
louder tone, but higher key.

(*e*) Beware of sustained loudness. Keeping a high
pitch till everybody is tired, in pew and pulpit, will
certainly tend to do two things—diminish the
audience, and kill the preacher. Besides, if one is
loud and vehement where the sentiment is quiet, what
is he to do but to bawl and be boisterous when he
comes to passages demanding intense expression!
Great actors know how to *whisper* so as to be heard
by everybody in a large theatre. And indifferent
preachers know how to shout so as to be heard in-
telligibly by only a very small number even in a
moderately-sized church. Remember Hamlet's advice to the players: " Oh, it offends me to the soul
to hear a robustious periwig-pated fellow, tear a
passion to tatters, to very rags. . . . I would
have such a fellow whipped for o'erdoing termagant.
It out-Herods Herod! Pray you avoid it." Clearness, distinctness—not loudness—is the great requisite.
Don't try to be impassioned or emphatic throughout
the entire sermon. If nature thundered all the year
round, we wouldn't think thunder much of an affair,
after all.

(*f*) To *preserve* the voice, maintain wholesome
habits of eating and exercise; keep a good stomach;
dash cold water against the neck and chest daily;
pump the air from the very bottom of the lungs; and
use a natural and not an artificial or strained tone.

This finishes the strictly physical side of the problem
of delivery in public speech. But between this and
the strictly mental side, are some things not to be

classed with either, exclusively, yet of peculiar value in good delivery. They may be properly designated as

The Intermediate Sources of Power in Delivery

They are emphasis, oratorical style, the use of Anglo-Saxon words, and familiarity with the manuscript.

Emphasis

(a) How *defined.* It is taking a word or clause out of the level, and giving it a prominent place in the sentence.

(b) How *determined.* Emphasis as to its location must be determined solely by the meaning of the sentence. The substantive " thought-word " is the emphatic word in the opening sentence. The *new* thought added in each subsequent sentence, should have the emphasis. But take the sublime opening verse of the Gospel by John, and nine readers out of ten will misplace the emphasis in reading it, some at one point, some at another, but probably the whole nine will hit the third " was " *hard,* as if it were a far more important " was " than either of the others !

Perfect possession of the thought or feeling to be expressed is, therefore, indispensable to true emphasis. We cannot render what we do not understand. And a sentence may be so arranged that one can put the emphasis anywhere, without being sure he has the meaning of the writer. Here is the oft-quoted illustration of this point, showing what possibilities are wrapped up in a seemingly simple sentence : " Do you go to town to-day ?" Barring the preposition, one can get five distinct and perfectly proper meanings from that sentence, according to where he places the emphasis.[1]

(c) How is emphasis given? One way is by increased *stress of voice*. Some speakers use no other; the result of which is a heavy thump, thump, thump in their delivery, which soon ceases to have any of the effect of emphasis or expression, and becomes insufferably monotonous.

But there are other ways of emphasis, and they should be used to give variety to delivery. There is not only emphasis by force or stress of voice, but emphasis by prolongation of sound, by emphatic pause, by change of pitch, by passing from vocalizing to whispering ; which last, by Dr. Parker of London, as I once heard him, was tremendously effective.

ORATORICAL STYLE

This is another element of value in effective delivery. The sermon is *to be spoken*—it is for the *ear*. It has a single main object, and must secure it; one leading point, and must carry it. The sermon is an oration, not an essay. Preaching is the noblest kind of *oratory*. But to be that, it must be adapted to *delivery*. And the best delivery is impossible, without an oratorical style. No intricate and involved processes of reason-

---

[1] Everybody knows—*almost* everybody—that the italicized words in Scripture are not for emphasis. But an elocutionist was once insisting upon a certain emphasis in drilling one of our students in a Bible reading, and he supported his contention by pointing out that the word was in italics. I told the student he should have shied 1 Kings 13 : 13 (old version) at the elocutionist : "And the old man said to his sons, 'Saddle me the ass' : and they saddled *him*."

ing, no long and complicated sentences. The sense must be conveyed at once and through the ear, as the speaker proceeds. Therefore, break up sentences; simplify trains of thought; go straight for the object desired; put an *urgency* into style. Write for the ear, that you may speak to the heart. Guthrie *wrote aloud*, and committed in silence. He said writing aloud led to a spoken style.

USE OF ANGLO-SAXON WORDS

This is another contribution to effective pulpit speech. Preachers often lose power over their hearers rather by their phraseology than by their thought. They overload their thought with polysyllabics, and take its vim and point and pungent directness all away. Hear the Bible: "There is no work in the grave." Change this into phraseology common to many a pulpit: Religious activity cannot be exercised in the sepulchre. Hear one of our terse proverbs: "It's an ill wind that blows nobody any good." Now change this into the supposed elegance and stateliness of some preacher who is more bent on sounding words than sounding thought: It's a truly diseased gale that puffeth benefaction to nonentity. The difference is apparent—and so is the point. Oratorical style is for *carrying* things. It moves in straight lines. It is bent on its object.

FAMILIARITY WITH THE MANUSCRIPT

This is another condition of effective pulpit delivery, but, of course, only prevailing where the sermon is written. The preacher must ordinarily look at his hearers, and get their eye, and hold it, if he would inspire them, and catch, as well as give, inspiration. He must break loose from the fetters of a close and constant attention to his manuscript. His glances at the paper before him must be momentary, and to a degree unconscious. If this sub-process of taking in the sense through the eye is prominent, if there is a constant effort to pick out and pick up the written words, the faculties are so preoccupied that an ideal delivery is simply impossible. Hogarth represented this absurdity of pulpit discourse in one of his effective pictures, where a preacher is spelling out the sense of his manuscript to a snoring congregation. Two things are requisite to familiarity with a manuscript—*bold, plain handwriting*, and *previous study of the manuscript.*

But, after all, the hidings of power in delivery are not here—not in posture, gesture, or voice; not in emphasis, oratorical style, Anglo-Saxon words, or familiarity with the manuscript. All these are important. They are conditions of most effective delivery. Delivery is better, is always better, with them than without them. But they are not the sources of that power which is mightiest over the human heart in connection with public speech. Men differ widely in these respects, with equal power. They violate all laws of posture and gesture and emphasis and inflection, yet have power. Some of the greatest oratorical effects are produced by men with no external graces whatever. John B. Gough was all action. Jonathan Edwards had no action. Each in his way was a great mover of men. Dr. Wadsworth, of old Philadelphia fame, had a way of turning his arm in the air like a great screw, and it often seemed a way of getting an argument in, where a logical sledge-hammer would have been of no avail. While some men, like Arnot of Scotland, at the close of important periods, throw the whole body forward, as if to smite the audience with the butt end of an argument.

What are we to argue from all this? That gesture and posture and voice are of no account? By no means. But that there *may be* power in delivery in spite of great defects along the lines we have been discussing.

We all know that a good voice is a mighty aid to effective speech. But men of thin, shrill, feeble voices have had great power in delivery. John Randolph's squeaking voice did not prevent him, with his concentrated earnestness, from moving in narrow lines with great intensity. Robert Hall's voice was thin and feeble, but he was eloquent.

This only shows us that the hidings of chief power in delivery are deeper than we have yet gone. The problem, as we have said, is not simply physical. It is also *mental* and *spiritual*. On the physical side, we have *posture, gesture, voice*. Intermediate, not to be classed exclusively with the physical or mental, but touching and connected with each, are emphasis, oratorical style, use of Anglo–Saxon words, and familiarity with the manuscript.

The Mental and Spiritual Sources of Power in Delivery

These, of course, are at the very core of our inner life—the soul of our soul. They are—*ideas, feeling, earnestness, and authority*.

IDEAS

Ideas are at the basis of effective delivery. If right delivery is the fit and true expression of thought, then a powerful delivery is not the child of weak thoughts. Power in thought *tends* to power in expression. It does not always produce it. And sometimes, as we all know, there is considerable power in expression, with no power in thought: a great clatter with an empty cock-loft—vox, vox, vox, and nothing more. "Was he soond?" asked the Scotchman, referring to the preacher's orthodoxy. "Soond!" was the reply, "he was *a'* soond;" referring to the preacher's noise. Weak expression and strong ideas may sometimes go together; but they do not naturally go together. A great sermon may be poorly delivered, and a little sermon may be most effectively delivered. But it still remains true that ideas are at the foundation of power in speech. Ordinarily, a man must believe that there is power in his sermon—that he has something *worth* saying, if he would have power in delivery. And that he may have the belief, let him have the ideas. They are the best inspirers of effective and eloquent action. If there is nothing in the sermon, no action is needed except to turn over the leaves of the manuscript—and the sooner the better, for both audience and preacher. If there is nothing to stir the soul and rouse to action, then a vigorous sawing of the air, and a terrible amount and weight of emphasis, will only remind the hearers of that oft-quoted street cry of Constantinople: "*In the name of the Prophet—figs!*" A great noise and a great name—and only figs after all!

FEELING

This is fervency—emotional outplay. Call it what you will. But it is a thing to be laboured for and prayed for. It is a prodigious source of power in delivery. And no man can be a great preacher without having this element in greater or less degree "coming and going between himself and his hearers." Passion is eloquence. "Till thought becomes a passion, it hardly ever becomes a power." The same truth spoken by different men, or by the same man at different times, will often produce very different effects: and the difference, to a large degree, is traceable to the amount of feeling experienced and manifested in its delivery. Surely to feel the power of the thought is indispensable to the most effective delivery of it. Cicero says, "I never yet, I assure you, tried to excite sorrow or compassion when speaking before a court of judicature, but I myself was affected with the very same emotion that I wished to excite in the judges." The want of this accounts for the failure of some men of even unusual talents. Their words have no power, for they themselves have no feeling of their power in the time of delivery. The emotion does not flash in the eye, nor tremble on the lips, nor betray itself in the tones of the voice.

Humboldt described Schleiermacher's preaching as "the *personal, penetrating, kindling effusion of a feeling.*" And this was the preaching that "shook Germany from its spiritual lethargy." Let us mark and weigh these words of a great student and a great statesman, and seek to have all our preaching pervaded with this "personal, penetrating, kindling effusion."

Two or three questions here suggest themselves that should have heed.

1st. Is it ever justifiable to *assume* feeling? It is better to have it. But the use of the *language* of feeling may sometimes be the very means of getting it and increasing it. Certainly it is our duty to pray, even when we do not feel like praying. And the effort to pray may rouse the spirit of prayer. And certainly it is our duty to give, even though we have no pleasure in giving. But the giving on principle and from sense of duty will issue in the joy of giving. So, it would seem, a preacher might sometimes assume the language of feeling to waken feeling. We are creatures of association. And *association* has a deal to do with all our mental and spiritual moods.

But let the preacher beware of the *habit of feigning emotion*. Sooner or later it will certainly be detected, and the discovered sham will end all possibility of effective appeal.

It may be urged in reply to this that actors on the stage simulate feeling, and show the absurdity of this rule. But the objection does not hold—and for two reasons. First, the actor is known as *acting a part*—that's his business. Hence this feature of the case does not affect his moral character. Secondly, the *true* actors, who stir men's souls and fire their passions, or melt them to tears, are those who so throw themselves into the characters they represent, that for the time being they *really are* what *they seem to be*. Instead of being feigned, the action and passion are intensely real. Quintilian says, " I have often seen actors, both in tragedy and comedy, when they laid aside their masks, after going through some distressing scene, quit the stage in tears." Talma, a great tragedian of former years, is reported as saying, " It has been imagined that, in studying my parts, I place myself before a glass; I gesticulate—shake the ceiling of the room with my cries, and in the evening, on the stage, I utter intonations I learned in the morning: prepared inflections and sobs of which I know the number. It is an *error*," he adds. " *Reflection* is one of the greatest parts of my labour." It was thus he sought to absorb himself in his subject.

Now while this argument is a terrible arraignment of the theatre itself for putting plays upon the stage whose leading characters make it necessary for the actors to really be, for the time, creatures of passion and hate and intrigue and lust, where does it leave the minister who is feigning an emotion he does not feel, and playing a sorrow that is not in his heart! No, brethren, let us be sincere. The *habit of simulating emotion*, all shifts aside, *is sheer hypocrisy*.

But a second question is suggested by this discussion. Should feeling in the pulpit ever express itself *in tears?*

There should be no weeping for *effect*. *Frequent* weeping is a weakness. So is wholly *unrestrained* weeping, however infrequent. It may show the violence of the emotion, but it also reveals the weakness of the preacher. But deep emotion that *will break out*, yet which is partially suppressed, upon which the preacher has the curb and bit, will melt an audience as no *violent* manifestation can by any possibility. " Nothing approaches nearer to the ridiculous than an attempt to be affecting which is at the same time violent and unsuccessful."

But argument with true pathos means mastery. And the pathos of tears is sometimes of resistless power. Yes, weep in the pulpit, when the weeping is for real grief of heart. Paul wept many tears as he warned men. He told the Church, " even weeping," of some who were the enemies of the cross of Christ. Augustine wept, and moved his whole audience to tears by his weeping. But these occasions were rare, and only when he could not keep down the sobs of his great heart. *Artificial* tears will only lead men to repeat the question once asked concerning a preacher by an unaffected auditor, " What is the man crying about ? " And the question will only evoke the same answer that was given then : " If you were up there yourself, and had as little to say, perhaps you'd be crying too ! "

A third question is suggested by this discussion. *How is feeling to be cultivated ?*

(*a*) By the true actor's way, is one answer. By *reflection*—by *meditating*, bringing the occasion, the object, and the subject repeatedly before the mind, getting the total meaning and bearing of the subject, vitalizing one's self with it, until it pervades the whole nature. To fill the heart with heat, one must fill the brain with the fuel of ideas.

(*b*) Another way to cultivate feeling is by *always exercising* the sensibilities. Choose *proper objects* for quickening the sensibilities ; and then, when aroused, let them go out in action. A sluggish nature will grow tender and sensitive by this process.

(*c*) Still another way to cultivate feeling is not to be afraid of it, nor of manifesting it. Let the lips quiver with emotion, let the eyes suffuse with tears, if they will. The man who resolutely fights down feeling, who represses it, is putting out the fire with which he can best kindle and inflame souls, and move them upward and Godward. He is in the pulpit, called there of God to help men and women to a better life. If he fail of this, he would better get out of the pulpit. And to be afraid of enthusiasm, to stamp out all feeling, is the surest way to fail.

There is danger, of course, that the feeling may not always have wisest manifestation; but there is a hundredfold greater danger of deadening all feeling and emptying heart and soul of it, both of preacher and hearer, by its constant repression.

EARNESTNESS

Earnestness is closely akin to feeling—but it is something more. Its best and most enduring basis is a profound conviction of personal responsibility to God; and a deep and affectionate solicitude for men. Its specific conditions are the presence of some definite and worthy object, and an earnest desire to accomplish that object.

These may not always make delivery effective, but there can be no truly effective delivery without them. All mannerism, all affectation, and very much of awkwardness, is at once thrown off when a man is in dead earnest. And mannerism, affectation, and uncouthness are among the chief vices of delivery.

Earnestness will grow in the preacher with the growth of deep, personal interest in the work. Particular occasions and special themes will develop earnestness. Clear and vivid conception of divine truth

tends to produce it.   But, above all else, in order to
earnestness in delivery, it is essential that the preacher
should be an earnest man!   A prevailingly trifling
spirit, having its joke at every turn, taking no serious
view of life, having no heart-piercing convictions of
the illimitable need of men, whose unvarying bent is
to levity and frivolity even in the presence of the high
aims and solemn responsibilities and eternal verities
of the Word and work of God—such a spirit is fatal
to all earnestness, and therefore, in the end, to all real
pulpit and spiritual power.

   This is not antagonistic to *cheerfulness.*   Cheerfulness should certainly mark the preacher.   He, of all
men, should be no sombre-visaged, sepulchral witness
to the beauty and joy and blessedness of the gospel of
glad tidings.   But the lightness and levity and inordinate trifling of some men, is but a travesty or mock-
ery of Christian cheerfulness and gladsomeness, and as
"the crackling of thorns under a pot."   To be truly
in earnest the whole spirit must be imbued—the
preacher must be an earnest man.   And this is a chief
element of power in delivery.

AUTHORITY

   This is not that so-called "dignity of the pulpit,"
which mistakes solemn mien for weight of character,
and which puts human arrogance in place of divine
sanction.   But it comes from a vivid sense of being
God's messenger, and speaking in the name of God the
things of God.

   Jesus spake "with authority."   It became Him.
And it becomes every man standing in His stead.   Paul

urges Titus to exhort and rebuke with all *authority*.
Not that the *person* of the preacher is anything ; but
that the *message* is *everything*.

And if the preacher can say, as he ought to say,
" That which we have heard, which we have seen with
our eyes, which we have looked upon, and our hands
have handled, declare we unto you ; "—in other words,
if he can speak from the experienced power of the
great truths with which he deals, happy is he, and
mighty is he. He cannot fail of power in public
speech.

Dante wrote and looked as if he had been in hell.
The secret of Edwards' power was here. He looked
and spoke as in the presence of God, and with a
weighty sense of the matter delivered. There was
nothing else whatever in his delivery to attract attention. But this was everything. Beecher has essentially this idea. He says, " The real root and secret
of power in the pulpit, is the preaching of the invisible
God to the people as an ever-present God." Surely
this will ever be, dynamically, superior to all else in
the delivery of sacred discourse. Hence the need of
the constant cultivation of a more and more vivid and
abiding sense of the divine realities of the gospel
message.

1. From all this it follows, first, that delivery is a
spiritual work, for which there is needed the constant
help of the Spirit of God. His aid is as essential in the
utterance of the preacher's message as in its composition. We degrade it, pervert it, rob it of all its distinctive and peculiar character, by ignoring the Holy
Spirit's agency. He must enter into the actual labour
of the public *presentation* of the truth, even as he en-

ters into the actual labour of the private *preparation* of the truth.

2. It follows, secondly, that the preacher should prepare for composition not only, but for delivery, by prayer. He should go to the secret place of prayer always, and be alone with God awhile, before going to the pulpit. He should pray that the Holy Spirit may move him to appropriate gesture and tone of voice, and so fill him with his theme and his object, that every part of the varied and subtle instrumentality of expression shall be fitted for the best and most effective utterance of the truth of God.

The peculiar vigour and vitality of Luther did not come simply, nor chiefly, from his anchorage in doctrine; but from his constant, direct, cherished, intimate intercourse with God. "To have prayed well is to have studied well," was one of his favourite maxims. But he proved that it was as applicable to delivery, as to study.

We all know there is a certain something in spiritual baptism which tells in posture and gesture and voice. It does not make men alike in their physical or mental qualities, but it puts a certain something into their delivery that spells power. *If the closet is a throne, the pulpit will be.*

XXV

THE IDEAL SERMON

SYLLABUS

If, of all men, the man in the ministry should have "ideals," and if the chief instrument in the ministry is the *sermon*, it is highly important that the minister should frame for himself a clear conception of the *ideal sermon*.

1. It has been defined, "The sermon that does the business." But this is no definition. It is simply saying the ideal sermon is the successful sermon. And the preacher must wait until next Sunday to find out whether it is ideal or not. The whole thing is *guess* work until the sermon is delivered.

Moreover, the sermon may be crowded with bad grammar, bad logic, bad exegesis. If God uses it, presto ! the sermon is ideal !

Moreover again: Where does this definition put some of Christ's preaching ? It certainly sometimes failed to do the business.

And still again : An ideal surgeon, with an old jack-knife, performs a successful surgical operation. Is the jack-knife thereby made ideal?

2. Nor does enumerating certain good qualities define an ideal sermon, unless those qualities are *indispensable* to a sermon. We may say an ideal sermon is logical, or illustrative, and these are good qualities, but a sermon may be ideal, without either a process of logic, or an illustration. Things not *vital* to a sermon should not appear in an ideal definition.

An ideal sermon is just what a sermon is, but *something more*. Put that "something more" into our definition of the sermon, and we have the definition of the ideal sermon.

So we define the ideal sermon, a formal religious discourse, founded on the Word of God, designed to save men, *and perfect in its adaptation thereto.*

This perfect adaptation involves four departmental characteristics, vital to ideal completeness.

1. *Perfect verbal form*, secured by *perspicuity, precision, energy,* and *beauty* of style.

2. *Climax.* Literally, a *ladder*—a way of ascent—a slope upward ; a *growth*—a progress—the sign and proof of life in speech.

What makes climax ? *Unity, order, movement.*

3. Perfect method of approach to the hearer. *Adaptation, adaptation.*

4. Born of the Spirit of God. The ideal sermon is not merely a human, but a divine-human product.

Two things would thus be made sure to the sermon. It would be true to the *truth* and true to the *man*.

The preacher has thus made two apostolic studies. He has studied "to show himself approved unto God"—and he has studied "how rightly to divide the word of truth. This means absolute surrender to the law of adaptation; and this means *the ideal sermon.*

XXV

THE IDEAL SERMON

WE open this chapter in the discussion of the ideal ministry with the very words with which we opened the first chapter. If our discussion has been worth anything, it has made the thought stand out with positive distinctness and emphasis that " of all men, the man in the ministry should have ideals." The ideal " consecration," the ideal " life," the ideal " stewardship," the ideal "Church ; " he can tolerate nothing less than these. They are set before him by his Lord.

Moreover, we trust it has been made clear that for the attainment of these God-appointed ideals, one of the God-appointed means, and the chief, is the preaching of the Word. Hence, as the chief *instrument* in this business of preaching is the sermon, the *ideal* sermon comes to supreme place in any comprehensive thought of the instruments to be employed in making Christ's kingdom come. Yet of those whose life business it is to preach the Gospel, how many have definitely set before their minds as a thing to be striven for, and more and more fully realized week by week, *their idea of an ideal sermon?* If, in any circle of clergymen, a dozen were asked to define an ideal sermon, would not the answer be likely to furnish some surprises of hazy indefiniteness ? Here are both the reason for this chapter and the inspiration of it. It is an effort to take the ideal sermon out of the clouds, and to give it flesh and blood, so that it shall stand out as a thing forever to be aimed at, and, if possible, realized, in holding forth the Word of life.

Comprehensively, as we have already seen, there are just two things to be done by the preaching of the Gospel : to make disciples, and then to make these disciples Christlike.   This is Christ's own unchangeable and unchallengeable commission.[1]   Every evangelical Confession of Faith embodies essentially these two ideas.   The Westminster Confession thus puts it : " God hath given the ministry for the gathering and perfecting of the saints in this life, to the end of the world." [2]

There it is—the twofold work; gathering and perfecting, the work of rescue and the work of transformation ; winning over an old creature in sin to be a new creature in Christ, and then changing that new creature, building it up into the divine image from glory to glory until it is " set before the presence of God's glory without blemish in exceeding joy."   This is the totality of the work of an ideal gospel ministry.   This is all a sermon should be made to do. This is all a sermon can do.

And it is just because this is the definite, conspicuous, indispensable business of the sermon, that the ideal sermon has been defined *the sermon that does the business;* the explicit business being to bring a soul to Christ or to make a soul more like Christ.   In other words, the ideal sermon is the successful sermon.   But this is no definition.   What

[1] Matthew 28 : 19–20.
[2] Confession of Faith, Chap. 25, Sec. IV.

makes it succeed? If you say because it is ideal—
there you have the vicious circle. The ideal sermon
is the successful sermon, and the successful sermon is
the ideal sermon. In a recent symposium on the
ideal sermon, the *effects* of the sermon, in one form or
another, were cited in every one of the papers presented, in proof, or lack of proof, of the sermon's
ideality. Whereas we all know that a sermon may be
bad in structure, faulty in logic, extravagant in
rhetoric and crude in thought, and yet be winged of
God to smite a sinner between the joints of the harness.

That is to say, a sermon may be to the last degree
faulty, and yet because God makes it effective, it is
an ideal sermon! But this plays sad havoc with
reason and common sense, and Holy Scripture. It
puts the ideality of the sermon outside the sermon, not
inside. It sets no *standard* before the young preacher
making his first venture. Yes, you say—"*doing the
business*" is the standard. But how is the preacher to
know that it will do the business? What is he to put
into it to fit it to do the business? Concerning this,
the ideal definition is silent. It answers not a word.
In other words, with this definition, ideal sermonic
work is pure guesswork, *until the sermon is delivered!*

Moreover, this idea that the ideal sermon is the sermon that does the business, is out of gear with the law
of *faith and works*. Faith without *works* is dead, we
all know. Now here is a sermon faulty in grammar, in
style, in logic, in exegesis. We are not only to trust
in God, but to *keep our powder dry*. Bad style, bad
grammar, bad logic, bad exegesis are *wet powder*.
God may use it—but His use of it doesn't make wet

powder the ideal thing in starting a conflagration, or
firing a congregation.

No, we are not quite ready yet to say, "Good-bye
to homiletics and the art of sacred discourse," and to
throw all laws of effective sermonizing to the winds.
Unity, *order*, and *movement*, the three prime requisites
of all mighty public speech elsewhere, are still the
dominant forces in constructive sermonizing. A
sermon cannot have one theme or a dozen themes, one
object or a dozen objects, or no object at all, and yet
be an ideal sermon.

God's Word says, "*Study* to show thyself approved
unto God, a workman unshamed by his work." This
command means, if it means anything, that God's ministers are to be *wise* in winning souls. They are to
make this business of soul-winning a *study*. They are
to study the law of adaptation ; and to study the hearts
and lives of the people to whom they preach : and to
study the Scriptures for the fittest word to meet the
ever-changing need. But of what use is all this if the
ideal sermon is simply the sermon that does the business ? We may hand out any old ramshack of a
sermon to God; and if God uses it, *presto !* the sermon is ideal ! Moreover, if *doing the business* in
preaching is the proof of ideality, where does it put
some of *Christ's* preaching ? Take the rich young
man who, after hearing Christ, went away sorrowful,
for he had great possessions. Take the Pharisees who
went away from Him gnashing their teeth. Hear
Christ's own sad lament over Jerusalem : "How oft
would I have gathered you and ye would not !"
Either His preaching on these occasions was not ideal,
or it plays the mischief with the notion that an ideal

sermon is the sermon that does the business. Let us understand once for all, that God's use of an instrument does not make that instrument ideal. A surgeon camping out in the wilderness, or present at a railway accident, without his tools, may flip out a jack-knife, and perform successfully a surgical operation. Yet would that make the jack-knife an ideal instrument in surgery? Say that to the surgeon, and he would laugh at you for your folly. But wasn't it an ideal instrument *in the circumstances?* No, indeed. It was the only *possible* instrument, and it did the business. But that did not transform a clumsy old jack-knife into an ideal surgical instrument. And what about the surgeon? It was the *ideal surgeon* that did the business. So God, in His *spiritual* surgery, sometimes takes a very poor sermonic instrument, and does great work with it; yet the sermon may be only a poor old jack-knife after all.

Moody's bad grammar and bald form and mixed metaphors and fearful leaps of logic did not hinder his *sermons* from doing a great deal of business for God, nor hinder *him* from being a great winner of souls. Yet one would hardly call " bad grammar," and " mixed metaphor " and " bald form " and " sad leaps of logic," ideal points in a sermon ; nor would one call any sermon " ideal " that was crowded with these points.

No. Very rude may be the *instrument*. But if God plays on it, out will come some heavenly music. We are not to get at the secret of an ideal sermon by noting and studying what any particular sermon *has done*. The man behind the gun has a good deal to do with the execution of the gun. The man behind the sermon is a tremendous factor in the problem of ser-

monic effectiveness.   And the Holy Spirit is never to be
forgotten in any case.   He can make a bird in the air,
or a half-idiot, or a little child tell the matter, to the
conquering of the worst situation and the softening of
the hardest heart.

On the other hand, the instrument may be perfect,
but the man handling it unfit.   Everything may be
right in the sermon, yet something may be so wrong
in the sermonizer that God will not bless it to the
hearers' souls.   And, still again, everything may be
right in both the sermon and the sermonizer, and yet
an Achan in the camp of Israel may stay the doing of
the King's business.   Moreover, God Himself tells us
He has chosen " weak," " foolish " and " despised "
things, yea, " things that are not," to bring to nought
" things that are."   Why ?   " That no flesh should
glory before God ! "   So we find Him sometimes withholding His blessing from the really eloquent and
scholarly, and naturally convincing discourse, and
making mightily effective the crude and stammering
speech of some unlearned and lowly preacher of the
Word—thus putting the treasure in a very " earthen
vessel," that " the exceeding greatness of the power
may be of God, and not from ourselves."

What then ?   Are we to infer that it makes no difference what kind of sermonic instrument we use in
preaching, so long as it is God's truth we preach ?   By
no manner of means.   Results are not arbitrary in this
business of soul-saving any more than they are arbitrary in any other business.   God is not always at war
with the nature of things.   Grace is not a perpetual
challenge of reason and common sense.   Trust in God
will not avail us much, if we don't keep our powder

dry. Let us hear again the divine injunction, "Give diligence to present thyself approved unto God, a workman that needeth not to be ashamed, handling aright the word of truth." That's the divine order. It is presumption, and not trust, that counts on any old blunderbuss to do execution for God.

But if we are not to define the ideal sermon as one that does the business, we are no nearer exact definition by enumerating certain specific qualities that may be good in themselves, but that are not indispensable to an ideal standard.

For example, we may say that the ideal sermon will be *logical*—logical being here used in the sense of proving a thing to be true. But whether the sermon is logical or not, will depend altogether on whether logic is wanted in the sermon. One point of an ideal sermon would be its logic, if the object of the sermon were demonstration. But if the object of the sermon were not demonstration, the logic would be good for nothing. In other words, logic in a sermon is a *dispensable* element. Some of the best sermons ever written have been without the slightest trace of logical process. They proved nothing. They simply exhibited truth—made it plain by clear statement and apt illustration.

Again : we may say that the ideal sermon will be marked by illustrations. But some of the mightiest and most inherently and naturally effective sermons have not had a single illustration from start to finish. They have been simply tracks of irresistible logic, fitted to convince the sinner, and so bring him to Christ ; or fitted to convince the believer, and so anchor him immovably in some truth of God.

Clearly the things that are not *vital* to an ideal sermon should not appear in the definition.

But what is a sermon? We need to have in mind precisely what a sermon is, before we can accurately define the ideal sermon. We have already defined the sermon as *a formal religious discourse founded on the Word of God and designed to save men.*

With this definition before us, we are surely at the door of the definition of an ideal sermon. An *ideal* sermon is just what a sermon is, but *something more.* For a sermon may answer to our ideal definition, and yet it may violate every known law of structure, and be ungrammatical, involved in style, jumbled in thought, and simply chaotic in its handling of material.

Therefore, into the definition of the sermon that distinctly separates it from all other discourse we must put the words that make the ordinary sermon an ideal sermon.

So we define the ideal sermon as a formal religious discourse founded on the Word of God, designed to save men and *perfect in its adaptation thereto.*

That is to say : it must be perfectly *adapted* to do the thing for which every sermon should be prepared, viz., to bring a sinner to Christ, or to make him more like Christ ; to save him from the penalty of sin, or from the pollution and power of sin. In either case, and in any case, to move his will and to move it Godward. If every sermon ought to be constructed that some man or men may be reconstructed—if every true sermon must mean, in its intent and aim, changed hearts and lives, then *perfect adaptation to do that thing* is the all in all of an ideal sermon. It then becomes an instrument without a flaw, a word exactly fitted to meet a specific definite need.

Is such a sermon possible? Not in the present limitations of the human mind. But approximations to it are the duty and the privilege of every man who preaches.

Let us see now if we can make this ideal sermon stand out before us as a distinct object of thought. Let us try to give it clear and positive characteristics by which it may be known—characteristics that shall lift it out of the level of the common, and make it a thing to be prayed for, and toiled for, while God gives us the power of utterance.

Manifestly, minute details here would only bewilder us. We want generic qualities, comprehensive of all excellencies, and covering groups of qualities. There are four departmental characteristics that go to make up the ideal sermon, and that must be present in every sermon laying any claim to ideal completeness. The first concerns the outward verbal form of the sermon; the second the inner structure of the sermon; the third the hearer it seeks to reach and save; and the fourth, the agency of the Holy Spirit in the sermonic process.

The first departmental characteristic of the ideal sermon is *perfect verbal form*. It must make *its meaning stare the hearer in the face*. In other words, the style will be so clear and vivid and energetic that it will let the hearer see the thought just as the thinker thinks it. The style of the sermon will have the quality of being seen through; that is, *perspicuity;* and the quality of definite, exact outline; that is, *precision;* and the quality that gives momentum to thought and makes it impinge; that is, *energy;* and

the quality that clothes thought with rhetorical at-
tractiveness ; that is *beauty*.   These are the elements,
perspicuity, precision, energy, and beauty, constituting
that perfection of style which does for the thoughts
what a pure atmosphere does for the stars—makes
them look at you with unwonted depth and breadth
of meaning, as if all their glory were in their eyes and
struggling for expression.

If the preacher would know whether the sermon
prepared for next Sunday had been given this ideal
verbal form, he can easily test the matter by asking
himself this question : If I were in the pew, with just
the mental grasp and culture of the ordinary hearer,
listening to this sermon, would its meaning from start
to finish be perfectly clear to me ? We fancy, this
test honestly applied, would transform many a sermon,
break up many a long sentence, drop out some big
words, and make people wonder what had happened
to the sermonizer !

A second vital and departmental characteristic of
the ideal sermon is *climax*.

What is climax ?   Literally, a ladder.   And a
ladder is for climbing.   It is nothing unless a way
upward ; a way of ascent.   Climax, in the sermon, is
just this : a way of ascent, a slope upward to some
higher and better thing.   Therefore, from introduction
to conclusion, the sermon must be a growth, a progress,
a gathering force, having possible recessions, like the
mighty river, but thereby only increasing in momentum
and inspiring power as it presses on.   This is real
climax—the sign and proof of life in speech, the
mighty thing that, under God, moves and sways and
uplifts and conquers.   It marks every great sermon.

The true preacher must therefore rid himself of the idea—the very common and erroneous idea—that somewhere in his sermon he is to reach his climax; *i. e.*, his highest, most impressive, point. This is a true meaning of the word climax; but a derived and secondary meaning. The primary and vital meaning of the word is that which makes the entire sermon a growing, cumulative force. So the sermon itself must be a climax; *i. e.*, an ascending ladder. And just as a man reaches a ladder for ascent when his foot touches the lowest round, so a preacher reaches his climax *when he begins his sermon!* And onward and upward he passes to the height of his climax, as with increasing intensity of earnestness and power of pathos he commands thought and expression for final victory.

Now, what makes climax? What are the secrets of it, that enter into it, contribute to it, and render it possible—that constitute the attending and animating genius of climax? They are the three cardinal, structural qualities of the sermon—*unity, order*, and *movement*.

Sermonic *unity* demands a single specific theme, developed for the exclusive accomplishment of a specific definite object, *i. e.*, it demands a *subject*, an *object*, and a *plan*.

Sermonic *order* demands that the sermon say just now what ought just now to be said; *i. e.*, materials all marshalled and arranged for the best effect.

Sermonic *movement* demands unbroken continuity and persistent progress; *i. e.*, not a halt, nor an aside, from start to finish.

We venture to affirm there is nothing in the entire

field of homiletic discussion that would so contribute
to pulpit efficiency as the constant and masterful command of these structural qualities of sacred discourse.
Humanly speaking, here lie the chief secrets of pulpit
power.   To have a single purpose dominate through
the entire sermon from the first word of introduction
to the final word of appeal; to have order reign
throughout—every thought and illustration, every incident and argument marshalled to its place; and to
have a constant flow—a steady onward movement in
the sermon, bearing resistlessly to the goal—these
three are vital to climax.   And climax is one of the
shining glories, as well as one of the essential elements, of the ideal sermon.   Instruction, only to persuade thereby; truth, only to transform thereby;
æsthetic and homiletic, only and evermore to move
the will, so that it shall be more and more like the
will of God—this is the essential function, as it is the
lofty ideal, of all true sermonizing.   A new creature
in Christ Jesus is its first and last and supreme intent.
And this is redemption's intent.   And thus the sublime purpose of God's whole plan of salvation crowds
itself into every true sermon, and gets its consummate
expression in the ideal sermon.

A third departmental characteristic of the ideal
sermon is *a perfect method of approach to the hearers
it is seeking to reach and save.*   The sermon must not
only be true to the truth it preaches, and to the man
that preaches it, but suited in its matter and method
to the man or men for whom it is especially designed.

As we have seen, in our discussion of the law of
adaptation,[1] men take in truth in different forms and
by different avenues or sides of their minds.   Some are

[1] P. 164.

unemotional. They do not like melting moods, or pathetic appeals. They delight in argument. And the less it is accompanied with emotional outplay, the better they like it. Others are full of pathos ; easily touched and moved. Truth comes to them through their emotions. They are seldom, if ever, reached in any other way. Some are, naturally, born battering rams, bristling with controversy. You will not conciliate a wild bull by flaunting a red flag in his face. Neither will you conciliate a lover of hot debate, by flinging to the breeze a logical battle flag. Some are stolid, and need heroic treatment. They will bear the thunderings of a big Sinai. On the other hand, those of excitable temperament, timid, shrinking, sensitive natures, cannot bear and do not need the thundering of any Sinai. It would rouse a fearful tempest in them, or crush all hope and heart out of them. Again, some delight in the play of the imagination : in the artistic touch of fancy. Now to insist on feeding such minds with bare syllogisms, as one would set a system of theological truth before an examining committee, would be like reducing " Paradise Lost " to a series of propositions in Euclid for the purpose of exhibiting its beauties to a lover of poetic forms.

Hence it follows that the ideal sermon to one hearer may not be the ideal sermon to another hearer. *Adaptation !* ADAPTATION ! A careful study of this word in its relation to pulpit and pew might reveal a multitude of homiletic sins. How it would show the preacher who prides himself on his logic, and who comes to his pulpit with a battering-ram of argument every Sabbath, that there are those in the pews who care nothing for his logic, and who are no more moved by it than they would be by a logarithm. And how

it would show the preacher who is forever letting his
soul "take wings and fly " in the joy and abandon of
a vigorous imagination, that there are plain matter-of-
fact hearers before him who are wondering what in
the world he is talking about. And how it would
show the preacher who is forever making a downy
pillow of the Gospel and shying it at people week by
week, that there are possibly listening hearers in his
congregation, whether from Millionnaire Avenue or
Little Hell, whose least desire or need is a gospel
lullaby.

A fourth departmental characteristic of the ideal
sermon is that it be *born of the Spirit of God*. If its
subject-matter is Holy Scripture, and if its object is salvation from sin, it is perfectly obvious that the making
of sermons is a business with which the Holy Spirit
must have vital connection. For to interpret the
Word of God, and to make men like God is the Holy
Spirit's exclusive office. And if God has determined
by the foolishness of preaching to save men, the sermonic instrument must be of the Spirit's fashioning,
to be best fitted to its end.

The ideal sermon is, therefore, not merely a human,
but a divine-human product. It is the truth of God
through human personality. And the Spirit of God
should sovereignly preside in its construction and use
from beginning to end : from the selection of the text
down through all the process of sermonic development, the choice of a theme, the formation of a plan,
and the collection and arrangement of materials, to
the final application of the truth to the hearer's heart.
We think too exclusively of the Holy Spirit's agency
at the contact of the sermon with the hearer's mind

and conscience in the public assembly. He should be an invoked and expected co-worker throughout the whole process of selection, analysis, composition, and delivery.

Two things would be made sure to the sermon thus born of the Spirit of God. First, it would be *true to the truth*. The Holy Spirit would see to it that it reflected God's mind, and kept the balances of Holy Scripture throughout all the path of discussion and appeal. By this is not meant absolute infallibility; but that general guidance which would secure the proportions and relations and significance of truth, so that truth should not suffer by human handling, nor mar the image of God being wrought out by it in the soul of the hearer. The presence and gracious guidance of the Holy Spirit, humbly and earnestly sought at every step of the sermonic way, would surely keep the sermon true to the truth.

But it would also be *true to the man*. For the Holy Spirit always preserves and honours the individuality of those through whom He speaks. Even infallible inspiration made no copyists. Paul never wrote like Peter; nor Peter like John; nor John like Isaiah.

The ideal sermon, therefore, born of the Spirit of God, will be stamped through and through with the individuality of its human author, and yet be kept utterly true to God's Word. The unwarped truth and the unwarped soul will go together. The person will be in the message, and the message will be in the person—divine truth through human personality; neither of them twisted or bent so as to be out of gear with the Book or the man.

Does not this group all that is needful to make the ideal sermon stand out before us as a distinct object of thought—a thing to be grasped, to be taken out of the clouds, and to be given embodiment in sermonic flesh and blood ? Here are the four indispensable marks of the ideal sermon : (1) It will let the hearer see the thought just as the thinker thinks it ; being stamped all through with perspicuity, precision, energy, and rhetorical beauty of style. (2) It will be adapted to reach the hearer with increasing power as it proceeds, being pervaded by the animating genius of climax. (3) It will be an actual adjustment each week to the ever-changing condition of the soul the preacher is seeking to reach and save. (4) And so it will knock at the door that is most likely to open to the truth ; whether the door of reason, or the door of imagination, or the door of conscience, or the door of the affectional nature, or the door of plain, straightforward, practical common sense.

And this suggests the answer to the charge that ideal sermonizing would allow no variety in preaching. If we all build after a certain model, it is asked, what possible room can there be for variety ? The answer is that the themes discussed, the objects aimed at, the condition of the hearers, all make room and demand for a large variety. Then also, tracks of resistless logic, wealth of imagination, appeals to the heart, to the conscience, to the judgment ; and plain, homely but mighty matters of fact—all these make possible an almost limitless variety. But however sermons may differ in these respects, every *ideal* sermon will have—*must* have, perfect verbal form, perfect climax, perfect method of approach to the hearers aimed at,

and the blessed cooperating agency of the Holy
Spirit. And what possible call or justification can
there be for variety that is secured only by bad
verbal form, or by anti-climax, or by unfit approach,
or by lack of the Holy Spirit's presence and guidance!

"Let us hear the conclusion of the whole matter."
Before the preacher begins his week's sermonic work,
before he starts on the search of a theme or a text,
should he not, by a distinct and positive act of surrender, submit himself to God, that God may lead him
through the whole process of preparation? Let him
make it his daily business to take God into the business,
that each sermon may be in a true and blessed sense
divinely born—the product, through the human spirit,
of the Spirit of God. Then let him gather and organize
his materials, fit each to each, make each point a step
to higher vantage and increasing force, and allow no
alluring by-path to tempt him to the least abandon-
ment of his single theme and his exalted purpose; so
that the sermon shall grow in power as it proceeds.
Then let him give his thought embodiment in words
that shall clearly and vividly and mightily tell his
thought.

He has thus made two apostolic studies. He has
studied "to show himself approved unto God," and he
has studied how "rightly to divide the word of truth."
He has fitted the arrow for its flight. God only can
send it home. Hear the greatest of human preachers:
"I planted, Apollos watered. God gave the increase.
So then, neither is he that planteth anything, neither
he that watereth, but God that gave the increase."
Be willing, O man of God, to become all things to all

men, that you may by all means save some. This means absolute surrender to the law of adaptation. And this means

The Ideal Sermon.

XXVI

THE CRUCIAL QUESTION IN APPLIED THE-OLOGY: WHY ARE NOT MORE SOULS BROUGHT TO CHRIST BY THE SERMON?

SYLLABUS

Question distinctly for the preacher. Broadly speaking there are only two kinds of sermons; soul-rescuing, and soul-building. And the challenging question is, Why are not more souls brought to Christ by the sermons ?

1. Does the reason lie in the divine *purpose ?*
2. Is it to be found in the present conditions of society ?
3. Is it because evangelistic preaching is thought to be not quite up to the level of the *teaching* work of the ministry ?

The characterizing features of a sermon that is after a soul.

1. Such a sermon is come, like the Master, to call a *sinner* to repentance.
2. Such a sermon is come, like the Master, to seek and save *the lost*.
3. Such a sermon has no "*to-morrow*" in it.'
4. Such a sermon is not a bow drawn at a venture. It means singleness of aim, knowledge of the actual human nature and adaptation thereto.
5. Such a sermon is filled with compassion.

Practical test applied to the sermon already preached.

The last command of the Master.

XXVI

THE CRUCIAL QUESTION IN APPLIED THE-
OLOGY: WHY ARE NOT MORE SOULS
BROUGHT TO CHRIST BY THE SERMON?

THIS question is distinctly and exclusively for the preacher. Whatever may be true as to the responsibility of the Church, or of any organized agency in the Church, or of any individual member of the Church, for the paucity of results in the effort to bring the world to Christ, this present inquiry is meant only for the man who is set apart to preach the Gospel; and it is meant for him only as a maker and deliverer of sermons. If each minister were to ask, Why are not *my sermons* bringing more souls to Christ, the question would take its most personal and practical form.

Broadly speaking, and in the sense of official Christian ambassadorship, there are only two kinds of preaching; soul-rescuing preaching and soul-building preaching—or sermons designed and adapted to win men to Christ, and sermons designed and adapted to make men like Christ after they have been won to Him. Each may sometimes do the other's work. Preaching addressed exclusively to Christians, may win an unbeliever; and preaching to the impenitent may prove very manna from heaven to some child of God. But each has its normal sphere of operation, and is likely to do its business in that sphere.

Why are not more souls brought to Christ by the sermon ?

1.   Does the reason *lie in the divine purpose?*   This view is not without its advocates.   More souls are not saved, it has been said, because more souls have not been elected to be saved.

But this places the responsibility of paucity of results in the ministry on God!   It makes *wisdom* in winning souls impossible.   It puts arbitrariness in the place of voluntariness.   It takes the heart out of Christ's word, " Go ye and compel them to come in." It clears every minister's skirts now and forever from the blood of souls.

Let us at once and to the fullest degree recognize, accept, and glory in the divine sovereignty.   God is sovereign.   He has ordained whatsoever comes to pass.   But He is sovereign in the midst of voluntary and responsible human agencies, and through them. His sovereignty does not make a Christian ambassador an automaton, nor the people to whom he preaches, lumps of putty !   God is sovereign.   But He is not always at war with the nature of things.   And the sermon fitted under God to do a specific thing is the sermon that is likely under God to do that specific thing.

When we have furnished the absolutely fittest sermonic instrument to do this work of rescue, and have furnished it often enough to show that unsaved souls lie as a burden on our hearts, and that we are ever trying to make disciples of them in obedience to Christ's last command ; when we have exhausted the possibilities of faith and prayer, and have so taken Christ with us into the study to prepare the sermon for rescue, and have so taken Christ with us into the pulpit to preach the sermon for rescue, that every demand of faith and love and devotion and consecration has been met— *then* we may fall back on the sovereignty of God and say, as Christ Himself once said in facing this same mystery, "Even so, Father, for so it seemeth good in Thy sight." But *until* all this has been done, what right have we to fly to God's sovereignty as a shelter for our inefficiency ? "Fear not," said God to Paul, when this great winner of souls was appalled by the obstacles before him, "Fear not, I have much people in this city." Suppose God had said, "Fear not ; the number of people to be saved in this city is fixed, and cannot be either increased or diminished by any effort whatsoever," would that have been a stimulant to this burdened soul ? If it is doctrinally sound to say, "Work out your own salvation with fear and trembling, *for* it is God that worketh in you to will and to work," then it is doctrinally sound to say, "Work out the salvation of others with fear and trembling, *for* it is God that worketh *through* you both to will and to work." In other words, that God is sovereign is a stimulant to all-abounding activity in soul-winning, and never, *never* a soothing salve to cover our failures in soul-winning.

No! It will not be by this road that we shall get a satisfactory answer to our question, Why are not more souls brought to Christ by the sermon ?

2. Let us then ask if the reason is to be found in the present conditions of society—in the difficulties that confront us, in the rush and roar of our modern life, in the fact that men are gone mad on their idols ? Concede all that may be claimed—the insane race for

riches, the hells of hate open-mouthed and rampant, belching out their sin and shame, the confederated iniquity that is taking colossal form, the subtle, insidious, wide-spread worldly-mindedness—concede it all, yet the Word of God is not bound. Christ is not dead. The Holy Spirit has not been shorn of His power to convince this world of sin. If souls cannot be won to Christ now, because of the embattled hosts of principalities and powers and rulers of darkness, then they can never be won, and the battle with sin is already and irretrievably lost. But souls can be won. Behind every minister of the Gospel is this assuring, triumphant, omnipotent word of Jesus Christ: "All authority hath been given unto Me in heaven and on earth; go ye, therefore, and make disciples." No, the reason why more souls are not brought to Christ by our sermons is not to be found in the giant and defiant iniquities that are on every side of us.

Where, then, shall we look for the secret of paucity of results in this work of rescue? If not in the sovereignty of God, nor in the hatred and hardness of human hearts, let us turn the search-light on the pulpit itself and see if it is not there.

3. Is it because of a belief, hardly confessed to our secret self and rarely, if ever, openly avowed, that evangelistic preaching is not quite up to the level of the teaching work of the ministry—the great business of unfolding and expounding the truth to God's saints? Is this the reason why our preaching is not more fruitful in soul-winning?

We all know that the estimate we put upon any work will go far to determine our joy in it, our power, and our victory. The man who thinks his work petty is not likely to spangle the heavens with the glory of it. If he counts it great and noble, nobility is likely to shine in the very crudeness of his endeavour.

So a low estimate of gospel rescue-work is likely to tell disastrously on the work of rescue. If we regard it as something minor and subsidiary and treat it as an "aside" of the great work of the ministry; if we go to it with the half-conscious conviction that it is elementary—"the word of the mere beginnings of Christ"—and that it does not allow us the full swing of our powers in grappling with the profound doctrines of God, and with the complex social and economic problems that now confront the Church, then we have lighted on one secret at least of our bringing so few souls to Christ by preaching. It is not in the nature of mind to be stirred deeply and moved to mighty effort by that which is deemed of comparatively minor importance. You cannot fly a kite as you would *seek to save a soul*.

What, then, is our view of gospel rescue-work? What estimate do we put on evangelistic effort? Do we hold that bringing souls to Christ is as much an obligation and as great a privilege as feeding the flock of God? Or do we regard it as an "aside"—something not to be wholly ignored indeed, but requiring only occasional attention, and that can very well be done at special seasons, and commonly by an evangelist?

The view we really hold in this matter has already had expression in our practice. Let us, therefore, have the testimony of the facts.

Evangelistic preaching is preaching whose exclusive purpose is to bring souls to Christ. Evangelistic services are everywhere understood to mean services exclusively for rescue. The announcement that a certain church will hold a series of evangelistic meetings is, therefore, the direct and clear proof that such meetings are out of the ordinary ; that they are special, exceptional, resorted to under a kind of stress, as if to give easement to conscience or to gratify a local desire, but to be soon dropped that the regular work of the church may be resumed. The regular work of the church, indeed ! Where is our warrant for interpreting the last command of our Lord after this fashion—putting the " making " of disciples into a corner and giving the " teaching " of disciples pretty much the whole field ?

And when evangelistic preaching has not been given a set season and a series of meetings, but has appeared in the regular and ordinary ministry, how has it been treated ? Some ministers have relegated it wholly to the evening service. Some have given it scant room even there. So that it has come to pass in many a church that sinners—highly respectable sinners often, but nevertheless sinners before God—have grown gray in regular morning attendance upon the sanctuary, who, because they were never out at an evening service, have never heard a sermon that was meant to bring them to Christ ! Think of it ! All their lives, once a Sabbath, in the house of God, before the man of God, hearing the Word of God, and never once told what they must do to be saved ! Never once appealed to with a personal gospel invitation, because, forsooth, evangelistic preaching has been assigned to another part of the day !

But the spirit and the method of this appeal are no

less important than the fact and the time of it. When direct appeal has been made to those who are not Christians, how has it been made ? For example : A sermon is preached on some general subject, with elaborate exposition, argument, and illustration, with some general object like instruction chiefly in view, and at the close the preacher says, "A word now to the impenitent." Candidly, is that the way to do this business of rescue ? No, no, brethren. We cannot crowd much eagerness into an inference !

Think of writing on the title page of such a sermon a characterizing word like this, "Filled with a mighty persuasiveness " ! Or this, "Intent on saving a soul " ! Or this, "Throbbing with eager desire for rescue " ! Oh, no ! Such a label, all shifts aside, would be a libel. Such a label, all shifts aside, would be a lie.

By what should a sermon that is in pursuit of a soul and bent upon rescue be distinctly marked ? It must have some characterizing features by which it may be known.

1. Such a sermon is come, like the Master, not to call the righteous, but a sinner to repentance. Like the Master, therefore, it will face the fact of sin, and deal with it without the slightest gloss or the faintest apology. It will not tone down sin's appalling features by euphemistic words or phrases. It will have little or nothing to say of "heredity," or "environment " or "the stream of tendency " or "the victim of circumstances." The soul that it is after is a sinful soul. Its sin is the only reason for seeking it. Its sin is the only thing from which it needs to be saved. Godly sorrow for this sin is a vital condition of salvation. And sorrow for sin is no more possible with-

out conviction of sin, than a shadow is possible without the sun.   The sermon that is after a soul will, therefore, seek first of all to give that soul a due sense of sin.   Tenderly and tearfully, but always faithfully, this will be done ; sometimes with the pathos and tragedy and appealing love of Calvary ; and sometimes with the awful majesty of offended law.   And herein the sermon will be in the direct line of the leading of the Holy Spirit, whose initial and exclusive work it is to convince of sin.   Surely to be making an open way for the Spirit's first and indispensable work—to so order the entire sermonic structure that both in thought and expression it will be the fittest channel for the Holy Spirit's convincing power, is to invite the mightiest Agent of the universe to cooperation with the sermon in the supreme effort to win a soul.   Possibly, brethren of the ministry—possibly here is the secret of many a sermonic failure ; that we did not tell the soul all the truth about its sin.

2.   The sermon that is after a soul, is come, like the Master, to seek and to save *that which is lost*.   Like the Master !   This lets in a flood of light upon what should be the tone and trend and dominating purpose of the true sermon.   The Son of Man never forgot.   He never allowed His hearers to forget.   He threw a world of meaning into the word "lost."   He made it present. He made it real.   He made it measureless.   His speech was weighty with proverb and precept, with symbol and parable, telling what it is to be lost.   And while His speech was both pathetic and tragic with the sanction of two eternities, He did not put the loss far away in the vast unknown future.   He said it was now and here. Think of the lost sheep and the lost coin, and the lost

boy; and the seeking Shepherd, and the seeking woman, and the seeking Father. This is Christ's own way of telling us that the sinner He is come to seek and save is lost already. So the sermon that is after a soul will tell in all its earnest and eager search that it is seeking a *lost* soul!

3. The sermon that is after a soul has no to-morrow in it. Its accepted time is "now." It means instant and absolute surrender; a decision at once for Christ; immediate entrance into the kingdom of God. Its invitation is a present, urgent, insistent invitation. It gives no hint to the soul it seeks that it will come again. It allows no evasions, encourages no delays, coddles the sinner with no suggestions that he is in a good way if he is seriously minded, and thinking about this matter of personal religion, and seeking more light, in the hope that by and by he will see his way to a full acceptance of Jesus Christ. It will not tell him to keep on reading his Bible for further light and guidance; nor will it send him to the church through whose gates he may at last find a Saviour; nor to the prayer-meeting where in continued prayer and meditation he may ere long be brought to a willing mind. No! But with imperious and compelling, yet most loving, urgency, it will tell him there is no "by and by" in which a soul may come to Christ. And, pointing to the cross, it will say, "Behold the Lamb of God!" "*To-day, to-day,* if you will hear His voice, harden not your heart."

4. The sermon that is after a soul, is not a bow "drawn at a venture." Haphazard shots, even though the arrows are drawn from the quiver of God's Word, and winged with prayer—are not the

most effective.　God uses them.　He has the direction of their flight; and, just as of old, He may send them to the smiting of some great sinner between the joints of the harness.　But neither here is God always at war with the nature of things.　His ordinary method of procedure is by the law of adaptation.　He that winneth souls is wise.　But what *wisdom* can there be in the winning, if results are arbitrary, or the fruit of chance?

The sermon that is after a soul will, therefore, have singleness of aim, knowledge of the actual human nature aimed at, all possible study of that soul's individuality, and an individuality in the sermon answering to, and adapted to, the individuality of the man. There will be a clear reason for taking one text rather than another, and for treating that text in one way rather than another.　And the reason will be found in the soul sought.　Men take in truth in different forms, and by different sides of their minds; by the reason, by the imagination, by the æsthetic nature, through the feelings, in plain homely garb, in poetic form, in syllogisms.　Truth must knock at the side of the mind by which truth is most likely to enter.　Truth is carried to some by tropes and metaphors; to others by the hard cudgels of logic; to others it is floated on the watercourses of their tears.　The sermon that is after a soul, means knowledge of the road, the way to get in, and "this one thing I do."　It has all the possibilities of a definite determined purpose, while it has all the possibilities of "a bow drawn at a venture." The true gunner firing into a flock, will not swing his gun and fire as he swings.　He will sight a single bird in the flock, and fire.

5. The sermon that is after a soul is, like the Master, "filled with compassion." It will have in it what was in Christ's eyes when He looked on Peter, with the curses and denials scarce off that poor disciple's lips. It will have in it what was in Christ's voice, when He stood weeping over Jerusalem, and said, "How oft would I have gathered thy children together, as a hen gathereth her brood under her wings, and ye would not." The severest rebuke will get its chief severity from this deep undertone of divine compassion. And whether it be warning or entreaty, command or invitation, the terrors of the law or the forgiveness of the Gospel, the pathos of a suffering and beseeching and pursuing love will bathe it all, and make it clear that if the sermon does not bring the prodigal home, it will be because he preferred to trample on his Father's heart and murder mercy.

Is this kind of a sermon a common thing in the pulpit of to-day?—a sermon that is after a soul; that dares to deal in affectionate fidelity with the sin of that soul; that makes it manifest that the soul it seeks is lost, and that the day of salvation is "now"; that pursues the seeking with intense and eager interest, never letting the sinner go, throughout the entire discourse from start to finish; and that exhibits a mighty passion of love behind it all? How many such sermons have been preached in recent years? What if each preacher of the Word should call the roll of his sermons, say five years back; the text, the topic, and the dominant purpose of each. How many of them would bear this characterization: "Filled with a mighty persuasiveness; a sermon that was after a soul"?

Brethren of the ministry, what are sermons "to the times" compared with sermons of the eternities! Sermons of instruction are indeed priceless. To feed the flock of God is the business of every man of God. But is it his whole business? God forbid that one word should ever be said in even seeming disparagement of the blessed work of building up the body of Christ. But given the conditions that are the preacher's peculiar privilege from forty to fifty Sabbaths each year of his active ministry, viz., the day of God, the house of God, the Word of God, the man of God and the Spirit of God—given these five supreme conditions each Lord's day, with a fairly approachable and a not unfriendly audience, yet few, or no conversions as the immediate fruit of the Sabbath service—what does it mean? Does it not mean that *something is the matter with the preaching?* This discussion is an effort to find out what the matter is.

Your last hundred sermons, O God-commissioned herald; or your last five hundred; how many of them could you mark with a red cross as a sign that each sermon thus marked brought a soul to Christ? And how many of these red crosses could be underscored to show that it was *some direct word to the impenitent* that did the rescue work. And then how many of these underscored crosses could be starred, to show that from start to finish the sermons thus marked *had the capture in view?* If not one—*not one*—does not our question, Why are not more souls won to Christ by preaching? find its partial answer in the *kind of sermons* we have been preaching? And should it not send us to our studies and to our knees with the cry to God to help us make sermons that throughout all their plan and purpose should palpitate with eager desire to find and win a soul. Who can doubt that God would put His seal on such a ministry? And what an answer it would be to the stinging taunt of a recent pulpiteer that "the sermon is a back number"!

Listen to our Lord:

"*All authority* hath been given unto Me in heaven and on earth."

That's *your* authority; and it is *heaven's own.*

"Go ye therefore and *make disciples.*"

That's your *business*—and it is the *King's* business.

"*Preach the Gospel.*"

That's the one instrument of rescue.

O, man of God, throw out the life-line!

Index

A

ACQUISITION of a good delivery, 414

Activities, Christian, their help in spreading the Gospel, 17

Adaptation, the law of, 159; the saying the right thing at the right time, in the right way, 159; an admitted prime necessity, 160; that the sermon should answer some end, 161; should have respect to men as they are, 163; also to differing minds and temperaments, 164–166; sorrow calling for wise and tender words, 169; the magic wand, 182

Aim, supreme (of ideal ministry), 29; in preacher's weekly sermon, 96; in sermon preparation, 100, 317, 350

Alexander, Dr., his query how a youth should be taught to paint and painter's answer, 219; his "Thoughts on Preaching," 296, 327; his advice to cut off superfluous studies, 300

Alienation, estrangement, and impenitency in the pew, 170

Ambassadors for Christ, characteristic marks of their stewardship, 14; distinguishing intellectual gifts in, 14; the preacher a herald, steward, minister, 108; must hold commission consciously from his divine sovereign, 109

Anglo-Saxon words, use of in effective pulpit speech, 429

Answering questions, method of, 187

Apostrophe, as an aid to style, 401

Applied theology, the crucial question in, 465

Approving judgment of the Church certifying to the call to the ministry, 115

Art, the exclusive business of, 14; the idolatry and contempt of, 306
——, divine, of preaching the Gospel: the four "Constants," 307

Assimilation and concentration desirable gifts in the student in the ministry, 127

Attention, Charles Dickens on the quality of, 125, 126

Attentiveness, a quality in the ideal student for the ministry, 125; Charles Dickens' attestation to the quality, 125

Augustine and Chrysostom, strong contrasts between, 14

Authority, speaking with, 438

B

BEAUTY in style, 401–403

Beecher, H. W., his paraphrase of Paul's noble avowal, 40; his "Lectures on Preaching," 328

Benevolent schemes and Christian giving, 369

Bible, the, familiarity with urged, 299; spirit in which it should be studied, 299, 300; methods in studying it, 301; reading the entire books of at one sitting recommended, 301

Biblical proportions, methods for securing varied, 373

Boards of the Church, topics of Christian benevolence as related to the, 368

Bookcase essential for the ideal study, 155; Albert Barnes' study, 156

Books in an ideal study, the, 141–

479

mentally before the preacher, 328; should not be patchwork, 329

Seward, W. H., an effective public speaker, 231

Shedd, Dr. G. W. T., quoted, 41, 203, 204, 250, 278, 279; his "Sermons to the Natural Man" recommended to be read, 293

Simplicity, dignified, in sacred discourse, 404, 405

Sin, conviction of, the preacher's work by his sermon, 93

Singleness of theme and object in sermonic discourse, 335

Skeletonizing, habituate the mind to, urged, 297

Skeletons, books of (pulpit helps), their use negatived, 298

Smith, Gypsy, 14, 294

Smith, Sydney, on reading discourses from the pulpit, 224; on method of preaching, 225

Sociological movements that have no thought of spiritual regeneration, 21

Sorrow, a special condition calling for wise and tender adaptation by the preacher, 169

Souls, why are not more brought to Christ by preaching? 465

Specialist, a, not the best material for the Christian ministry, 129

Speech of the pulpit characterized, 29; public, sacred, and secular speech, difference between, 29; facility of, attractive to men, 208; fluency of mistaken for extemporaneous ability, 218

Spirit, ruling, in the ideal ministry, 37; cooperation of in selection of the preacher's theme and the choice of a text, 94; spirit of God, the ideal sermon born of the, 458

Spirit's cooperation through faith, the, 91; assured by the great and precious promises, 92; in the construction and application of the sermon, 92; along the lines vital to spiritual power and victory, 93

Spirituality the vital trait of ministerial character, 121

Spurgeon, on an empty mind and its gift of saying nothing, 24

—— and Beecher, strong contrasts between, 14

Storrs, Rev. Dr. R. S., on "The Future of the Protestant Pulpit in American Society" quoted, 18

Story, the sculptor on facility, 222

Student in the ministry, the, 121; quality of intellectual character possessed by the, 122; should be receptive, attentive, concentrative, assimilative, and many-sided, 133

Study, the minister's, 139

Style, ideal qualities of, in the sermon, 379; value of a good, 380; important for the pulpit, 381; objections to, 381, 382; Paul paid no attention to, 383; different properties of, 384, 393, 394

Subject-matter of the ideal ministry, 45, 238

Success, essentials to, in extemporaneous preaching, 211

Sugden, Sir Edward, his testimony as to reading, 150

Supreme aim of the ideal ministry, 29

Symbol and sacrament, preaching for God, 17

Syrophenician woman, influence of the story of the, 246

T

TALENTS, the parable of the, 86

Temperament of the sermon-writer, 328

Testimony of the Church, argument from the, 110

Text of Scripture, what fidelity to it will secure, 52

Text-book, the, in the minister's study, 145; a classified, 297

Texts, and their explanatory, propositional, and observational discussion, 259–272

Theme, preacher's, chosen and sermon written to suit some present